Gordon Burn was the author of four novels, *Alma Cogan* (winner of the Whitbread Award for Best First Novel), *Fullalove*, *The North of England Home Service* and *Born Yesterday*. He was also the author of the non-fiction titles *Somebody's Husband, Somebody's Son*, *Pocket Money*, *Happy Like Murderers*, *On the Way to Work* (with Damien Hirst) and *Best and Edwards*. His last book, *Sex & Violence, Death & Silence*, was a collection of his essays on art.

Denise Mina is the author of fourteen novels, three plays, five graphic novels and a bucket and half of short stories. She has won lots of prizes, important ones, precious ones, foreign ones and the Gordon Burn Prize in 2017, which made her cry because she loves his work so much. She regularly presents television and radio, and lives in Glasgow.

Further praise for *Somebody's Husband, Somebody's Son*:

'Quite possibly, alongside Martin Amis's *Money*, one of the most important British books of the decade . . . [A] stunning non-fiction masterpiece . . . You can only imagine its power on first reading. We're talking a good few years before 'true crime' had successfully entered the lexicon of British literature . . . In Burn's dependably insightful hands, the form was elevated. Throughout, he never flinches; neither does he wallow. His sentences are neat and informative. He understands the weight of keeping it simple, of racking up the facts.' Austin Collings, Th

'The dank, stultifying Britain that Burn depicts so intimately in this book is, I think, gone for ever . . . Of course it is dark . . . But its author's refusal to deal in anything other than the facts means that the atmosphere is somehow pristine, too: wholly reliable, deeply moral . . . Its righteousness stems not from judgement, but from paying attention to things as they really are, however much he (and by extension, we) want to look away.' Rachel Cooke, *Guardian*

GORDON BURN

SOMEBODY'S HUSBAND, SOMEBODY'S SON

FABER & FABER

First published in 1984 by William Heinemann Ltd
First published by Faber & Faber Ltd in 2004
Bloomsbury House
74–77 Great Russell Street
London WC1B 3DA

This paperback edition first published in 2019

Typeset by Faber & Faber Limited
Printed and bound by CPI Group (UK) Ltd, Croydon CR0 4YY

A CIP record for this book
is available from the British Library

ISBN 978–0–571–34727–8

2 4 6 8 10 9 7 5 3

To my parents

. . . and the power to light the room came from another country, well to the north, where snow had already fallen.

John Cheever, *Bullet Park*

Contents

Introduction

by Denise Mina

For readers who already enjoy true crime, this book is a shocking delight, like finding a gold ring in a packet of Hula Hoops. For others, it's a profoundly discomfiting read. Gordon Burn not only wrote a true crime book well. He didn't just research his subject. In *Somebody's Husband, Somebody's Son*, he challenged the foundational premise of crime writing.

This book was startling when it was first published in 1984. Even thirty years later, true crime is still regarded as slightly distasteful. Crime fiction aficionados often draw a lip-curling line between what we do and the lesser form of true crime. While crime fiction has recently come to be regarded as rather worthy, true crime is still cast as salacious, prurient, intrusive, mean.

True crime is one of the oldest and most universal story forms. It comes from an oral tradition rather than a written one, as does poetry. The narrative shape is often quite odd because it doesn't come from a rigid literary tradition but developed higgledy-piggledy from court reports, newspaper journalism, and penny broadside sheets which were printed and sold loose in the streets on the occasion of a crime or execution.

But it isn't the shape that makes it low. It's the subject matter. This distaste is almost superstitious; as if reading about violent crime could invite it to your door. Or else, it's soiling; as if the writer or reader is somehow implicated in the crimes themselves. To counter this, true crime writing is sometimes defensive and condemnatory.

It takes the time out from the story to tell the reader that the writer doesn't approve of this series of cannibalistic murders *at all*. Sometimes they are needlessly ponderous and research-heavy, to differentiate them from less serious books, quickly cobbled together from newspapers shortly after a case.

With all of these many limitations and disadvantages, true crime was an odd choice for Gordon Burn – an established and well-respected writer. Several commentators wondered why he would stoop to literary slumming of this sort. Having written a true crime novel myself, I've been asked if I did it 'to make a fast buck'. Trust me: none of those bucks were fast.

Even the most grudging reviewers had to concede that the book was beautifully written. Most referenced Truman Capote's *In Cold Blood* and Norman Mailer's *The Executioner's Song*. These are the totems of respectability in true crime writing; a flag that the reviewer doesn't like true crime but understands that there is something interesting there, beyond the smoke of their own distaste. *The Executioner's Song* won a Pulitzer, after all. For me, coupling them to *Somebody's Husband, Somebody's Son* is wrong, because this book is both more radical and more difficult than either of them. It offers no bogeyman to lock up. It does not leave us feeling safer because the case is solved.

In Cold Blood and *The Executioner's Song* predate the publication of *Somebody's Husband, Somebody's Son*: Capote by eighteen years and Mailer by five. It's inconceivable that a reader as avid as Burn wouldn't have read them – just as it's inconceivable that a writer as radical as Burn wasn't building on what they were doing. He did something far more radical. Those two books were both immersive New Journalism, they were both genre-defying and brave, but they were not *Somebody's Husband, Somebody's Son*.

What they all have in common is that they are all true crime, all well written and well researched, and they are all by white men looking at the crimes of other white men. But *In Cold Blood* is always about Capote, and *The Executioner's Song* is an attempt by Mailer to investigate Gilmore's motivation.

What sets *Somebody's Husband, Somebody's Son* apart is that it examines the Yorkshire Ripper case holistically. It examines the context of how it happened, who the crimes were committed against, how it could happen, and the socio- and geopolitical site of the crimes. It's both grander in scale and more profoundly honest. We don't know why Peter Sutcliffe did it. We don't know because motive is ultimately unknowable.

The traditional question posed by true crime is why the criminal did what they did. Superficially, it's a fairly simple question, often with a self-evident answer. They did it for kicks. They were evil. But this does not satisfy because this is facile. In the commission of brutal crimes, the perpetrator's motives are often so muddied by expectation, justification and legal defences, that all we can do is speculate, and we do that through the prism of our own time and values. Burn did not pose that question in this book. He asked a more difficult question: where could this happen and among what sort of society could it keep happening?

It's one of the fictions of all crime stories that murderers exist in a vacuum, untouched by social attitudes, their criminal careers unshaped by police incompetence and false assumptions or family loyalties. These are comforting fictions.

Of all the obvious fictions in the way we talk about crime, the most all-pervasive is that of the criminal individual.

Serial killers have a scientifically defined pattern of offending. They are masterminds of avoiding detection. Gradually, they get sloppy and leave clues because they want to get caught. That is the individual construction of criminal events.

The social construction – taking context into account – is that the police don't catch serial killers because the police are a bit rubbish at that. Killers become serial killers because the police don't catch them the first, second or third time. They leave clues because everyone gets less vigilant if they do the same thing over and over again.

Deciding to site criminality in an individual is a fiercely political act. It only appears neutral because it mirrors the status quo.

Devoid of social context, dreadful people do awful things for reasons we normal, good people may never understand. Perhaps they decided to do wrong things. Perhaps they lost control or were predestined to do them because of Current Reason X. Reason X changes over time and it always reflects the age and culture from which it springs.

The most popular Current Reason X is childhood head injury. In other times demonic possession or childhood sexual abuse could be the cause. For a long time an Oedipal complex of one kind or another was the favoured explanation. It's a maxim in most true crime stories: *cherchez la mère*. But although these monolithic explanations go in and out of fashion, they remain sited in the criminal individual. Crime is not about context. It's not a social event. Cops, family and culture are always reactive, never complicit.

Somebody's Husband, Somebody's Son doesn't do that. It contextualises the Yorkshire Ripper case, and because of this it's a strange and melancholy book, challenging the individualistic assumption at the very heart of crime storytelling.

Burn vividly explores the contempt that the culture Sutcliffe was living in had for sex workers. He looks unflinchingly at machismo and class divisions. When Sutcliffe's younger brother, Carl, was brutally beaten about the head after coming out of a nightclub, Peter offered him brotherly advice: 'Always carry a sock in your pocket and all you need is a stone or some other solid object to turn it into an effective weapon.' In contextualising Sutcliffe's life, Burn robs the reader of all of the comforting, distancing fictions around crimes of sexual violence.

To research this book, Burn moved to Bingley, where Peter Sutcliffe grew up and his family still lived. For three years, he interviewed family and friends, got to know the landscape and the world Sutcliffe lived in, the mindset and world view of the workplaces, discos and clubs that Sutcliffe grew up around. This is more than establishing a personal connection or showing his working out on the page. This is a sociological and political inquiry of context. It's a compassionate attempt to fully understand incomprehensible events.

I left school early, and it's the privilege and misfortune of autodidacts to have their world view shaped by fundamental misunderstandings. I had no one to explain to me that Marcel Duchamp's *Fountain* should be read as a comment on the intervening hand of the artist. I saw in it a statement about the ubiquity of beauty. Reading Genet, again without being told what to think about it, I knew I was right. Beauty and grace are everywhere, if only we can peer into the gloom and see it.

Beauty is in the supermarkets, in petrol station toilets, in all the small, grim places. Great writing can be a one-line tweet with perfect rhythm. It can be graffiti. It can be a sonnet by John Donne. Or it can be a true crime book that doesn't lie to make the world palatable. It just tells you the truth about what happened.

Reading *Somebody's Husband, Somebody's Son* is a lesson in truly great writing, all the more beautiful for being found in the small, grim places.

Denise Mina
2019

PART ONE

House

Although less than six miles along the Aire valley from Bradford, the enduringly Victorian 'Worstedopolis' whose dormitory it has increasingly become, Bingley is in many ways a country town, distrustful of, and often hostile to, what are all too easily interpreted as slick city ways. It is a conservative community, tolerant of mild eccentricity but more given to 'shamming gaumless' than to acts of flamboyance or outward display.

Travelling north to prepare a biography of her friend Charlotte Brontë almost a century and a half ago, Mrs Gaskell, whose train would have called at Bingley en route to Keighley for Haworth, only a short distance down the line, was immediately struck by the sullen and suspicious demeanour of the people 'in such a new manufacturing place':

'The remarkable degree of self-sufficiency they possess gives them an air of independence apt to repel a stranger . . . Their accost is curt; their accent and tone of speach blunt and harsh . . . a stranger can hardly ask a question without receiving some crusty reply if, indeed, he receive any at all. Sometimes the sour rudeness amounts to positive insult. Yet, if the "foreigner" takes all this churlishness good-humouredly, or as a matter of course, and makes good any claim upon their latent kindliness and hospitality, they are faithful and generous, and thoroughly to be relied upon,' Mrs Gaskell concluded in 1857, and little that has happened in the intervening years would cause her to radically revise that view.

'Foreigners', in fact, which meant Bradfordians as well as southerners and those from further afield, were probably a less rare occurrence in Bingley in the mid-nineteenth century, when the railway and the canal were both bustling thoroughfares, than they have become today.

Shoppers and commuters are the only passengers likely to alight these days at Bingley station; and the holidaymakers who are the only cargo that the Leeds–Liverpool canal now carries linger just long enough at the top of the Five Rise Lock overlooking the town to bemoan the unsightly concrete bunker erected by the Bradford and Bingley Building Society, and the 'Damart' sign defacing the handsome chimney of the former Bowling Green Mills, before opening the throttle on their rented narrowboats and gamely chugging on.

As recently as the early 1960s, however, when the Arts Council was still a warren of cobbled streets staggering down to the river, and the shopping precinct was still the site of the Myrtle cinema, Bingley, because of its advantaged position, was regularly choked with visitors from the surrounding towns, come to seek a breath of fresh air.

From Main Street, once part of the principal road from Bradford to Lancashire and the North, Bingley very quickly climbs up the steep sides of the valley, until the blackened stone of the semi-detached villas and Victorian terraces on the gentler slopes is overpowered by the paler brick of the post-war estates which provide the physical link between the heart of the old town and the scattered hamlets and villages high up on the moor's edge.

It was to places like Gilstead and Eldwick that the hikers and bikers would come on August Bank Holiday Mondays and at Whitsuntide, toiling up the hills to the town's outer boundary in their hundreds, and then on, past High Eldwick, across Rombald's Moor to Ilkley, a sight as predictable as the rain that beat down on the Airedale Agricultural Society Show, held in Myrtle Park, every summer, and the Round Table's 'Moonlight Express' which left Bingley station for Morecambe illuminations at 7.01 p.m. on the first Friday of every September.

These and other seasonal certainties – the St George's Day parade, the Children's Gala, 'progging' for 'Plot Night' (Guy Fawkes), the Sunshine Christmas Club – loaned a steadying rhythm to the Bingley year which in its turn has proved a reliable

4

ballast against unwanted – always referred to locally as 'unnecessary' – change.

John Sutcliffe has benefited all his life from the stability and sense of continuity that a small, semi-rural community like Bingley provides, and he has always endeavoured in his own way to guarantee it for the future.

On 11 November 1960, for instance, Mr Sutcliffe, a good-looking man, well-known locally for his achievements on the cricket and football fields, was a featured soloist when Bingley Musical Union, the town's male voice choir, performed with Hammond Sauceworks Band in the Princess Hall. Highlights of the evening, as that week's Bingley *Guardian* duly recorded, were 'The Lord Is My Light' (27th Psalm); 'In the Gloaming'; selections from *South Pacific*; 'Comrades in Arms'; 'Plantation Songs'; 'Land of Hope and Glory'; and 'Abide with Me'. A collection taken for Bingley Blind People's Association and Bingley Children's Gala raised £20 10s.

Fifteen years on, the setting was different – the main hall of the recently completed Bingley Arts Centre. But on the evening of Sunday, 7 March 1975, Mr Sutcliffe was again one of the soloists when the Musical Union again appeared with Hammond Sauceworks Band, performing by and large the same programme, and was prominent in the photograph that accompanied the Bingley *Guardian*'s notice hailing it as 'without doubt one of the most successful combinations of sounds to which music lovers in the Aire valley have ever been treated.'

It was around this time, however, that dark rumblings started to be heard about the unlikelihood of the Musical Union surviving beyond its centenary, then only fifteen years in the future: young men were no longer following their fathers into the choir as the present members had followed their fathers before them; young men didn't want to spend their Monday nights in an underheated room rehearsing 'Love Divine' and 'Some Enchanted Evening'; life was full of too many other distractions.

Peter Sutcliffe was third-generation Bingley, a chain that he would finally break himself by moving out to Bradford after he was married. His greatgrandfather, John 'Willie' Sutcliffe, an imposing presence, head of the accounts department at Bradford Co-operative Society, had made the move in the opposite direction with his young wife in the 1890s; and once settled in Eldwick, then little more than a scattering of grey stone terraces easily mistaken from a distance as merely a hilly outcrop of the local millstone grit, had quickly established himself as something of a figure in the community.

J. W. Sutcliffe's uncle was already installed as church-warden at St Lawrence C. of E., Eldwick; his wife became a stalwart of the church Ladies' Committee and it seemed natural that, when the time came for their first grandchild to be born, John Sutcliffe would be born in the large, plain house with a view of the moors that had seen his own father grow up.

A gradual descent down the side of the valley towards the centre of Bingley and a lifetime in manual labour have left John Sutcliffe full of nostalgia for both the scenery of his childhood and the exalted position enjoyed by his grandfather.

As a child he'd ride the tram into Bradford with his grandmother sometimes, and there the two of them would marvel at the sight of his namesake, big John 'Willie' Sutcliffe, at work. 'He must have had a staff of about twenty girls in his office. It seemed to stretch as far as the eye could see, and there were all these desks all the way down with girls scribbling away at them. And me grandfather's desk was at the top of the office, high up, facing them all. I met a man who worked for Bradford Co-op, many, many years after me grandfather had died, who told me they used to tremble in their boots when they saw him coming. He said he were a proper tartar.'

This picture of his grandfather in his public role, familiar from retelling to succeeding generations of the Sutcliffe family, is indelibly linked in John Sutcliffe's mind with a second, more informal one: his grandfather at the dinner table, at home, working his way through huge platefuls of offal that seemed all the more delicious to the small boy watching at his elbow because it was food that his grandmother, in common with most women of her acquaintance, couldn't bring herself to cook, much less eat.

'He used to eat some of the most esoteric stuff that you ever saw in your life, and he had to be who he was to get it in the quantity and quality that he did. He was a great man for tripe and pigs' trotters and best beef sausage, chicklins [chitterlings, pigs' intestines] all stuff like that . . . He absolutely loved offal.

'And when I was a kid, I used to stand at the side of his chair when he was eating his evening meal and I used to look up at him, just like a little pup watching somebody with food. And he'd just go on eating away and eating away, a very well-built, well-made feller, with a great full moustache, until all of a sudden he'd look down as if he hadn't noticed me till then and say, "Hello, would you like to try a bit of this?" And he'd chop me a lump off. It didn't matter what it was; it were me grandad's dinner; and it were beautiful.

'And it's stood me in good stead to this day that I can eat *anything* out of a butcher's, be it trotters or be it cow-heel or be it tripe or chicklins – anything at all in the offal time. I *love* it.'

This appetite for what he'd very quickly identified as 'man's food' did little to dent the reputation John Sutcliffe enjoyed even at that early age for being what is known in West Yorkshire as 'a real lad', or just 'real'. Constantly in scrapes, one of his earliest memories is of an incident that he says happened when he was just eleven months old, at the cottage in High Eldwick that was his parents' first home.

His mother had taken a tin of gravy out of the oven and left it on a table under the kitchen window to cool. Hoicking himself up with the aid of a table-leg and a chair, he'd somehow managed to make contact with the rim of the tin and had pulled the hot, clinging gravy down all over himself. He'd be reminded many times in later life how lucky he was not to be permanently disfigured; but, although he was fortunate not to get it full in the face, the left side of his chin and his left shoulder are still noticeably scarred. 'I can remember doing it,' he says. 'I can remember screaming me head off when it happened.'

Not the sort of man to easily forget anything – he's always ready with the time of day, correct to the nearest second and carries the local bus timetables around in his head – John Sutcliffe's memories of his first six years, spent on the edge of a farm in the middle of nowhere, are especially acute. After a period of neglect, he has taken to revisiting the scenery with which he was on such intimate terms as a child in order to remind himself, so he likes to tell his friends, that times haven't always been so bad.

'Up there, the summers were always summers and the winters were always winters,' will begin a typical reminiscence of the 'real' weather enjoyed on the moor-top. Such as the times when all you'd be able to see going to school was the top of an old dry-wall sticking up above the snow, which you would have to lead your little sister along by the hand. Or the fireballs which, another time, the same stone wall served to protect them against, sending them blazing into the tops of nearby trees in the premature dark.

'And in the summer I can remember the . . . the *heat* of the sun and the smell of the hay and everything about life in the country. It was so . . . lovely and warm and brilliant. Not so long ago I went to watch a cricket match up at High Eldwick, just up where I used to live, and when I left Bingley it were absolutely bucketing down; it was coming down like stair-rods: when I got up to where the cricket field is, you could see right down over the Aire Valley, and from Keighley, right through Bingley, Saltaire, Shipley, there was a thick white cloud hanging low over the river that never moved. Up where I was, though, it were beautiful. It was a glorious, sunny day.'

In similar vein, he can wax lyrical about the generosity of the farmer on whose land their cottage stood: '"Now then, lass," he'd say to me mother, "anytime tha wants a tunnip, go over t'field and get yersen one."' And even about the earth-toilet, located some distance from the house on the far side of a dirt road. He says he dreams of returning permanently, to see out his days. 'I've always said I'd like to finish me time back up there again. I really would. I'd really love to go back and live in that cottage where we lived.'

And yet, based on what he always told them while they were growing up, John Sutcliffe's children never thought of his upbringing as anything but 'hard': in the emotional, if not the purely physical sense, he always seemed to them to have been deprived. It was certainly an impression that their own experience of his mother, a difficult, demanding, undemonstrative woman, tended to bear out.

Only Peter, the oldest of John Sutcliffe's six children, would ever find anything resembling a welcome at his grandmother Sutcliffe's door. For the rest, whether they'd been sent up on an errand or just happened to be passing, she'd keep them standing outside, and in all weathers.

It had registered with John Sutcliffe at an early age that his mother was his father's social inferior. Returning from summer holidays spent with his grandparents in Mrs Cannon's very proper 'holiday home' on Queen's Promenade in Douglas, Isle of Man, he'd be especially struck by the fact that his mother was from cruder stock – 'from right at the lower end of the social scale,' as he'd describe it later; 'as low as you possibly could be in a town this size.'

The daughter of a foundryman, she'd been brought up in what is still known as 'the bottom of the town', meaning the terraced cottages in the shadow of Bingley Parish Church which the antique collectors who come to browse there now consider 'picturesque'. Unlike her husband, who had been a pupil at Bingley Grammar school until the age of sixteen, Ivy Sutcliffe had left school when she was twelve and gone straight into the mills which, in the first half of the century, was where virtually everybody went.

Mrs Sutcliffe allowed marriage and the birth of five children to only briefly interrupt her career as a box-minder; the responsibility for minding, feeding and generally bringing up the four youngest fell on the oldest boy, John.

In characteristically bravura fashion, John Sutcliffe would boast in later years about how he'd conned his way into the village school at the age of three by telling a local farmer's daughter that his mother had said she was to take him: 'I were bored. I

9

were fed up being up there on me own all day. I used to see the kids, all considerably older than me of course, trotting off to school of a morning, laughing and carrying on, and it seemed real. So eventually, off me own bat one day, I just followed them. And I went to school ever after.'

It is a fact, nevertheless, that this conveniently freed his mother to go on earning the money of which she was to become more and more fond. Although he held down a decent job as a textile 'designer' – really a sort of night foreman – in a mill in Shipley, her husband had never capitalised on the grammar school education that his scholarship had won him. And, unlike both husband and son, she couldn't wait to swap the moorland cottage for a modern home with the latest in modern amenities.

This finally happened in the late 1920s when the Sutcliffes were among the first to move into a terrace of semis whose leaded lights and dainty porches stood in marked contrast to the scenery in which it had been set down: the U-shape of Rylands Avenue seemed to have been branded on to the otherwise unspoiled Gilstead hillside as baldly as it might have been on to the haunch of a cow.

John Sutcliffe continued to make the two-way hike to his old school in Eldwick every day until the age of eleven, when he transferred to the 'Modern' school down in the town. At the beginning he was regarded as a bit of a 'country cousin' by the other pupils, who had nearly all grown up surrounded by the sound of clogs on flagstones and the whoop of factory whistles. But an outgoing nature, combined with a fairly strapping build, quickly won him friends. He was a natural at all sports, especially football and cricket, and first choice for all school- and, later, town-teams.

He also showed some talent for acting, particularly comedy, and had played 'Idle Jack' in *Dick Whittington* and 'Buttons' in *Cinderella* with amateurs at the Victoria Hall, Saltaire, as well as Wackford Squeers in a school production of *Nicholas Nickleby*, by the time he was fifteen.

His mother, however, had little time for such frivolities, and preferred to see him delivering papers to her far-flung neighbours morning and night and at weekends: if he begged hard enough she might sometimes give him the odd sixpence back out of his 4/6 weekly wage.

There was no question of him staying on at school past the age of fourteen even if he had been able to: his mother wanted him out earning, which he took to be no more than her due: 'She weren't really concerned where I worked so long as I was bringing in a wage. Which was natural. She'd spent her life working hard to give us a decent home to live in, and she wanted some contribution back. By gum she got it as well. She med sure of that. Oh yes.'

Ivy Sutcliffe exercised an equally tight control over the wage packet brought home by her husband, Arthur. The move to Gilstead had coincided with a downturn in the textile industry that saw Arthur Sutcliffe in a new job. He'd go back into textiles much later in life, in his fifties, but for twenty years he'd work for the Co-operative Wholesale Society in Bingley, as the door-to-door collector for their credit club.

Unlike his wife, who'd be remembered as 'fat' and 'slobby', Arthur Sutcliffe was a dapper little man with a love of dancing which, together with the miles he was obliged to walk (later cycle) every day, kept him looking fit and healthy.

He was a member of the choir at St Wilfrid's, Gilstead, and when his oldest son, John, started accompanying him at the age of seven, it set the seal on what was to be a lifelong friendship. Mrs Sutcliffe was a notable non-attender at St Wilfrid's, and she started turning up less and less at the popular Saturday night dances at the Princess Hall. Her husband, however, was always there as, indeed, he had to be, in his semi-official capacity.

Princess Hall was a swimming baths during the summer, but in the winter months the pool was boarded over for dancing to the likes of Bert Bentley and his Astorians. As a steward it was Arthur Sutcliffe's job to see that the floor was completely cleared between numbers, a task he performed with great efficiency and, as many of those present couldn't help noticing, not a little relish.

11

John Sutcliffe, though, who had inherited his love of ballroom dancing, was always pleased to have him pointed out as his father.

And there would be plenty of other occasions on which he'd be proud to say that he was Arthur Sutcliffe's lad. One of them was the day they padded up and walked out on to a cricket pitch together for the first time.

'Our mill's getting a team up to play Harrison's printers. Will you mek one in wi' us, we're a bit short-handed?' Arthur said to John Sutcliffe one day, which surprised him because, by then, his father was already well into his fifties. But of course he agreed, and he was never to forget it.

'It were one of these twenty-over-a-side games, where you hit out at almost everything: I mean, I laid about me and got forty-odd – I was caught on the boundary. But not me dad. He didn't show a lot of shots but, purely from memory, hit everything in the middle of the bat, right correctly, so the ball just dropped dead on the wicket in front of him. "Coom on!" he'd say, and we were off like hell, snatching singles. We played quite a few games that year with that mill side of his, and we had some right good times.'

It was the kind of relationship John Sutcliffe had always imagined having with his own sons, should he be lucky enough ever to have any.

2

John Sutcliffe's first thought when he heard his wife was pregnant was that he hoped it would be a boy: he knew it was the done thing to put on a big act about not caring about what a baby's sex might be, but he did care and it never occurred to him to pretend that he didn't. It might not matter all that much to a woman what she gets, he argued, but, deep down, every man wants his first to be a son: 'They pretend to be delighted when it's a girl, but they'd have been much more delighted if it had been a boy, the first one. It's the sort of thing that fellers do.'

John Sutcliffe had finally married Kathleen Coonan in March 1945, a year before finishing his wartime service in the Merchant Navy, while he was home on a month's leave. He was twenty-three, she was two years older, and they had been engaged since the very early days of the war. When it actually came down to tying the knot, however, he would always tell himself afterwards that it had been a very close-run thing: the home-town girl and Bingley versus an itinerant theatrical career.

He'd had a not particularly hectic war, stationed for the most part in Gibraltar, where he was one of the backbones of a garrison concert party which performed for and broadcast to the troops, usually in support of professional entertainers who had been sent out by ENSA: he was particularly impressed by Sir John Gielgud, who arrived wearing a dinner jacket one time to deliver well-known speeches from Shakespeare.

For his own part, John Sutcliffe prided himself on being a good all-rounder: he could do a bit of singing, or play the harmonica a bit if they wanted it, or recite monologues – 'Albert and the Lion', 'Nelson Gets His Eye Back', that sort of thing.

It was enough to bring him to the attention of ENSA's permanent organiser on the island, who suggested that he might be able to get Sutcliffe a start on the boards should he ever think about taking it up professionally. He did think about it but decided that, all things considered, his responsibilities lay elsewhere. He had a girl at home who'd spent years waiting for him faithfully, and it wouldn't have been fair to suddenly kick the whole job into touch.

Apart from the fact that he had a wife of just over a year whom he had never lived with but who was already seven months pregnant, John Sutcliffe picked up the strings of his life pretty much as he had left them, when he came home from the navy for good in April 1946.

His first job when he left school at fourteen had been in a joinery, but he'd given that up after only a few weeks because something else had come his way that he *really* wanted. He'd started as an apprentice at the Co-Op bakery in Bingley and had stayed there quite happily until his call-up five years later. And, now that the war was over, he walked straight back into his old job.

He was also lucky when it came to finding somewhere to live. Unlike most young couples who were having to fall back on the goodwill of in-laws and parents, he was able to rent a little place for not much money from a man in the office at work.

It was a stone cottage built into the hillside on Ferncliffe Road, one of the steepest inclines out of Bingley town centre and the western boundary of what only ten years earlier had been allotments and hen-runs but was now the nucleus of a sprawling council estate.

Every penny John Sutcliffe had earned during his years in the Merchant Navy had gone straight to his mother; and his mother being what she was, he'd neither received, nor expected, anything – not a chair or a secondhand carpet – in return. With the little they had, though, and with help from the Coonans, Kathleen's family, they did everything they could to make the place habitable in the two months before the baby was born.

On the morning of Saturday, 2 June 1946, Mr Winston Churchill opened the victory celebrations at Woodford in Essex with the exhortation that 'It is a poor heart that never rejoices.'

14

And 200 miles away in Bingley in the West Riding, Kathleen Sutcliffe went into labour at 10.00 a.m.

Although she'd wanted to, she had decided, on the advice of her doctor, not to have her first baby at home. And, by the time John Sutcliffe got back from phoning for a taxi, he found her with her coat buttoned and her case packed, ready to go.

'Norman Ray's', which is how everybody still thought of Bingley and Shipley Maternity Hospital even though Mr Ray, a former owner, had long gone, was still in the early throes of nationalisation in the summer of 1946; and an unpleasant atmosphere, underscored by reams of unreasonable rules and restrictions, was the matron's way of communicating her displeasure to the patients.

John Sutcliffe very quickly got the message that his presence would not be required and, having seen his wife installed safely in a bed, wandered off to look for some way of occupying his time. Normally on a Saturday he would have been playing cricket, but he'd felt obliged to scratch from that. So, back in Bingley, he threw himself into helping his father's youngest brother, Harry, strip the walls in the back room of his greengrocer's shop.

He stopped to call the hospital at 4.00, when there was no news, and once more at 7.00, when there was still nothing. When he rang again at 10.30, though, he was told that he was the father of a son who had been born about two hours earlier: visiting would be allowed the following afternoon.

It was a short walk from the telephone box up at Gilstead that he was standing in to Rylands Avenue where his parents still lived. They seemed mildly diverted by the news of their first grandchild but really more interested in what was on the wireless; no celebratory drink was forthcoming because they kept no drink in the house. John Sutcliffe decided he might as well stay the night.

He was the only visitor at 'Norman Ray's' on the Sunday afternoon because he had arranged it that way: he'd told Kathleen's mother and her sister, Mary, that they could go in and see her on their own in the evening.

He had been advised that the baby was small, only five pounds, but he was still unprepared for the scrap of life that he was only allowed to look at through a glass screen. This wasn't because his son was in danger or in any way ill, but just another of the matron's rules: no father was allowed to so much as touch his baby in the first few days, and babies were only taken to their mothers for feeding.

Peter Sutcliffe would be ten or eleven days old before his father picked him up; and when he did, set against his own big hands and powerful forearms, he seemed even tinier. There was a saying, though: 'They've got all the world to grow in,' and John Sutcliffe was encouraged by the doctors to believe it. He was also reassured on the pronounced egg-shape that characterised the lefthand side of his son's skull: it would even out to nothing in time, they said, but Mr Sutcliffe kept an eye on it over the years and it never seemed to; it just disappeared gradually under Peter's coarse second-growth hair.

Kathleen Sutcliffe, meanwhile, a conscientious Catholic who had given him the name 'Peter', and had it formally registered while still at 'Norman Ray's', under another hospital rule (her husband had contributed 'William', his own second name), was exercised by only one thing: she'd felt perfectly fit within a couple of days of the baby's delivery, yet her confinement seemed to be never-ending.

She had been in the hospital fifteen days when the Sunday finally rolled round for her husband to collect her. Instead of going straight home, though, the taxi dropped them first at the terraced house where Kathleen's mother lived with her older daughter, behind Dubb Lane Mills in the centre of Bingley. An aunt and uncle and two or three cousins lived in the next street over from where Kathleen herself had been brought up, and they were all there waiting to greet the new addition to the family. The baby, not unnaturally, was the cause of many loud and sustained expressions of concern and a lot of faffing and fussing that John Sutcliffe put down to it being a mainly female company. 'Women,' he thought, watching them all dancing attendance on his son.

*

With her abundant black hair and striking good looks, Kathleen Coonan was thought of as something of a 'catch' locally: she had been able to take her pick of the young men queueing up to partner her at the dances that were then almost a nightly event in the church and village halls and mechanics' institutes all over the district.

She was in munitions, working at a bullet factory, when she started courting John Sutcliffe from Gilstead, and they made a handsome couple. They became engaged in 1941 before he left to join the Merchant Navy, and were married four years later.

It was a white wedding, conducted by a formidable old priest called Father Hawkswell at St Joseph's, Bingley. There was a reception at Bingley St John's Ambulance Hall, to which Arthur Sutcliffe, the groom's father, had become attached in a voluntary, but smartly uniformed, capacity. And there was even time for a week's honeymoon in a boarding house in Morecambe which coincided with the armistice being declared and the slow return to 'normality'.

'I'd be a wealthy woman today if my grandfather hadn't killed himself,' a mature Kathleen Sutcliffe, wearied by the constant struggle to feed a growing family or by the prospect of another night's office-cleaning, would sometimes tell her children. And her mother, who spent the last years of her life living with them, would once again reminisce about the posh pony-and-traps they used to go to church in when she was a girl growing up in Devon.

All that had disappeared with the crash of the porcelain and ironmongery business which her father had painstakingly built up in Dawlish. He'd ended up on the road as a travelling salesman and, in these reduced circumstances, had somehow found himself with his wife and children in the attractive and thriving woollen town of Bingley. Here, having made modest provision for his family, he very soon did away with himself in the canal that ran conveniently close to their new home.

Perhaps as a result of the upheavals and traumas that thrust

17

her prematurely into adulthood, Lottie, his eldest daughter, remained unmarried long enough for her to be written off as an 'old maid'. She was thirty when she married Thomas Coonan, a Connemara man whose route to Bingley had been as unpredictable as her own.

Coonan, a textile worker, was a staunch Roman Catholic, and his wife became an enthusiastic and lifelong convert. Their three children would all be educated at St Joseph's, the catholic school in Bingley, but, unhappily, Coonan didn't live long enough to see it: he died after they'd been married for only seven years.

Nevertheless, with the Church as a support, Mrs Coonan dedicated herself to bringing the children up singlehandedly with, it was generally recognised, creditable results. The two girls in particular, Kathleen and Mary, always gave the impression of being 'quiet' and 'refined', 'good Catholics' who attended mass regularly and were always well turned-out.

Pressure had been intermittently brought to bear on John Sutcliffe in the months and years leading up to his marriage to embrace the Roman Catholic faith, and the subject would go on being brought up regularly in the first few years of his life with Kathleen. But the suggestion was always firmly resisted, even mildly resented. He was C. of E. He'd been born C. of E. and he intended to stay that way: it was beyond him why one Church should always be after stealing converts from another.

A religion that totally banned contraception, however, very quickly made its presence felt in his life: following his first spell of leave after the wedding, his wife had written to say that she was pregnant.

3

Within a few months of Peter being born in June 1946, Kathleen Sutcliffe discovered that she was expecting a second baby. It was news which, given his often-stated intention of having a large family, should have delighted her husband.

John Sutcliffe was always a great advocate of the 'old-fashioned' virtues of family life, regardless of the fact that, as he liked to point out, in his case his wife's religious convictions made such an old-fashioned family almost inevitable. 'To me, to live a life and not have children,' he'd say, 'would mean that that life had been *nothing*. After all, aren't children and a family worth more than money? I mean, there must be very, very wealthy folk who can't have any family who'd willingly forgo all the wealth they've got just to have a family – an *actual* family – of their own.'

Any pleasure he felt at the news of the new arrival, however, was seriously qualified by the state of his own health. Thanks to his sporting pursuits and a naturally sturdy constitution, John Sutcliffe had hardly known a day's real illness in his life. But within weeks of coming home from the war and setting up house with Kathleen in the cottage on Ferncliffe, his health started to deteriorate alarmingly. Even casual acquaintances commented on the change.

In the eight months from his demob in April 1946 to the end of the year, his weight dropped from over fourteen stone to just nine stone six and there seemed to be no way of calling a halt. The pounds were dropping off him visibly; he'd come home from work so weak he could hardly stand; in the morning it was as though he was putting on another man's clothes. And what made it all the more worrying was that nobody, including his own doctor and the doctors at the hospital, could give him any clue as to why it was.

Finally, in desperation, he gave up his job. And, miraculously, it worked. He'd worked in the bakery with no apparent ill effects for five years before the war, but now, as soon as he left, his skeletal frame once again started to flesh out. By the time their second son was born in September 1947, he was back up to around twelve and a half stone.

Just as his sickly self had seemed to find its echo in Peter, who at fifteen months still looked at least six months younger, so his renewed sense of well-being seemed to be reflected back at him from Thomas Arthur, named after his two grandfathers. The new baby was plump in all the places the first one was hollow; he was as pink as the first one had been rickety and pale.

And then, as mysteriously as Peter Sutcliffe had hung on and survived, Thomas Arthur Sutcliffe was dead. Born at home, as all the succeeding Sutcliffe children would be, he'd started refusing food when he was three days old and had finally been rushed to hospital in a taxi by his father. Three hours later a policeman was sent round to tell them that he had died. The undertaker took a small coffin to the hospital the following day and the baby was buried without ceremony in a common grave.

By the time Peter was brought home from his grandmother Coonan's where he'd been staying, it was all over. His mother was pregnant within four months with his sister, Anne, but for the time being he had her all to himself again. It seemed to John Sutcliffe impossible that they could but, in the following months, mother and son seemed to grow even closer. It was a relationship that, as it developed, increasingly unsettled him.

Everybody was always very gentle with Peter because he was so much on the 'weak and weedy' side and always so sensitive; and, at least in the first eighteen months, this included his father, who of course understood that it wasn't the lad's fault that he'd been born that way out. It used to amuse him at first, some of the queer ways he had of going on – such as the habit he developed of shuffling round the house on his bottom with one leg stuck out in front of him and the other dragging underneath. He was a good talker but, because of his tiny little ankles which hardly seemed up to bearing the weight, very slow to walk.

Thinking that they might get him on his feet, John Sutcliffe went out and bought Peter a pair of lace-up leather boots, specially reinforced over the instep and ankles, when he was about a year and a half. And they seemed to do the trick. Instead of shuffling, his mother encouraged him to toddle round the house with her, holding on to her skirts. The trouble was, once he was walking, he wouldn't let go.

Whatever room in the house she was in, and whatever the time of day, he was with her, clutching on to her clothes. She only had to make as if to get out of a chair and he'd be there attaching himself to her dress, his face half buried in the folds. And it went on not just for weeks or months, but for years.

There was another boy the same age who lived only a couple of doors down the row, but Peter would never go out and play. He hardly ventured outside on his own at all, in fact, preferring to stay quietly indoors with a game or a book or, quite simply, dog the footsteps of his mother. As somebody who had very quickly carved out an independent existence for himself on the hills and moors that still swept down to his back door, John Sutcliffe found this very peculiar.

'I would set off across those fields on me own when I was only a couple of years old, and walk as far as me legs would carry me on nice days, then sit down, have a rest and come back again. I knew every inch of those fields up there when I was a kid,' he'd tell his son encouragingly, but to no avail. Peter never became the sort of lad who'd jump up from the tea-table and be off messing about. He'd just have his tea, go into the front room, open a comic and read or listen to the wireless.

'On a nice evening they should *want* to be out. It should take you all your time to get them in when it's time for bed and the sun's shining and all the other kids are playing out. It's part of a child's life to be like that,' he'd say to Kathleen and she'd agree, but next time he came home there'd be Peter still hanging on to her skirts.

The best way to cure this chronic shyness, they decided, was to put him in a situation where he'd be forced to mix. It had been agreed between them long before they were married that the children would be brought up Catholics, and Peter had been going to St Joseph's on Sunday mornings with his mother since being able to walk. 'The Sacred Heart', as it was better known, was a small, moss-encrusted Victorian building, as plain inside and out as the back-to-backs by which it was surrounded and not 200 yards away from where the Sutcliffes lived. The infants' school adjoining the stone church was long and low and equally utilitarian and, it was felt, was the perfect place for Peter to be brought face to face with the outside world.

Surprisingly, although he was barely four and had led such a sheltered existence, he went off to school on his first day without a murmur and would never be known to complain, even though his skinny legs were an obvious and, as it proved, irresistible target for the mockers. It was a passivity that was to characterise his whole school career, so that at the end of it very few teachers, head-teachers or priests attached to his schools would be able to associate the name with a face.

Several of his classmates at the Sacred Heart, as the sons and daughters of Eastern European and Italian refugees still struggling to establish a foothold in their new country, had far greater reason to feel out of place. But at playtimes in the schoolyard, it was Peter Sutcliffe who was taken for the 'foreigner'. Where the other children were noisy and boisterous and unselfconscious in each other's company, he seemed unapproachable and withdrawn. He'd never voluntarily get involved in the ordinary rough-and-tumble or take part in any games, preferring to stand in the corner formed by a heavy stone buttress and one of the school walls, observing but unobserved.

This was where his father would invariably find him in the afternoons, whenever he wandered down to check on how much school life was achieving its objective of bringing him on a bit. 'Pete!' he'd call out to him over the damp black wall that just about came up to his waist. 'Peter! Why are you just *stood* there, lad?' Although of course he knew: he was still no size at all and the other kids were just too rough for him. It would all be different, though, once he got a few years on his back; then he'd soon shape up. As he'd tell him sometimes in an effort to gee him up.

For instance, there'd been this lad at his own school, Jack Ratcliffe, a walking matchstick-man until he'd gone into the army, gangly and skinny and not over-tall, a right weed. But what a size he was by the time he came out; fifteen and a half stone and an all-in wrestler: 'I could've eaten him for breakfast when I were at school. Later on though, he would've made mince-meat out of me.'

By the age of five Peter still hadn't got out of the habit of clinging limpet-like to his mother's hems. And even when he was seven his father would look out of the window and see him and his mother and, usually, another woman coming up the road from school: the other woman's children would be walking by her side, casually holding her hands; Peter, though, would be largely invisible in the camouflage of his mother's skirts.

Shortly before they were due to take possession of their first council house, however, Kathleen had presented him with another son, and this one had inherited his father's name. Michael John Sutcliffe was born on 6 September 1950. Anne was just two; Peter was in his first term at school.

Although it was old and cramped and totally lacking in what were coming to be regarded as the basic modern amenities, John and Kathleen Sutcliffe had both been happy in their first home. The way it had been built, on a narrow terrace hacked out of the dirt of the hillside, meant that the back walls were constantly damp, but 'little inconveniences' like this didn't particularly bother them: the previous tenants had put some floorboards up to provide an extra layer which largely prevented the wet coming through the wallpaper.

Besides which it was handy for the new shops that had been built for the people on the expanding Ferncliffe estate, as well as for the shops in town and Peter's school; and Kathleen's mother and sister lived just a few minutes' walk away at the bottom of the hill. Mrs Coonan was always ready and willing to help out when she was needed or to babysit on the rare occasions that John and Kathleen went out together on a Saturday night.

But it was John's mother who, on one of her almost unheard of visits, decided that the cottage was no place to bring up a young family. She made it her business to go and see the man in charge of housing at the Town Hall and, within months, they found that they had been assigned a new house on the other side of the valley, in Cottingley. This turned out to be a mixed blessing.

Neither John nor Kathleen had been aware up to that point that there were such things as council schemes for rehousing people, let alone how to qualify for one. So they were as much bemused as thrilled by the brand new, three-bedroomed semi-detached with outside and inside toilet that they found themselves moving into at the end of 1950.

Tacked on to the hills that rise like walls from the west bank of the river Aire, Cottingley was one of the last rural outposts of the area covered by Bingley Urban District Council: the new council estate, which was as foreign to the natural environment as most of the people selected to live on it, petered out eventually to reveal a panoramic view of the 'select' northern suburbs of Bradford, held at bay only by wild tracts of moor.

From Manor Road, which was to be the Sutcliffes' home for the next eight years, the scenery offered nothing but open fields interrupted by a few scattered farms. There was a working-men's club, a butcher's and a small post office-cum-general dealer. The shops and Bingley were near enough to be easily accessible in theory, but theory hadn't taken into account the lack of public transport, the climate and the back-breaking hills.

Because of its exposed position on the 'wrong' side of the valley, Cottingley was wide open to whatever weather happened to be coming down from the Dales. And, even in summer, one ingredient of this weather was usually a biting westerly wind – 'as salt as if it came straight from the middle of the Atlantic' as J. B. Priestley once wrote. Cottingley was consequently a landscape populated by huddled figures in constant battle against a downdraught which was either preventing them from getting home or blowing them there faster than they wanted to go.

The impact of their new surroundings on the Sutcliffe family was immediate: Peter started to be taken to, and brought home from, the Sacred Heart every day in a taxi, for which the local authority footed the bill; and his father was much less often in the house.

After leaving the Co-op bakery on account of his health, John Sutcliffe had been taken on as a weaver in a mill on the far side of Bingley from where he now lived; and most of his interests outside work tended to keep him in or around the town.

His wasting illness had at first left him too weak to play his usual full part in Bingley's sporting life. But two of the men he worked alongside at the mill were keen enough body-builders to have started a small club in a garden shed behind one of their homes. They also kept a set of weights at work which they trained on during break time when they were on night shift, and

John Sutcliffe didn't take much encouraging to join in. He was gradually able to restore the balance between his body-weight and his strength by firming his muscles up again.

Working nights, as he mostly did, meant that he couldn't always make the twice-weekly training sessions with the Bingley Town team with whom he played football at weekends in the Bradford Amateur League. But he compensated for that by turning out on Wednesdays with various 'half-holiday' teams. He never had any difficulty getting a game and, in fact, was thought by many at the time to be good enough to turn professional; there are still those who believe he could have made an England-class goalkeeper.

Equally, in the summer months, he was in great demand as an opening batsman. He played for three different clubs in his first five years home from the navy and, even in late middle-age, was still in a position to be able to pick and choose.

Bingley Musical Union, the all-male choral society, also occupied a great deal of his time. As well as rehearsals on Monday nights in an upstairs room at the Fleece or the Ferrands Arms, and concert performances around the locality, there were social evenings (including a Ladies' Night once a year when members could bring their wives) and 'mystery tours' out into the surrounding countryside: unsuspecting drinkers at places like the Commercial Hotel, Cockhill Moors, would be regaled with full-blooded versions of sentimental favourites like 'Shenandoah' and 'The Little Drummer Boy', and the choir would then sing their way home in the dark.

He allowed his interest in the legitimate theatre to lapse for some years after the war but then was drawn back into it in the mid-fifties by a cricketing pal whose wife harboured theatrical ambitions such as he had once known.

'Operas, musical comedies, farces, dramas, the place hums with them. Every second typist is an *ingenue* lead somewhere, every other cashier a heavy father or comedian . . . The local papers print whole pages of amateur stage photographs. Nearly every organisation appears to run a dramatic society as an offshoot . . . There are soubrettes and tragedians in all the shops. The very factories produce their own reviews and pantomimes. All the town's a stage . . .', Priestley wrote of the Bradford of the 1930s, at the height of the Depression. And, twenty years later, John Sutcliffe was among those helping to keep the tradition alive.

Idle and Thackley Amateur Dramatic Society was the first to harness his talents: he'd bicycle to Fisher's Mill, where rehearsals were held in the canteen two nights a week, straight from work. His services were also called on by another amateur group in Shipley, whose productions frequently overlapped with theirs. And, when word eventually got back to Bingley about his appearances in other towns, he was recruited for the Amateur Operatic Society there.

He was never given any of the principal leads which, he realised before he ever joined, were subject to a 'closed-shop': Jack Bailey, a local businessman, and Audrey Whitwham, the daughter of the tobacconist in Main Street, always had first claim on the best parts. But he wasn't in it for the glory, as he often commented, but for the fun.

He'd be given a taste of what life might have been like occasionally when a production transferred to the Bradford 'Alhambra' for a week's run. He appeared there with the Bingley Amateur Operatic Society in *Oklahoma* in 1960 when the audience included Kathleen and a family that now numbered five: Peter, at fourteen, was the oldest; Jane was the youngest at four. Maureen, who was eight at the time, was thrilled to hear two women in the row behind them single out the 'gorgeous man' who was her father for special praise.

On top of all this he never stopped being a member of the choir at St Wilfrid's, Gilstead, where he had started with his father as a boy. Even after the move away to Cottingley, he continued to cross the valley twice a day for the Sunday services, with a lunchtime session at the Fisherman or the Ferrands to slake his thirst in between.

Kathleen's attendances at the Sacred Heart, however, gradually started to fall away. The children were always sent but, with the breakfasts to make, the house to clean and the Sunday lunch to cook, the slog from Cottingley, involving steep hills in both directions, became too much. 'Then in the evening, by the time she's seen to all the teas and everything, it's probably too late for church,' as her husband always patiently explained.

From the smart 'looker' of her youth, Kathleen Sutcliffe had slipped imperceptibly into the cosier role expected of a woman of her age and class. 'Warm' and 'kind-hearted' were the epithets now applied to a woman on whom the birth of six children in ten years (she was never to forget 'our Tommy', the baby who died) was beginning to take its toll. Part of what made her such a 'good mother', though, was the way she hardly ever complained; she gave every appearance of being quite content to live in her husband's shadow.

Months of constant night shift, which was slightly more rumunerative than working days, together with an active social life, meant that John Sutcliffe didn't see as much of his family as he might have while they were young: he was never around enough for his presence to become taken for granted. When he was in the house, however, his children were left in no doubt at all who was master: he brooked no contradiction, and his word was law.

On the rare occasions when they did go out together as a family it was usually by coach to a cricket ground in one of the northern counties, to watch John Sutcliffe play. Unlike the sons of his father's team-mates, however, Peter never used to pay much attention to the game; he'd invariably disappear with his mother to go for a walk around the shops. 'To him, it's just a crowd of idiots banging a ball about with a piece of wood,' John Sutcliffe would later explain, a bit shamefacedly, to his pals.

When Peter was ten and coming up to leaving his junior school, his father made a last-ditch effort to cure him of this aversion to sport. He made a leather football and a football strip his main present that Christmas and, on the first fine day of the holidays, decided it was time he tried it on. There was a pitch

28

straight across from their house in Manor Road, so they were perfectly placed.

'Coom on lad, get your football gear out,' he said, trying to drag him away from his comic. 'I'll go over and have a game wi' yi.' Which brought the expected response: 'Oh it's too cold . . . I'm not bothered . . . I don't want . . .' Until his father came close to losing his temper in the end. 'There's no point having a football and a new set of gear if you're not going to use it. So, come on. Frame yerself.'

He started off by demonstrating how to dribble the ball and follow it and keep it under control, running up the pitch in his own well-dubbined brown boots, shouting instructions as he went. Then it was Peter's turn.

'Well, he took to that ball as if he'd been born wi' one tied to his toe,' John Sutcliffe would say when retailing the story in the years to come. 'He took it the full length of the field, no bother. Never lost control. So I says, "Right, let's go back now." So he dribbled it right back again the full length of the field, and kept it under control all the way. So I thought, Well, he's a bloody natural. I thought: He's going to enjoy this.'

Back in the house, though, Peter took the strip off and never put it on again. A couple of years later his mother gave it to a boy in the same street who was interested in football and regularly watched Mr Sutcliffe taking part in matches that his son, in the house only fifty yards away, studiously ignored.

Peter Sutcliffe's embarrassment about anything to do with his body, pronounced throughout his youth, became particularly acute in the summer when, streaming with hay fever, he had to accompany his family on holiday.

For the last thirty years of his life John Sutcliffe's father kept a caravan at Arnside, a small, rather genteel, coastal resort on the southern edge of the Lake District, about a two-hour drive from Bingley. He used it all year round as a refuge from his wife, with whom relations had grown more and more strained as they'd grown older. But in summer, his children took it in turns to stay there with their families.

The Barbers, the owners of the site at New Barns Farm, had gone to great pains to ensure that it wasn't a blot on the landscape: the caravans had been distributed throughout a wood in a way that guaranteed privacy for their occupants and an unpolluted view from the far side of the river estuary into whose waters the Barbers' land eventually disappeared. Many of the owners had erected rustic fences with lychgates around their mobile homes, whose names – 'Haven', 'The Hollies' – were spelled out in poker-work over the doors.

John Sutcliffe and his family were unusual in that they arrived from the station on foot, after a considerable route-march, whereas most of those staying at New Barns owned their own cars. But, once they were unpacked, they quickly made themselves at home.

The Sutcliffe caravan was parked in a good spot, on the edge of 'White Creek', a pebbled beach in a small bay sheltered by the surrounding hills. And John Sutcliffe never lost any time in stripping down to the trunks or army-surplus shorts that were his uniform for as long as the weather held up. He'd wade across to Grange-over-Sands at low tide, bringing back flatfish that he'd located with his feet, and was hardly out of the water. But, self-conscious as he was about a body that he knew to be weak and skinny, Peter could hardly ever be lured in.

Even on the hottest day, when the river was alive with noise and splashing and the beach littered with towels, Peter was reluctant to take so much as his shirt off and often, in fact, wasn't anywhere to be found.

'The wind always blows strongest on the tallest tree' is the maxim by which the show-jumper Harvey Smith, who was born in Bingley and now owns much of the town's outer fringe, has always claimed to live his life, but he is not loved for it locally. Bingley people like their trees, if not quite felled, then at all times ruthlessly cut back. Which is where John Sutcliffe first fell foul of that part of the community in which he lived.

On his regular visits to the holiday caravan, Arthur, John Sutcliffe's father, was seldom alone: Jack Hawkes, a man who worked with John in Bingley and was himself a frequent visitor to Arnside, had spotted him in the company of various 'lady-friends' and, back home, the word had slowly got around about Arthur Sutcliffe's 'passion wagon'. But eyebrows were also starting to be raised at the behaviour of his oldest son, who was seen to be a regular caller at the home of a single professional woman in Cottingley, and seemed increasingly to believe he was the small-town version of his famous namesake, Herbert Sutcliffe, the great Yorkshire and England opening batsman who had a reputation for dousing his flannels in eau de cologne before going out to play.

Not content with having his name in the paper every other week in connection with the Musical Union or the operatics or the cricket, he was forever getting up at Cottingley Working Men's Club to perform one of the 'turns' he'd perfected in the Forces. He also contrived to have the most colourful front garden in Manor Road.

Getting up one morning to find what he considered a 'superb display' of tulips – different colours in all four corners and a big centre-piece made up of diagonal black and white blooms – half-flattened and half-stolen, helped nudge John Sutcliffe towards the decision to try and leave Cottingley and return to 'his' side of the valley.

5

The teachers at St Joseph's R.C. Infants and Juniors were the envy of their colleagues at other schools in Bingley: whenever they encountered them at the swimming baths or anywhere else in public, the Catholic children, it was noted, were always 'immaculately behaved', and Peter Sutcliffe was no exception.

As a ten-year-old he looked very like the boy in the peaked cap featured in Bradford and Bingley Building Society newspaper advertisements under the headline 'His future is in your hands'; but, apart from a quiet smile and a constant 'yonderly' look, there was nothing about him that made him stand out.

Academically, too, he was undistinguished, routinely bringing home respectable but far from glowing reports. His father, though, who only ever seemed to see him with his nose stuck in a paper or a book, thought that he must do well at the 11-Plus and, when he didn't, took it as a more or less personal affront. The day after the results came out, he went storming up to the school.

How was it, he wanted to know of his son's teacher, that he hadn't passed to go to St Bede's? Surely if *any*body at the Sacred Heart was brainy enough to get through to the grammar school it was Peter? He was above average in everything except physical activities. He was always down at the children's library with his sisters. He was *extremely* bright.

The answer, when it finally came, frankly astounded him. 'Oh,' he was told, 'you don't want him to go to St Bede's, Mr Sutcliffe. You've got four other children. You want him out at work when he's fifteen.' Try as he could to disabuse her of this notion, it was her final word.

Cottingley Manor, the Roman Catholic Secondary Modern school, was a grimy, porticoed mansion surrounded by acres of

32

playing fields at the town end of Manor Road. Which meant that, when he started there in September 1957, Peter Sutcliffe had less far to travel than many of the other pupils, who came down from the outlying villages and from as far away as Shipley and Saltaire. The inevitable territorial rivalries that resulted had always formed the basis of school gangs, and new boys always had to be careful not to find themselves caught between sides.

Although two years his junior, Anne Sutcliffe had quickly overtaken her brother in stature and established herself as his 'protector' while he was at the Sacred Heart. This had put paid to most of the taunts about his timidity and his skinny legs but, from the age of ten, he had been pestering his mother for a pair of long trousers to hide them in and his pleas took on a special urgency with his imminent transfer to the 'rougher' Secondary Modern school.

Long trousers, though, as his father kept telling him, didn't grow on trees. If they bought him long trousers they'd have to cut at least four inches off the bottoms. He'd just have to put up with it until his legs grew long enough and then they'd buy him some grey flannels. And that was an end to it. He was to stop worrying his mother silly.

'Blue jeans' were one American import that hadn't infiltrated as far as the West Riding in 1957. But *Rock Around the Clock* reached the Myrtle Cinema, Bingley, in August that year and the Bingley *Guardian* was moved to run an editorial the following week decrying the new breed of 'delinquents' the film had left in its wake: a gang of them 'dressed in the silly "Teddy" clothing' had disrupted a dance organised by Bingley Round Table at the Princess Hall, overturning and ripping up seats; 'decent people', it concluded, 'must be protected from these morons who believe in nothing but their own right to do as they please in their own small-brained way.'

They were sentiments which, within a very few weeks, Peter Sutcliffe would have cause to wholeheartedly endorse. As he'd suspected, he had remained friendless at Cottingley Manor Secondary Modern, and his isolation, together with his 'weedy'

33

appearance and his obvious fear, had made him an irresistible target for the aspiring 'hard cases' and embryo 'Teds'. At the beginning he'd tried to handle it in his usual way, by disappearing into the walls. But that hadn't worked and he'd been forced to take more drastic action: he stopped going to school altogether.

At the top of the Sutcliffes' house at 79 Manor Road was a small loft or 'underdrawing' that was easily accessible from the landing at the head of the stairs, and Peter adopted this as his own private 'burrow'. By standing on the bannister-top it was a simple matter to push open the wooden trap-door and hoist yourself in. And, without anybody ever suspecting anything, he did this every day for a fortnight.

Every morning he'd shout 'good-bye' and bang the back door the way he always did when he went to school. But instead of disappearing down the hill, he'd wait until the coast was clear and then secrete himself in the underdrawing where he'd wait patiently all day until it was time to reverse the pretence.

Lying alone in the dark he'd listen to the weather or the birds, or to the sounds of the house – his mother moving around cleaning, his father, home from the night-shift, snoring in the bedroom below. Mostly though, as he'd tell his parents later, he just slept, something for which he had an apparently boundless appetite.

Whatever day of the week it was, whatever the time of year, Peter was always the last one down. 'That little bugger's got to learn to get his backside off the bed in the morning,' John would endlessly complain to Kathleen, but he never did. 'Bad timekeeping' would lose him job after job when he was older, and his sleeping wasn't confined to the beginning of the day: workmates would arrive, as arranged, to go out with him for the evening, only to find themselves exchanging small talk with his mother for an hour while Peter slept soundly upstairs. Sometimes he'd 'pass out' for five or ten minutes more or less in mid-conversation and prove, as his father was again always complaining, the devil to wake up.

The first his parents knew of his absconding from Cottingley Manor was when a letter arrived from the headmaster asking why he hadn't been at school for two weeks. Confronted with this, Peter's immediate reaction, as when sensing any displeasure, was to dissolve into tears. But then he quickly owned up. The pressure the bigger lads were putting on him was too much, he said. They were at him and at him and wouldn't leave him alone, but he knew it would get even worse if he complained. He'd taken it all until he couldn't take it any longer and then had started hiding in the underdrawing instead. He *hated* that school, he said. He didn't want to go there any more. But his father was quite firm: 'It's your school,' he told him. 'You've *got* to go.'

A long meeting with Mr Battersby, the headmaster, got the whole thing satisfactorily sorted out – at least, as far as John Sutcliffe was concerned. Although he suspected that Peter might have been occasionally bullied in the three years that he had left at Cottingley Manor, he never truanted and he never came home complaining again, which was the important thing: it marked the beginnings of 'character' that his wife's 'cossetting' and overprotective attitude had always denied. Even so he couldn't stop her regarding Peter as the little one who needed extra care and protection right into his early teens.

Not long after this episode, Kathleen Sutcliffe, whose fifth child, Jane, was only two and a half, found herself pregnant once again. Another baby was another reason to add to the growing list for leaving Cottingley, and at the beginning of 1959 John Sutcliffe managed a quiet word with the churchwarden at St Wilfrid's, Gilstead, who also happened to be Chairman of Bingley U.D.C. Sutcliffe was somebody who needed a bigger house because of a growing family; he supported his local church and wanted to be nearer to it, was the basis of their special pleading, and it paid off. In June, six months before Carl was born, they crossed the valley for the second and final time and moved into a four-bedroomed pebbledash at 57 Cornwall Road.

Like the rest of Ferncliffe Estate ranged above it, Cornwall Road

had been built on the hillside which it was now helping to oblit-
erate in the years immediately preceding the war. Made up of
uniform rows of brick-and-stucco boxes, it fell away steeply at
both ends so that, whatever way it was approached on foot, it
was impossible to arrive without feeling out of breath. Turn left
out of the Sutcliffes' new home and you were soon surrounded
by the woods and meadows bordering the canal. Turn right and
you were descending into the smoke issuing from, and blurring
the outlines of, the tall mill chimneys in the centre of the town.

As an estate-dweller, John Sutcliffe found himself part of a
small minority in the church choir, as in most of the other organ-
isations to which he belonged. And, as if to prevent further
incursions, St Wilfrid's and the equally solid, equally coal-black
Gilstead Wesleyan Chapel stood like twin guardians at the brow
of the hill where Ferncliffe Estate ended and the old Gilstead village began. Posters hanging in Gilstead Post Office offered the
visitor further clues as to what kind of community this was.
'"Lovely Things" will be the subject of an address given to the
members of the Gilstead Methodist Ladies' Pleasant Hour by
Mrs C. Walker of Keighley on Thursday,' said the elegant cray-
onned script; 'Eldwick Ladies Choir will give a concert in aid of
the British Heart Foundation at the Eldwick Memorial Hall on
Friday, artists to include Doreen and Ronald Lee (vocal duo) and
Gerald McCauley (tenor).'

But back down on Cornwall Road and Queensway and the
Oval the signs were just as easy to read: threadbare curtains and
botched windows, rusting cars jacked up on bricks, ribby dogs
scavenging in the gutters, and pasty-faced, mongrel children
waiting for their parents to get home.

Ferncliffe Estate was not entirely populated by the 'rough'
working-class, however; there were many hard-working,
'respectable' families and John Sutcliffe instinctively placed
himself at this end of the spectrum. 'Our kids were different to
the majority of them who lived round our way. They were
always properly clothed and well-fed. Peter went to school in
his grey blazer and grey flannels right up to the last day. *They*

never had to have free school-dinners or anything,' was to be his proud boast in later years. 'They had love and care at home. They weren't brought up rough-and-ready. They had so much protection.'

The back garden at 57 Cornwall Road had been ruined by motorbikes belonging to the previous tenants. 'I'd be better off digging for oil than trying to grow owt in that lot,' was one of John Sutcliffe's favourite jokes. So he concentrated on the front instead, growing vegetables in the borders, planting conifers in each corner, and making a putting-green on the lawn. On summer evenings he'd often be out there on his own with a putter, somewhat to the embarrassment of his older children, playing 'clock-golf'. But then, two and a half years after returning to Gilstead, John Sutcliffe suffered a sudden fall from grace.

Jack Hawkes, a neighbour of the Sutcliffes at number 71, had always been unimpressed by the debonair face that 'his nibs', as he always called him, showed to the world. The two of them had once worked nights together at a mill in the old part of Bingley, and Jack Hawkes wasn't alone in noticing that, during fine weather, John Sutcliffe never brought anything to work to eat: he'd disappear down a fire escape in the early hours to help himself to tomatoes, lettuce and whatever else was growing in the allotments that ran between the railway line and the canal.

So it came as less of a surprise to Jack Hawkes than to many when he woke up on Christmas Day 1961 to learn that John Sutcliffe had been arrested in the middle of the night and charged with burglary at a house further along the street.

'39-year-old weaver, John William Sutcliffe, admitted stealing foodstuffs valued at 19s 7½d and was conditionally discharged for twelve months on payment of costs,' the Bingley *Guardian* began its account of the magistrates' hearing, two weeks later.

He was on his way home from a Christmas Eve party which lasted until 4.30 a.m. on Christmas Day. Some young people in another room were having a party which was just about breaking up. On hearing a light switch in the kitchen they went to investigate, just in time to see Sutcliffe, whom they recognised, making a dash for the door. Some youths chased him down the road, caught him and sent for the police. As he ran, Sutcliffe left a trail of packets of raisins, sweets etc behind him, which he had stuffed into his pockets.

He was genuinely sorry for the theft because the complainants were distant relatives of his and hitherto he had had a perfectly clean record.

Christmas Day was John Sutcliffe's one big day of the year, when he liked to 'impose' himself on the kitchen and, characteristically, although it was after 8.00 a.m. when he was finally let out of the police cells, he carried on as if nothing untoward had occurred. But that year a pall inevitably hung over the proceedings.

When, on 27 December, Mr John Taylor, a retired school-caretaker living alone at 28 Cornwall Road, gassed himself and his pet cat, it set the seal on a memorably miserable Christmas.

6

Unlike his father, who was mostly either out or asleep but un-ignorable, Peter was nearly always in and yet nowhere to be found.

He'd left school in the summer of 1961, aged fifteen, and gone straight into the engineering works of Fairbank and Brearley in Church Street, Bingley, as an apprentice fitter. But, even as a seventeen-year-old, he was conspicuously shy: to most of the people who knew him then and found him perfectly pleasant, he seemed to be looking at the world from a distance, as if it was just so many images, flickering on a screen.

He tended to be so quiet at home that none of his family was ever sure whether he was in or out. He could enter a room or leave it without it registering with anybody that he'd been or was gone. It was possible to walk into a room in which Peter was sitting and not even notice that he was there. 'I've walked into the house many a time and he's been just sat quiet in the kitchen without me realising for ages,' his sister, Maureen, says. 'Not reading or anything; just sort of sat there staring at space. Pete were one of these who could sit for hours on his own without getting restless, like some blokes can't; they've got to be either watching television or talking to somebody or going out for drinks with their mates. Pete were quite happy in his own company. He didn't get bored.'

The hours he spent shut away in the toilet – he'd sit there all afternoon if nobody disturbed him – became something of a family joke. And his monopoly of the bathroom was tolerated as merely another idiosyncracy until his sisters started to grow up. Then the charge that he spent more time in the bathroom than all the women in the house put together, which meant five, including his grandmother and his mother, was one that was incessantly heard. There was a pellet-hole in the bathroom door, and sometimes Carl would secretly watch his big brother snipping millimetre after millimetre off his curiously electric black hair. He could stand rooted for half an hour or more in front of the mirror, lost to the world.

So 'meticulous' was a description that, half-compliment, half-criticism, attached itself to him as an adolescent, and another one was 'deep'. Apart from the hours when he was out working, he seemed to spend the whole of his mid-teens alone in the room that he slept in at nights with his two brothers, with the rest of the household kept at bay on the other side of a firmly locked door.

On the evidence of the ledger which he kept doggedly throughout these years, in which each week's Top Twenty hits were recorded in a neat, almost prim hand, he had all the makings of the sort of clerk the Wool Exchanges in Bradford had once been full of, but which was now a fast dying breed.

It very quickly became clear that the industrial environment certainly didn't suit him, although lack of prospects and unpunctuality, rather than temperamental unsuitability, were always the reasons offered for his frequent changes of job. He left Fairbank and Brearley after less than a year, complaining that, far from being taught anything, he was being 'exploited', and for a short time worked alongside his father in the mill. It took him just a few months to discover that his future didn't lie in weaving, and Fibre Products, a firm on the small industrial estate just outside Bingley, was his next stop.

There the masks that the employees had to wear as protection against the dust from the rags and asbestos that they spent all day chopping and grinding kept communication to a minimum; but even so Peter Sutcliffe would be remembered as 'a queer bugger' with the look of 'a frightened animal'. In this case, however, it is possible he decided that silence was the safest option.

Some of the hardest nuts in Bingley worked at Fibre Products, men like Ken Eslin who, when he threatened to shoot your legs off, was rumoured to mean it and was to spend most of his life 'inside'. And Sammy Foulds, so innocent-looking he always carried his birth certificate, but whose appearance was deceptive. 'The Weasel', as 'little' Sammy was better known, was notorious for provoking fights in the pubs around Bingley so that his 'protectors', the brothers Geoff and Jack Southgate, might keep their hand in at beating people up.

Gradually, though, as he approached his eighteenth birthday, it was noticeable that Peter was starting to harden up a bit; at long last he was starting to come out of his shell. He had bought a motorbike as soon as he was old enough, which meant he had at least something in common with the men in whose company he was obviously about to spend his adult life. And it was gratifying to his father to see that, as well as motorbikes and motorcar manuals, he was starting to take an interest in 'health-and-strength' magazines.

He put himself on a course of one of the 'bulk-builder' foods advertised in the body-building periodicals and acquired the 'Bullworker' which was to be assigned a permanent – for a time, central – place in his daily routine. Every night after work he'd spend an hour or two locked away with it, returning it to the back of the wardrobe when he was finished. None of the family, not even his brothers, ever saw him training with the Bullworker; he was always very private. But the results soon started to become apparent and he was assisted in his quest for a new body by the manual labour involved in his new job.

'Bingley cemetery is one of the most popular places of resort, and is justly accounted one of the prettiest and most attractive places of the kind in England,' Harry Speight, a local historian, recorded in 1904. 'The mezereons, lilacs, roses and flower-beds . . . present in season a fine and varied show. But to lovers of botanical treasures the extensive range of rockery, which bears hundreds of curious and beautiful Alpine plants, will prove the chief attraction.'

Although less popular as a 'place of resort' when Peter Sutcliffe started work there as a grave-digger in the summer of 1964, the cemetery was still as formal in design and as fussed over by its gardeners as the surrounding countryside was wild. Standing on Bailey Hills, next to the nineteenth-century Bingley Grammar school, the view was of dense, permanently black woods beyond the river on one side, and of Five-Rise Locks beyond the main road and the livestock auction mart on the other. From the Catholic section, which marked the cemetery's highest point, cars and buildings were insignificant specks on the moors and hills that lurched and tumbled towards the horizon.

Beautiful in the summer months when cemetery 'business' was at its slackest, the same scenery would prove unnerving, even to experienced grave-diggers, at the end of the year when the nights started to set in and the distant lights in Harold Street were the only signs of life. Billy Moore, for instance, whose last months at the cemetery coincided with Peter Sutcliffe's first, was never ashamed to talk about the afternoon when the flickering lamps and the whip of the wind and the encircling darkness became too much for him and a veteran helper, and they'd dropped their spades and fled.

Shortly after joining the staff, he witnessed Peter being shaken in much the same way: 'He were digging an earth grave, were lad, just by the side of the grammar school wall an' he were using an iron prodder to locate the top of an old coffin that were already in. He were having to keep his feet to the side because it turned out there was no lid to hit, when suddenly he let out this scream which were really more of a yelp. By the time I got there he were still shakin', standin' wi' this skull on his spade. He couldn't let go. It does jump you a bit.' On occasions like this the diggers would douse themselves in Jeyes fluid or whatever else was handy, in an attempt to get rid of the stench.

The nature of the work, and the attitude of most outsiders towards it, made for the sort of camaraderie that few of those working at the cemetery had known in other jobs. There was a preponderance of young men and some of them could be a bit wild. 'But if you didn't do something to take the steam off, you'd blow the top off your head,' was always Gary Jackson's excuse, every time he was collared by the superintendent for going too far.

Somebody was always pouring water over somebody or dropping a brick on somebody's head, and Gary Jackson was usually standing by with his camera to capture the results. He took pictures of people getting up to mischief with the statuary and being dunked in the horse-trough and posing as what would be passed off on the more gullible as 'corpses', with dried and cracked mud all over their faces.

But it was one of the 'old-timers', a man called Eddie Bishop, who was on the receiving end of most of their stunts. 'Bish-bosh', as he was known, was a creature of habit and was therefore regarded as a sitting-duck: the only smoker in the stone outhouse where they all gathered to eat their 'jock', his ash-tray was alternately nailed to the table and primed to blow up; the cupboard he went to religiously every evening was booby-trapped with whitewash, and every time he slurped his tea half a dozen others slurped in unison with him, every time he folded a slice of bread into four and pushed it into his mouth, half a dozen others did the same.

The curious thing was that Peter seemed quite close to old Bishop, who had shown him how to brick out a vault and board up a grave and the other basics of the trade. If he took exception to the 'dogging' that his workmates found so amusing, he showed it no more than Bishop did himself. In fact, nobody was ever sure what Peter was thinking because his expression hardly ever changed: from arriving at work in the morning until packing up for home, he wore what some chose to interpret as a sneer of superiority and others as a conspiratorial half-smile. Billy Moore tended to side with the former: 'He never gave you an answer to anything, just his grin, as if to say, "Balls. You're talking rubbish."' But Gary Jackson wasn't so sure: 'He'd come in late every morning, nice and quiet, as if he had his day planned out, always with this right pleasant smile.'

'You had to be present at commitals, "ashes to ashes" an' all that,' another workmate, Laurie Ashton, remembers. 'You had to follow job right through to finish and sometimes, if it was a kiddie, say, I'd get right upset. But never Peter. He'd help old ladies away from the graveside right polite, like, help them down off the boards. But Pete wasn't a lad for showing his feelings in any shape or form. For instance, you couldn't get him mad, ever. All you ever got were just that daft smile.'

The only thing that drew any comment at the time, however, was his modesty, the way he'd always wander off into the bushes to relieve himself rather than stand up at a tombstone like the others; and the fact that he never removed the black leather-look jacket that he always wore, even at the height of summer, much less his shirt. He hardly seemed to perspire at all, in fact, and, back in the cabin, only rolled his shirt-sleeves up to his elbows to have a wash, whereas the rest of them stripped off and got under the 'Ascot' for a good scrubdown.

But nobody attached too much importance to this and before long he was being referred to familiarly outside working hours as 'our Pete'. He'd tag along if some of them went down to the White Horse at lunchtime, although he never really took to drink; and he'd stand by while they all whistled at the girls going past the top of Park Road in the centre of Bingley, although never joining in himself.

The working day at the cemetery always ended with a game of darts in the 'mess-room' whose stove and coal fire glowing in the permanent semi-darkness helped sustain a relaxed, almost clubby atmosphere. Peter gained in confidence enough to bring his own electric tape recorder on which records from his collection were interspersed with family noises and snatches of his father singing party-pieces such as 'Molly Malone'. And Laurie Ashton got permission from Mr MacTaggart, the cemetery superintendent based in Myrtle Park, to tow up the old Chevrolet he'd got his hands on so that they could work on it in the yard.

The twin passions in Laurie Ashton's life were, and even in middle age were to remain, 1950s American music and 1950s American cars. Two years older than Peter Sutcliffe, he had nevertheless been born too late to be part of the first full flowering of the Teddy-boy style that, disregarding passing fashion, he had adhered to rigidly as soon as he was out of short pants. For work this meant ice-blue 'circulation-stoppers' (trousers), heavy suede 'brothel-creepers' (shoes), black tee-shirts, a quiff that looked top-heavy on his wiry but small-boned body, and brass rings. Twenty years on, it is a look still much favoured in Bingley, where Elvis Presley continues to be the yardstick by which most women measure their men.

As a result of 'going pals' with Laurie Ashton, Peter was soon borrowing his father's dress-waistcoats, pale shadows of Laurie's spangle-fleck ones, and affecting bootlace ties. What really drew them together, though, was an interest in engines, and in this they were joined by Eric Robinson, another throwback Teddy boy and one of Laurie Ashton's oldest friends.

A neighbour of the Sutcliffes, Robinson had been in and out of institutions since adolescence for the sort of misdemeanours endemic to Ferncliffe Estate: his last conviction had been for breaking and entering and stealing butter, lard and a jar of pickles worth 4s 4½d from one of the Main Street shops. For this he was thought to be 'shook to feathers' or 'rajjed' or just 'thick' by many people; but those who considered him 'shrewd as a cartload of monkeys', like Douglas MacTavish, the cemetery superintendent, who wouldn't employ him for this reason, were probably nearer the mark.

When Eric bought a Vauxhall Wyvern, Peter loaned him £20 towards the cost of it and, although not licensed or insured himself yet, taught him to drive it up on Baildon Moor. In 1964 the two of them went with Laurie to buy his '57 Plymouth Fury and Pete demonstrated how much bolder he was becoming by tipping a three-wheel Reliant up on to its single front wheel and pushing it like a barrow across the showroom floor. Little things like this could start him off laughing uncontrollably and, reliving it later, he was even worse.

Such small adventures were nothing, though, to what Eric sometimes got up to after he'd 'necked' eight or nine pints. Eric and Laurie were gun fanatics, like most young men in Bingley, but Eric didn't confine his activities to 'squirrelling' and 'ratting' on the council tip. He owned Lugers as well as air-pistols and when he wasn't taking aim at the television, pretending to fire, he was taking aim at his mother. On one famous occasion he finally drew his gun in the middle of a western and blew the set to bits. Another time, Laurie had to stop him killing his step-father bare-handed for having a whippet puppy put to sleep: by the time he managed to pull Eric off him, his stepfather was blue in the face.

Peter always found this kind of thing hysterical, and the high spirits that he was learning to give free reign to in the company of his two pals inevitably started to spill into his job. The grave-diggers often earned a bit of extra money by acting as pall-bearers for the undertaking firms who used the cemetery's Chapel of Rest, and the long black coats they had to wear while carrying coffins never failed to start Peter off. 'He had a right laugh with 'im, if you got him going,' Laurie Ashton remembers. 'A right catching laugh.' But his sense of humour and the sense of humour of the others slowly started to diverge.

Peter hit old Eddie Bishop quite heavily over the head with a mallet one day while Bishop was boarding up a grave, and quite soon afterwards was spotted in the Catholic section hurling a rock on to a coffin that had just been set down in the earth. 'Now then, that'll waken you, you bugger,' he said, and laughed the way he did, through his nose.

A part of the job that most of the men particularly dreaded was being asked to go into the Chapel of Rest to clean or re-creosote the floor, particularly if, as the registrar would warn them when he handed the key over, there happened to be 'one in'. The only two who didn't seem particularly bothered were Peter Sutcliffe and Gary Jackson, who was to go on to take charge of a cemetery himself. 'It's not the dead as what can harm you, it's the living,' as Gary so often said. But knowing the others' feelings neither he nor Peter could resist the occasional morbid joke: before the duplicate key to the Chapel had been issued, one or other of them would position themselves on a slab under a shroud; then, when the man cleaning the floor crawled within touching distance, they'd allow an arm to swing slowly, heavily down . . .

Because of their unsqueamish attitude towards the 'customers', Gary and Peter were able to supplement their £9-a-week basic wage occasionally by helping the undertakers out in various ways. 'They only had about three undertakers,' Gary Jackson says, 'and five-bob were five-bob in them days. You'd do things like change their pyjamas if they'd died in bed, wash them down, that sort of thing. It were a bloody good way of earning a few shillin' in the lunch-hour.'

There were pitfalls, however. There were two chapels in Bingley cemetery, Church of England and Catholic, and it was part of the Catholic chapel that served as the Chapel of Rest. The etiquette was that you'd lock yourself in and draw heavy blue velvet curtains to screen off the body to which you were attending. 'It were very private, which obviously were a good thing. But one time I were washing a girl down who'd been in a bad accident when suddenly her mother came tearing at me from behind. She thought I were molesting lass.'

Hearing that they were looking for somebody to do similar work on a part-time basis for an hour or two some evenings, Peter went after, and got, a job in the town morgue. The morgue was in the gas-lit maze of streets at 'the top of the town', behind the King's Head; and in the pub afterwards he would be full of the white marble 'billiard table' with its plug-hole 'pockets' and 'the bad 'un from a car smash, all mangled', that they'd just got in. He was always going on about showing them round sometime, that is, if they wanted, and finally one night Eric Robinson called his bluff: 'But soon as we were round corner, Peter says, "Oh hell, I've forgotten the key." So we never actually got in.'

The next time Eric went missing up at the cemetery, however, Peter showed him something designed to impress. 'There'd just been a funeral, all mourners had gone and Pete an' Laurie were left to do filling in. Anyway, Peter were straight down, opened coffin lid up an' started delvin' in. It were a woman of about sixty-four. "Oh there's nowt on that," he said after a couple of minutes, an' that were that.'

Peter had already boasted to Eric about the 'loot' he was taking from bodies, and in particular about the recent occasion when he'd offered his sister Maureen a choice of half a dozen rings. '"Oh you've no need to go to jewellers," is what he told me he said to her, "you can have one of these." When she asked where he got them he'd said, "Off the bodies at work," and had a good laugh at the way she flinched. It seemed right comical to him.'

Tales about what was supposed to be going on at the cemetery gained a wide circulation in Bingley, and one man, a workmate of Peter Sutcliffe's father, with relatives buried on Bailey Hills, even went to the local police to complain.

Laurie Ashton knew what was happening, although he didn't like to dwell on it too much. He stood by and watched Peter open coffins on a number of occasions, but he never saw him touch any rings: 'He'd help any women off the boards right gentle, like, but soon as they were gone he were down into the grave. He'd loosen the wing nuts, which would take about three minutes because there were six of them and he were always very deliberate, then he'd slide the lid back slowly until you could just see the face. Very carefully, he'd lift away the square of lace they used to cover it and stare hard for about thirty seconds, concentrated, intent like, like he was waiting for something to move. When he were finished we'd do back-filling, put muck back in, an' that were it.' Peter would seem quietly content then; he would wear a look of calm, quiet satisfaction on his face.

There had been a seven-month hiatus in Peter Sutcliffe's graveyard career, when he'd been sacked for constantly coming in late. And just before the end of 1967, he was sacked for the second and last time. 'He accepted that he was on his bike,' Douglas MacTavish says. 'There was no problem about it. "Can't wake up in the mornings," he said quite cheerfully. He was never an awkward bloke.'

7

Peter's interest in motorbikes had soon become evident in the room at Cornwall Road that he shared with Mick and Carl. The first cheap bike he bought ended up in hundreds of parts spread out on newspapers on the floor, which is where it stayed because, having got it completely stripped down, he never worked out how to put it together again.

Tinkering with engines was all the neighbours ever saw the teenager Peter Sutcliffe do. Every night until dusk he was out at the front of the house, occasionally chatting to another boy from the estate in his jumpy, desultory fashion, but usually alone. He'd nod a polite 'hello' to any older neighbours who happened to pass, but he only had to see a girl or a courting couple coming to instantly 'colour up'.

Even to those who only vaguely knew him, Peter was immediately associated with grease and bikes. It was surprising, therefore, that when the time came for him to take his driving test, he failed. The reason, or so he claimed when he got back from Keighley, was that he hadn't looked in his mirror when turning a corner, when in fact there was no mirror on his bike. He crashed into the house in the closest he'd ever get to a rage, made a great show of ripping up his 'L'-plates in front of his father and swore that he'd never wear them again. Which he never did.

Although motorbikes and cars were to remain a major pre-occupation and virtually his only topic of conversation throughout his life, he drove them for many years without the benefit of a licence. Most of his vehicles also went untaxed and uninsured much of the time, a fact from which Peter appeared to derive some small, obscure thrill.

Out for a run one night in his green Morris Minor with another youth called Keith Sugden, he volunteered to walk to the nearest police station for help when they found they were out of petrol. Knowing that not only did he not have a licence, but that the tax disc on the front windscreen would be revealed, on closer inspection, to be nothing more than a Guinness label, all seemed to add to the fun. Sugden was certainly impressed by his friend's gall: 'He went to the station and the copper brought him back wi' two gallons of petrol in car an' dropped him off an' he never blinked.

'I think that was his kick. 'Cause when they'd gone he used to say, "Stupid bastards!" and have a right grin on his face. That's how cool he were. I'd call it "self-disciplined". He used to giggle. He thought it were great.'

Long before Peter started 'going mates' with Eric Robinson and Laurie Ashton, Keith Sugden, an apprentice at Harrison's printers in Bingley, had become the first real friend that he ever made. Unlike the crowd they both found themselves perfunctorily a part of, they were passive and quiet, positively reflective, given their surroundings, and Peter started to look almost comfortable in somebody else's presence for the first time.

'He were a loner, y'see. Pete would be in company but he'd never say anything, he'd still be totally on his own,' Keith Sugden says. 'He were always very remote. Always. And I can be the same, which is probably why we got on. I mean, he were company without being pushy, old Peter. If there was nowt to say neither of us used to say owt, and that were okay.

'The others would be shouting and bawling and piss-arsing around, but not us. We could have a good laugh; Pete could have his odd moment. But he were never vulgar. I don't think I ever heard him swear in all the time I knew him; "whores" and "scrubbers" is about the strongest he got. He were never *loud*.'

Apart from pubs there weren't many places for young people to go in Bingley, or even Bradford, in the early 1960s, even though London, if television and the newspapers were to be believed, was turning into the 'swinging' capital of the world. The C and D milk bar in Main Street – the Cat and Dog to regulars – boasted a juke-box and was open in the early evenings for hot and cold drinks; and there was the occasional 'Hot Dog Hop' at the Victoria Hall. But the Myrtle cinema had shut its doors for the last time, there wasn't even a Chinese take-away to go to after closing-time, and a sign outside the Mecca Locarno in the centre of Bradford indicated how slowly the tide of 'permissiveness' was creeping north: 'Because of the character of our particular entertainment, where men without previous introduction talk to any lady, a coloured gentleman must bring his own lady partner with him to any dance session,' it began and ended: 'Let us live together peacefully and let us be fair to all people and realise that nature has made us different.'

Because Peter Sutcliffe and Keith Sugden were both 'half men', as those who considered themselves 'big boozers' in Bingley pointedly put it, they preferred to drive out into the surrounding countryside rather than sit about nursing drinks. Once or twice Peter's Morris travelled in 'convoy' to Arnside with Dave Brearley's spoke-wheeled MG roadster and Richard Varley's old Standard with the white stripe across the top. But usually the two friends just drove to the coast on their own for the night, sometimes returning in the early hours after a scout around Blackpool; other times sleeping in the car – and once in a boat – on the promenade at Arnside, the resort of his childhood that kept drawing Peter like a magnet, until the gulls woke them up.

As teenagers they were both strikingly good-looking. 'Smashing. Dark black hair all swept back, an Elvis Presley type,' is how Maureen, Peter's twelve-year-old sister, saw Keith. And, with his olive skin off-set by the pastel-coloured suits he started wearing in his late-teens, Peter wasn't without admirers himself. Both of them, though, were awkward around girls. 'One's scared and the other daren't,' was the sort of thing that made Keith's ears burn when he heard it whispered behind their backs.

'I found it difficult to pull birds; or, at least, put it this way, to do the initial chatting up. But, whereas I wasn't willing to go forward an' mek a fool of meself, Peter would. He'd leave it up to me, though, to lead conversation after he'd got 'em; once he'd got 'em he'd just stand there with that smile on his face, hardly saying a word.'

When he was nineteen, Keith decided to kick over the traces and moved in with a girlfriend in Shipley who had her own flat. It turned out to be a short-lived rebellion, however: his mother came and dragged him home with her after just two weeks. But he made the most of it while it lasted and so did Peter who, basking in the reflected glory of his friend's bold step, virtually became a lodger himself.

It was a big house and a lot of girls lived there, but Peter stubbornly refused to be tempted even though they were considered an 'easy touch'. His disinterest finally revealed itself as distaste one morning when one of the tenants threw herself across the kitchen table with no clothes on and, only half-jokingly, offered herself as 'breakfast'. He didn't say anything, but then he didn't have to; it was written all over his face.

At the end of this brief interlude, Keith and Peter, who seemed especially relieved that the threat to their friendship had abated, drifted back into their old routine. Like millions of others touched by 'Beatlemania', Keith Sugden had bought a cheap guitar and taught himself the rudiments, and so had Patrick Slater, the mutual acquaintance through whom Keith and Peter Sutcliffe had first met. And after work every Friday Keith and Patrick would take their guitars and a small amplifier up to Cornwall Road to 'rehearse' for a couple of hours in the Sutcliffes' kitchen. Peter didn't play anything himself but he didn't seem to want to; he was perfectly content to watch and listen to the 'group', although his father on odd occasions wouldn't be able to resist getting his harmonica out and joining in.

Although Peter always did his best to exclude them, the audience for these sessions sometimes included his sisters and their friends from a few doors away, Jacqueline, Colleen and Maureen, the Hawkes girls. At sixteen Doreen, their oldest sister, was too old to be running in and out of 57 Cornwall Road the way they always were, but Maureen Sutcliffe had an idea she would like to have been. Maureen had noticed Doreen Hawkes hanging around his motorbikes making him uncomfortable, and it had occurred to her that she might have her eye on their Peter. As it happened, though, it was Keith Sugden with whom Doreen finally took up.

Keith and Peter were coming home late one night, tearing up the steepest part of Cornwall Road more recklessly than they should have been, when the car suddenly rammed the kerb. Keith was badly shaken but Peter, who had been behind the wheel, thought it was a great joke. 'I thought he was going to bloody kill us, but he couldn't stop laughing. He thought it were hilarious. "Bugger car" was all he could find to say.'

It was next day, while they were changing the buckled wheels on the Morris, that Doreen Hawkes engaged them in conversation; and that night, the first of many, they went out as a threesome. Peter had just started working at the cemetery and he was quick to use the line, picked up from one of the older men, that was to be his stand-by on numerous future occasions. 'I've a *real* job,' was his reply when Doreen asked him what he did. 'I've five thousand under me and not one of them complains.' The little giggle that punctuated this remark was one that, repeated endlessly over the coming weeks and months, would begin to set Doreen's teeth on edge. Peter's only answer to anything, even the most innocent question, was that nervous, high-pitched, preoccupied laugh.

Although he didn't seem to mind in the slightest playing 'gooseberry' on their nights out at Dick Hudson's, a pub high on the moor, Doreen wondered why he bothered to come, when all he did was 'hear all, see all and say nowt'. Even when he gave her a lift up to Keith's house, he'd sit in the car and not say a word. Keith, feeling that his loyalty was being tested, explained that it was just Pete's way: 'I think he gets summat from people, does Peter. Something he needs. He's no good at mekkin' conversation himself, so he either sticks to a character that can or somebody that has a bit of personality in other ways. Something in him stops him being able to put his self forward, Dot. That's why he clings.'

But if Doreen came to a sort of grudging acceptance of Peter's odd little ways, her mother and her oldest sister never did. Mrs

Hawkes, who for a long time only knew him as the Sutcliffe lad who was always out messing with bikes, starting off thinking of Peter as 'the nice, quiet, sensible type'. The more she saw of him, though, the more she was irritated by his giggle and unnerved by the power of his dark, penetrating gaze, the more uneasy she became. And no amount of reassurance on her daughter's part could make the unease go away. It got to the stage where they started having rows about him coming to the house.

After Buddy Holly, the whimsical English 'folky', Donovan, was one of Peter's favourite singers and he used to love to sit in the Hawkes's living-room listening to Keith strum the guitar to some of Donovan's songs. The expression on Peter's face used to be so admiring that the women in the Hawkes family, judging this to be the perfect spot to drive in the wedge, started to pull Keith's leg when he turned up unaccompanied, asking him where his 'boyfriend' was tonight. It turned into such a running joke, it occurred to Keith that Peter, always so sensitive to atmosphere, so quick at weighing situations up, must know what was going on.

But whether he did or not, he suddenly did something totally out of character for him. Although neither of them had ever seen him on his own with a girl, he turned up to collect Keith and Doreen at Doreen's house one night with not one but two girls in tow whom he had picked up earlier at a pub in Keighley. Keith and Doreen recognised his companions at a glance for what they were – 'scrubbers'. But Peter seized on the first opportunity that came up to spell it out: 'They're on the game, y'know,' he grinned when the two women went to the toilet, which was enough for Doreen who, feeling that her own reputation was at stake, very coolly asked to be taken home.

'His idea were for me to kip wi' one, to be quite honest,' Keith remembers. 'He were supposed to go in bedroom at Cornwall Road with her mate an' I were supposed to stop in living-room. But I weren't right bothered an' her mate weren't right keen on him. She wanted to go home. Anyway, he took 'em back to Keighley and I went back round to Dot's. What he were trying to do was split me an' her, y'see. That were the thing.'

Doreen only ever went into the Sutcliffes' house with Keith once, and the visit helped terminate what was anyway becoming an impossible relationship with Peter. It was a Sunday afternoon and there was a pleasant atmosphere owing to the fact that Peter's father, replete with half a dozen pints and his usually huge Sunday dinner, was in an especially expansive mood. Keith was playing guitar and John Sutcliffe was singing, but Doreen, still only sixteen at the time, became increasingly agitated until she knew that she had to leave. 'He were eyeing me up and down and I felt so uncomfortable I had to get out,' was the only explanation she could offer Keith later. She said she felt Mr Sutcliffe was undressing her with his eyes.

Keith and Doreen became engaged soon afterwards and from then on they hardly ever saw Peter. They moved in with Doreen's parents after their marriage in 1968 but, although they were only living six doors away and lived there for eight months, they didn't see Peter once in all that time. It was as if, as they often remarked to each other, he'd disappeared off the face of the earth.

Peter's mother used to like it when he went around with Keith, as she once confided to Doreen after she'd become Mrs Sugden: Peter was very easily led, she said; he was influenced by who-ever's company he happened to be keeping, and Keith had always been so steady; Keith never ever brought any trouble home. Doreen took this to mean that Mrs Sutcliffe would have liked to have been able to say the same about Peter's current friends.

Keith Sugden knew Eric Robinson although there had been times when he could have wished this hadn't been the case. In the two weeks that Keith was 'sacking down' at the flat in Shipley, for example, Eric had gone berserk and half demolished the basement kitchen with a sledgehammer when he was 'stoated', and he also almost got them both locked up. Keith had answered a frantic hammering at the door at 2.00 one morning

55

to be confronted by Eric, who was in desperate need of a favour: he'd broken into the garage around the corner from where Keith was living, he explained, and had managed to drag the safe clear of the building, but now he needed a match to light the oxyacetylene set before he could proceed any further.

The result of his labours was a cash-box full of Balkan Sobranie packets which, in turn, were shown to contain nothing but dozens of Durex sheaths. The safe ended up in the canal, which is where most of the incriminating evidence from Eric's midnight sorties tended to come to rest: it was full of the bikes he'd stolen to ride back to Bingley from Saltaire on, after he had been to see his pal Laurie Ashton.

It was a consequence of such petty – sometimes farcical – crimes that Eric was repeatedly being sent to prison, where Peter would write keeping him abreast of the goings-on in the small world which they'd mapped out for themselves and which they'd reinhabit as soon as Eric was returned to freedom.

Eric, Peter and Laurie Ashton struck most of their contemporaries in Bingley as an odd threesome. When they weren't sitting in the bashed-up Chevrolet of Laurie's, running the electric windows up and down, they were parked by the juke-box in the King's Head or the Ferrands 'like three owd lads', elbows on knees, staring at the floor. They tended not to hang around Bingley too much, however, which reduced the likelihood of them getting involved in the brawls that were an essential feature of the town's social life.

Peter in particular liked to escape to Bradford or Halifax or Keighley, to one of the pubs or coffee-bars that had been added to their circuit of regular haunts. He wasn't a big drinker: three or four bottles of 'light' would do him, compared to Eric and Laurie's eight or nine pints, but he didn't need much to get him going: he'd get intoxicated on the atmosphere generated by the other two and seemed happy enough to enjoy himself vicariously through them.

Laurie, for instance, knew every song in the rock'n'roll canon after years of dedicated listening and sometimes, if he was drunk enough, would get up on the stage at The Bridge or Green Gates Working Men's Club in Bradford and give them his Gene Vincent or his Eddie Cochran. 'By God you've missed your way. You're better than Gene Vincent. Why don't you make a go of it?' Peter would enthuse afterwards, his already high-pitched voice rising higher with the excitement. And the same at the Ryshworth club at Crossflatts, just outside Bingley: Peter always stayed out of the limelight himself, but he loved to see Laurie and Eric get up in their crepes and drapes and do some 'boppin'.

The only area in which he allowed himself any sort of self-expression was his appearance, which was not only eye-catching but 'immaculate'. Off-white and black suits were his favourites, worn with drainpipe trousers and Cuban-heel boots, although for a few months, Peter, Eric and a married friend of Eric's affected a uniform which consisted of matching black trilbies with white bands, and black shirts with white 'slim Jim' ties, all from Greenwood's 'the men's outfitters' in Main Street in Bingley.

But whatever he wore, Peter still couldn't disguise his shyness. He came to Eric once with a story about being discovered in a friend's garage with a girl off the estate; and he told Laurie that he'd taken a fifth-form girl from the grammar school to Arnside for the weekend. And, while it was true that Laurie had seen him chatting to one of the pupils who used the cemetery as a short-cut, it was the first time he had ever seen Peter in conversation with any girl, and he turned crimson when he knew he'd been spotted.

It was in fact very easy to make Peter blush. 'Nuddy' books were always doing the rounds of the men at the graveyard but Peter never seemed sure what the appropriate reaction should be. He was even more thrown by the pictures that one of the older diggers carried in his wallet of his wife in a number of provocative poses in their bedroom.

Even out drinking with Eric and Laurie, usually in less-than-salubrious spots, he would try and observe the proprieties. He grew very uncomfortable if they started telling what he considered

57

dirty jokes within earshot of a woman; and any woman daring to 'come on strong', as he saw it, threw him into terrible confusions. 'Those two mates of yours are bloody useless,' a girlfriend of Laurie's reported back to him after a night out in the car with Eric and Peter. 'I stripped off last night an' neither of them would climb in back wi' me.' The most embarrassed Laurie ever saw him, though, was when a girl accused Peter, who was below her working in a grave at the time, of staring up her 'clouts': it seemed to Laurie that he would have liked to have buried himself in the hole.

Behind the wheel of a car or on the back of a bike were the only times Peter seemed even vaguely unselfconscious. He enjoyed the journeys to and from the 'Tomato Dip' in Skipton, the Gardeners' Arms in Keighley and the half a dozen other places where they were regulars, better than the 'socialising' that he merely endured in between. He was at his happiest 'doing a ton' on the Golden Mile outside Skipton on the racing-style Norton Dominator 600 that he ran for a while, with Eric hanging on behind and tears streaming off the back of both their heads.

With Eric, he took to siphoning petrol out of cars in and around Bingley and stealing wheels, which started to fill the coal shed at Cornwall Road. The two of them were apprehended tampering with the doors of a Bentley which was parked outside the White Horse one night but got off with a warning from the police and a piece of advice from Peter's father, who told them to be more careful in future.

Often in the course of an evening in one of the pubs, while Eric and Laurie were casting an eye over the 'talent' and daring one another to make the first move, Peter would slip away for an hour, scouting, as he explained to them later, for new places to go. This is how they became, first, regulars, and then virtually permanent fixtures at the Royal Standard, a handsome Edwardian pub on Manningham Lane in the cosmopolitan, northern part of Bradford.

Unlike other formerly elegant buildings in the area, which had been allowed to fall into neglect and disrepair, the Standard's engraved windows and mirrors and brass and mahogany fittings had been preserved intact, although, in order to attract younger customers, the landlord had been obliged to convert the long, central room of the pub into what was starting to be known as a 'disco'.

'Fisherman's Cove', as it was called, was the sort of place that would soon be reproduced in the backrooms of pubs the length and breadth of the country: there was a juke-box standing on a small platform, and a tiny linoleum dance floor; fishing-nets and corks hung from the walls; and there was a permanent, not unpleasant pitch darkness only barely relieved by a few strips of ultraviolet light. But in 1965 it was different enough to send Peter hurrying back to his friends in a state of some excitement with the news that he'd found a 'cracker' of a pub.

Within weeks, they had colonised one of the tables and sets of 'buffets' nearest the juke-box and christened it 'Gravediggers' Corner', because of the work that they all did: not only were Peter and Laurie digging graves together at Bingley, but Eric had been taken on at a cemetery in Bradford where he shared a house with a workmate who joined them most weekends at the Royal Standard, along with another gravedigger from the same cemetery, which in all made five. This, of course, gave them a ready-made 'line' when it came to approaching girls; and they literally carved their identity on the corner by scratching small black skulls and crosses and coffins all over the luminous green and orange plastic panels behind their heads.

For a long time, Peter seemed as at home in the half-dark at the Standard as they had ever seen him, and was even a party to their frequent practical jokes: Eric took advantage of the bleaching quality of the ultraviolet one time to free two or three white mice which achieved the intended aim of creating chaos; and on another occasion, Laurie, aided and abetted by Peter, succeeded in having the pub evacuated by setting off fumigators from the cemetery in the men's toilets. Gradually, though, the detachment which had always been Peter's main characteristic started to reclaim him.

He was well known for remembering and remarking on things that none of the others had even noticed. 'Hey, look at her,' he'd say, quite out of the blue, indicating a couple on the other side of the pub. 'He's talking to her and she isn't taking a blind bit of notice. She's looking at him over there.'

Similarly, other people's small vanities or physical peculiarities could start him off chuckling happily, even convulsively, to himself. 'I remember one day we were sitting in the King's Head in Bingley and this bloke walked in an' it were right amusing to Peter because he had his hair cut halfway up his head. He laughed like hell at this. In fact he were almost hysterical,' Eric Robinson says.

'You wouldn't really take much notice of these things, you'd be talking away to each other, but he'd just sort of sit and observe. I never actually saw him chat anybody up. I never actually saw him approach anybody. He was just generally observing all the time.'

It was when he was about nineteen or twenty that Peter's abstraction started to deepen into what to his friends seemed like semi-trances. Most of the time Peter's moods went unremarked, and usually unnoticed, but on one occasion in the Royal Standard his 're-entry' was memorably dramatic: for no apparent reason, he crashed a glass down violently on to the table in front of him, sending splinters flying in all directions. When he made no move to explain or apologise, a youth at a neighbouring table tipped a full pint over him, but he still just kept on staring ahead.

Shortly afterwards, again in the Royal Standard, Eric Robinson saw him do something equally irrational: 'Pete was walkin' behind this right big fat 'un who was on her way to toilet, followin' on with that stiff walk of his, when suddenly he just went boomph! Kicked her up the arse and sent her reelin'. And he got a right laugh out of that, did Pete. He found it rather funny.'

Peter was less 'purist' in his musical tastes than Eric and Laurie who, for the most part, lived through the English 'beat boom' of the 1960s as if it wasn't happening. Besides Donovan, he liked Bob Dylan, and in particular a song called 'Rainy Day Women

Numbers 12 and 35'. And he also liked the Rolling Stones – or, more exactly, a single record by the Rolling Stones that he played almost beyond endurance on the juke-box at the Gardeners' Arms in Keighley:

> Sittin', thinkin', sinkin', drinkin',
> Won'drin what I'll do when I'm through tonight
> Smokin', mopin', maybe just hopin'
> Some little girl will pass me by . . .
>
> Don't say Hi! like a spider to a fly
> Jump right ahead and you're dead
>
> Sit up, fed up, low down, go round
> Down to the bar at the place I'm at.
> Sittin', drinkin', superficially thinkin'
> About the rins'd over blonde on my left
>
> She was coming flirty, she looked about thirty
> I would have run away but I was on my own
> She told me later, she's a machine operator
> She said she liked the way I held the microphone
> I said my, my, my like a spider to a fly,
> Jump right ahead in my web.

Peter couldn't go to the Gardeners' Arms and not play 'Spider and the Fly'; and once he'd played it, he had to play it again.

Conversation at the Royal Standard tended to be sporadic because of the noise, but what little there was was nearly all about cars and bikes. And in the 'mess-room' at Bingley cemetery it was similarly unfocused chit-chat 'about summat an' nowt'. The only topic which, by an unspoken rule, never came up was the work: death and the dead were rarely, if ever, mentioned. On one occasion, however, a few months before Peter Sutcliffe was sacked from Bingley cemetery in 1967, that rule was broken.

The men were getting ready to start the day when Trevor Mitchell, the cemetery superintendent, stopped by the cabin with some sad news: old Ellis, one of the greenhouse staff, was dead, killed by a car the night before, walking home in the dark from Dick Hudson's, the pub on Rombald's Moor. His body was in the top chapel, the superintendent continued, if anybody wanted to go and see him to pay their last, private respects.

Nobody was very keen, Gary Jackson remembers, because, frankly, they were expecting the old man to be in a bit of a mess. Amazingly, though, they found Ellis lying on the slab as though he was just resting: Trevor Mitchell raised his head gently to show them how the single blow had killed him almost instantly, fracturing the back of the skull like an egg: 'Even his clothes weren't muckied or anything; none of us could get over the lack of blood.' Conversation kept returning repeatedly to this conundrum over the following days, and how it could be so.

8

Just after 11.30 a.m. on 22 April 1966, Fred Craven was battered to death in the betting office that he ran above an antique shop in Wellington Street in the centre of Bingley. Despite the hour and the widely circulated advice of the police that the attacker would be covered in blood, nobody was ever charged with Craven's murder. But Michael Sutcliffe, John Sutcliffe's second oldest son, was held for two days for questioning before being released.

He had come under suspicion because his blue denim cap had been spotted in the area at around the time Fred Craven had been killed, but it was eventually established that he hadn't been involved: he had simply happened to be in Wellington Street fetching fish and chips for the men at the factory where he had recently started work as an apprentice joiner. Nevertheless his detention came at a time when he was busy staking his claim to being one of the town's new 'hard men', and in this respect it did him no harm at all.

At sixteen, 'Mick' Sutcliffe, as he was always known, was more than four years younger and nearly five inches taller than his oldest brother, a fact which, usually good-naturedly but on occasion more forcefully, he never let Peter forget. He had first demonstrated that he was capable of 'dropping' Peter in the course of a tussle over two fish suppers that their mother had left in the oven one night, waiting for them coming home from the pub: being the first one in and being 'stoated', Mick had hurriedly cleared both plates and then denied that there had been anything to eat at all.

Hearing him coming upstairs, though, Mrs Sutcliffe had called out from her bedroom to ask Peter if he'd enjoyed his supper, which sent him flying back down to the kitchen. 'He took a swing at me, so I dropped one on him. I dropped him,' was

Mick's casual explanation for the damage inflicted by a right hand that within a very few years would floor the British professional heavyweight champion, Richard Dunn, although not in an orthodox fashion.

When he was twenty, a couple of friends persuaded Mick Sutcliffe to start training with them at Keighley Leisure Centre, where he soon found himself recruited as a sparring partner for the up-and-coming Dunn. He didn't take kindly, however, as he often recalled later, to being treated as a punchbag: 'Outside, I'd have knocked seven kinds of shit out of him. But in the ring it's different. He had all head-guard on an' gum-shield in because he couldn't afford to get broken nose off any of us; you couldn't get at his head for paddin'. An' he were jabbin' me an' jabbin' me till he bust me nose. So I thought, Fuck this, an' I gave him one. I went to dig him in his guts but instead I hit him in the bollocks an' he were straight on his arse. He were curled up wi' pain.'

It confirmed what, after years of practice, Mick already knew anyway to be true: that in fighting there's only one rule, and that's to win. 'Once you get him down, mek sure he stays that way. Use your feet, use anything you've got to keep him there,' was what he was repeatedly telling Peter. But a fight he had with a youth called Varley suggested that Peter was incapable of taking this advice in: he came back bruised and bloody when in his brother's opinion he could easily have won. Some months later, as it happened, Mick had the opportunity of showing Peter how it should be done: while Richard Varley was reaching for the card that proved he was a black-belt in karate Mick 'smashed' him in the face then 'booted' him for good measure to keep him down.

Mick Sutcliffe didn't exactly court trouble, but he didn't go out of his way to avoid it either – unlike Peter, whom Mick only ever actually saw in a fight once, when he was about nineteen. It was on the Waltzer at the fair that came to Bingley every year and was explosive but brief: Peter's nervousness had communicated itself to a gang of youths from Shipley who had taunted him so remorselessly that he'd uncharacteristically let fly at one of them with a punch that was powerful enough to lift the troublemaker clean over the barrier and at the same time break his own wrist.

Working with two railway wheels slotted on to either end of an old axle, as well as with the Bullworker, had given him the beginnings of what in time he'd develop into a 'power-house' physique, but he was still a stripling compared to Mick. Mick's boast was that he could put anybody in Bingley down in thirty seconds, and few were rash enough to try and make him prove it. Even Ken Eslin, who had successfully intimidated Peter Sutcliffe and most of the rest of the workforce at Fibre Products, learned not to tangle with Sutcliffe's younger brother.

He turned up at the door at Cornwall Road one night because Mick had taken his car and got mud on it, and lunged at him with a knife: 'He wasn't bothered about stabbing somebody or hitting them with a pick shaft. If he took a swing at you it'd be with a glass, an' he'd twist it right in an' think nothing about it. But once I got the knife off him, I told him, I said, "Next time, I'll fuckin' kill you. I'll beat you to fuckin' death." And I meant it, coming to the house and upsetting me mother like that.'

From their earliest days it had been as obvious to John Sutcliffe as it was to everybody else that Michael was made of tougher stuff than Peter. Peter was the one who'd half-choke on a boiled sweet watching his father perform in *Oklahoma*, whereas if Mick was going to choke on anything it would be – and was – a penny that he'd tossed up and caught in his mouth. 'Mick's always been a hard lad: big, robust, happy-go-lucky, the very antithesis of Peter, who was always the shivering wallflower, the bloke who would avoid confrontations with the rougher end.

'Mick was a different type of person altogether. He was the little devil you'd find ripping his leg open on barbed wire; the little rough lad who used to love to go out and play with the other kids. He always had a crowd of lads round him; there were always half a dozen of his ilk all screaming up and down the road. He was a lad who could always stick up for his self because he was always among the weight for age class, was Mick. He's never feared anybody in his life, whereas there's plenty round this way fear him.

'I mean, lads his age who fancy their chances don't tackle Mick. No way. Because, when it comes to throwing his weight about, he can throw it. And this town knows it.'

Academically, Mick Sutcliffe was always a non-starter. But, given his other attributes, his father didn't worry too much about it. There were always jobs around for big, healthy young men, was how he looked at it. And so it proved: Mick followed the money from site to site as a casual labourer and was able to say without a trace of self-pity that he'd spent his whole life 'digging holes'.

His lack of ambition showed itself in his appearance, which was as shambling and uncoordinated as his distinctive, forward-tilting walk. Unlike his father and his brother, who both cared about appearances and put a lot of thought into their clothes, Mick tended to throw on whatever came to hand, even if it wasn't his. He bought his annual suit from the back of the van that toured Ferncliffe Estate every year just before Christmas, but more often than not ended up going out in one of the jackets that Peter would have selected after much deliberation at Marks, the tailor in Bradford.

One of the reasons Peter favoured Marks was that they often gave something like a 'gold' watch away with purchases over a certain amount, and he was known for having an eye for bar-gains of this kind. He was famous for being 'careful' with his cash. It was a source of wonder to Eric and Laurie, as well as to his family, how he would always seem to have plenty left long after they were all 'spent up'.

Just how 'careful' Peter was was made graphically clear to Mick one night when he slipped on one of his brother's jackets to go down to the pub: 'I had about three quid on us, like, but you could get ten pints for a quid then. Ten pints an' twenty cigs. Anyway, first thing I noticed were a little note in one of jacket pockets which seemed to be a list of dates. Then in the inside pocket I noticed this bulge. When I took it out there were about twelve or fourteen wage packets, full, unopened, saved from previous weeks, which tallied wi' list of dates.' Judicious snipping removed the first entry on the list and guaranteed Mick a whole week of 'reet throw-jobs' – his definition of a good time.

By his late teens Mick developed a hiatus hernia which proved inoperable and caused him to be frequently sick. But he was a prodigious drinker and, after several hours 'suppin' – pints, usually, plus brandy-and-ports if he was in funds – would make himself vomit so that he could go back and sup some more. It was the sort of behaviour that got him frequent 'tongue-lashings' from Peter, especially as he grew older, but Mick's reply was always the same: 'You live your life, an' I'll live mine.'

Peter's 'responsible' outlook on life was as genuinely baffling to Mick as Mick's fecklessness appeared to be to his brother. 'He allus liked money,' Mick says. 'But, whereas such as me'd blow all lot in over weekend, he never seemed to get out and spend it so much. If he did go out he'd tek a quid an' probably bring about ten bob back with 'im. He were like a squirrel. He were allus a right bloody hoarder.'

Quiet, careful and dependable, Peter Sutcliffe drifted along unnoticed in the mainstream of Bingley life, while Mick was absorbed just as effortlessly into the other Bingley that the casual visitor didn't, and many of the permanent inhabitants preferred not to, see.

Along with West Royd Estate in Shipley and Eccleshill in Bradford, Ferncliffe Estate was regarded by the police as a forcing-ground for petty criminals. It was the boast of many older Bingleyites that they had never set foot there, while the younger ones daren't because of the estate's reputation for casual violence.

Not a few estate-dwellers, on the other hand, could make similar claims about their unfamiliarity with certain shops in the centre of town, like Beehive Modes and Luscombe's, and even certain town-centre pubs: they tended to keep to the Working Men's and Ex-Servicemen's clubs, and the more out-of-the-way pubs like the Granby, behind Dubb Lane Mills, and the Fisherman on the canal.

In all these places a thick skin, a sharp tongue and a strong stomach were the equipment necessary for survival, plus a more or less total disregard for what used to be called the 'tender virtues'. Any man who wore an earring, for instance, could expect to have it ripped out and the lobe daubed in whisky for 'healing'; anybody who betrayed any attention to the way he looked or any affection for the woman he nominally shared his life with – always referred to as 'the dragon' – could expect to be the target of derision.

Shared prejudices and a shared interest in 'fur and fowl' and firearms meant that the 'generation gap' supposedly rending the rest of the country was never apparent. Young men like Mick Sutcliffe and older men like Jack Hawkes, president of the British Whippet Racing Association, could go off to a dog show or on a trip to Blackpool together in perfect accord. 'Women are for frying bacon and screwin'' is the sort of thing they could both chuckle over while buying the big sticks of pink seaside rock known as 'wife-beaters' to take home.

'Laddish pranks' were something that nobody was disqualified from taking part in on the grounds of age, and few people were better at thinking them up than Jack and Mick. Jack acquired a parcel of guts one time from his brother who worked in the slaughterhouse and sent them to one of their crowd who'd been waiting patiently to hear from an 'old tart' that he'd had a dalliance with on an organised day-out.

On another occasion they'd enjoyed themselves at the expense of one of the pleasure-craft owners who'd steeled himself and stopped off at the Fisherman on his way down the canal. A group of them had engaged him in pleasant conversation and watched while he tried to work out a way of pocketing a wallet bulging with scraps of newspaper that Mick had planted by the leg of his chair. Once he'd left they'd followed at a discreet distance and roared at his discomfort when he finally sneaked a look, only to find the message 'We've been watching you, you bastard' scribbled inside.

For more than a hundred years the mills and the other activities associated with the woollen trade had tended to obscure the fact that a significant number of Bingley people earned their living on the land. But as the industry had declined throughout the 1960s and weeds started to choke once thriving mill yards, so conversation in the pubs seemed to increasingly turn around 'lamping' and ferrets and other rural concerns.

Even in the seventies, a pony tethered to the bar at the Fleece or to a fence in Cornwall Road could go virtually unremarked. And a surprising number of the old ways hung on. An old woman who was an immediate neighbour of the Sutcliffes, for instance, believed that even factory-farmed chickens should be buried in the garden for a few days to get them 'ripe', which was also the thinking behind hanging hares out in the open to let the maggots do their work. The washing-line outside the Hawkes' house was often hung with rabbit-skins, and inside many a handbag and trouser pocket all over the estate was the inevitable 'lucky' rabbit's paw.

Mick Sutcliffe was the odd one out in his family in that he was the only one who was a countryman at heart – or a 'yokel' in the words of his father, who felt that a gamekeeper or a farmer's lad is what Mick should really have been. 'His pride and joy was to get up in a morning at half-past-four and take his dog out in the country and catch half a dozen rabbits while the dew was still on the grass. And it still is, actually. It's his way. He puts more effort into doing a bit of rabbiting while it's still dark than most working men put into an eight-hour day.'

There was nothing John Sutcliffe liked better than a nice rabbit freshly gutted and skinned and cooked into a pie or a stew but, in common with the rest of his family, he couldn't stand the ferrets whose smell seeped in through the back of the house, or the lurcher that was constantly getting under his feet: Mick was forever having stand-up rows with his father about him kicking the dog.

Peter, too, was less than fond of it, but then he could claim to have good reason. Even as adults the two brothers slept in the same double bed which, whenever he could get away with it, they also shared with Mick's dog: 'If I went to bed an' our lad hadn't come in, if he were out down Bradford or summat, I'd get dog in, get him against wall side, right cuddled up there, then Pete'd arrive. "That dog isn't in there, is it?" he'd say, an' I'd say no; it'd be just laid right quiet there until he pulled back the clothes, when it'd start. I used to jump at our lad then. If they don't like them, okay, but there's no need to bloody hurt them.'

On the nights when he was planning to get up in the early hours to go poaching Mick would flop into bed fully clothed, right down to his wellington-boots with a ferret writhing inside its draw-string bag on the floor beside him; by opening time he'd be dumping upwards of a dozen rabbits on the bar counter, ready cleaned but unskinned to prove that they were the genuine article and not, as had been known to happen, 'moggies'. Poaching was one way he had devised of supplementing his income when he was working, and his dole money on the increasingly frequent occasions as the years went on when he wasn't; and picking over the rubbish on the council tip was another.

Within minutes of the gates being closed at the 'waste management site' at Dowley Gap, on the canal bank opposite the Fisherman, the skips were alive with people 'rooting', but few of them had Mick Sutcliffe's nose. Gold bracelets, cigarette lighters, solid sliver picture-frames 'wi' dogs' heads an' all that all the way round' were some of the 'finds' that he reckoned brought his accumulated earnings from this source up to something like £2,000. Strictly speaking, of course, he was breaking the law, and John Sutcliffe received a great deal of sympathy from his friends in the Musical Union and at the cricket club for the antisocial behaviour of his son. Combing the tip, however, was one of the least illegal activities in which Mick was involved.

He had been arrested for the first time when he was thirteen for breaking into a youth club and stealing boxes of crisps and 'pop', and had been in trouble with the police more or less constantly ever since. He had convictions for robbery, assault, actual bodily harm and grievous bodily harm, and by his mid-twenties would have spent four consecutive Christmases in Armley jail. It should have been five, however, as he is the first to admit:

'The way I worked it most of the time is, I'd spot something handy that was worth a bit of summat and just put me boot or a rock through shop window at night on the way home. I didn't tek it back wi' me to Cornwall Road, though. I had a little storage place an' lads who wanted gear used to come an' collect it there. I had buyers all over an' there was never any come-back off of any of them.

'This particular Christmas Eve, though, I were with another three an' it were about ten o'clock at night when we kicked window through an' just climbed in. I ended up wi' a pile of boxes up past me chin – shirts, jumpers, pants, boots – an' they must've thought I'd just been shopping because nobody took any notice of me as I were walking home.

'"Here," I said, an' I gave me father a jumper, for Christmas, like, an' our Peter an' me mother an' the lasses, an' I kept one mesen. But two of these other silly cunts that were wi' me, they walk straight into King's Head wi' all their clobber an' start floggin' it in there. Naturally it's only half an hour afore they get done. It's two days before they oppen their mouth on me though, so it's Boxing Day an' I'm wearing one of the jumpers, which they fail to notice, when they pull us in. Me lawyer put it down to high spirits of the season an' we got away with a fine.'

Occasionally John Sutcliffe would express his half-hearted disapproval of the way various members of his family were conducting their lives, but his own occasional, aberrant lapses meant that he had forfeited the right to criticise anybody, at least in Mick's eyes. 'He turns round to me an' says, "You're goin' crackers, you; you're getting worse as you go on." An' two weeks later he gets fuckin' caught nickin' a load of silver hissen coming down Sherriff Lane, coming home from some cricket do in early hours of the mornin'. I can remember me mother shoutin' and bawlin' an' playin' hell. He'd even tekken a kettle for some stupid reason. He were pissed up.'

In the same way that he'd stood up to the priest at Cottingley Manor Secondary Modern, whom he accused of trying to 'indoctrinate' him, Mick stood up to his father, who had a tendency to throw his weight about in the house when he was drunk, in a way that Peter couldn't. But this only partly explained the grudging admiration, almost bordering on envy, that those who knew both brothers detected in Peter. Certainly they could hardly have offered a greater contrast in styles: Mick ebullient, profligate, loose-limbed, staggering home broke; Peter taciturn, temperate, inhibited, perched nervously on the edge of his chair.

His inability to relax, even when sitting in front of the television, was something that had come to seem so much a part of Peter's nature that it had long ago ceased to be commented on at home. Nobody could ever remember seeing him just lounging around: he always sat up erect with both feet firmly on the ground, swivelling his eyes to left or right whenever anybody spoke to him, rather than turning his head.

Just how tense Peter was was always particularly apparent to Mick on the rare occasions when he joined him in the Fisherman for a drink. 'I allus knew he were a bit tensed up. He'd come in an' sit with his hands on his knees, right sort of stiff so's you'd feel like saying, "For fuck's sake, relax!" On the other hand, after he'd had a few beers he used to go to opposite extreme.

'He didn't sup much because he couldn't handle pop. He only used to sup a few light bottles. But if I got him on pints, that were it. He'd get right over-excited more than owt, laughing and talking and telling jokes. And once he started laughing you might as well forget it then, because it'd be a ten-minute job. It were one of them laughs where it screeches out; he'd shout out like a right shrill shriek an' the whole pub'd look round. He'd just let it go when he were popped. He didn't bother then.'

In the company of his brother Peter enjoyed a sort of delayed adolescence, travelling up to North Yorkshire on poaching trips in an old van packed to overflowing with town tearaways and guns from Mick's 'armoury' (although it was clear to anybody that Peter didn't know a curlew from a pheasant). Drinking also became less hazardous in the pubs around Bingley for Peter and his pals Eric and Laurie, given Mick Sutcliffe's growing reputa-

72

tion. But Peter would also try and impress his brother with his own 'credentials'.

Mick got the story about the bag of rings collected from bodies in the graveyard, although he was never shown any hard evidence; and he was given a late-night tour of the town mortuary where Peter walked fearlessly up to a body in a shroud, his footsteps echoing off the cold stone, while Mick prepared to run.

It was riding pillion behind him on one of his motorbikes, though, that made Mick realise that Peter had a daredevil side: 'It's okay if you go on a motorway or summat, but it were ridiculous the speeds he used to go up and down these roads. I've seen him come round on to Cornwall Road at ninety after he's tekken us out for a spin round, then ride bike into the house an' up stairs.'

When Mick was about seventeen, Peter decided to introduce him to Bradford and to the city-centre pubs that he'd spent the past two or three years discovering for himself. After a couple of drinks he'd demonstrate how to go about chatting up a girl. 'If you play your cards right tonight you could have me,' was his usual tack, and Mick usually wasn't the only one who remained unimpressed: 'It didn't exactly come to him as if he had a born ability to do it.' Occasionally, though, he'd get far enough to arrange a date and come home a few nights later raving to Mick about what a good time he'd missed.

Mick, in fact, had had sex for the first time when he was sixteen, which he was confident put him several years ahead of his brother; and he'd gone with his first prostitute when he was seventeen, several years before Peter was to drive him through the red-light district of Bradford with the triumphant air of someone revealing a secret world.

The overcrowding and their mother's perpetual presence should have made the conduct of a private life difficult, if not impossible, at Cornwall Road but, to Keith Sugden, Laurie Ashton and other visitors, the opposite seemed to be the case. 'Come up any time you like, lad, and bring a girlfriend,' was an invitation that, coming from John Sutcliffe, caught Laurie slightly off-guard; but Keith had already taken advantage of the prevailing permissive atmosphere to consummate a relationship with one of Maureen Sutcliffe's older friends.

When Maureen became pregnant herself at sixteen, however, her mother reacted in what she couldn't help thinking was a wholly unreasonable way; she couldn't have been unaware, after all, that for some time Maureen had been sleeping with the baby's father: 'In lots of ways she were an exceptional person, me mother. She were right patient and a right good mum. But you couldn't sit down and talk to her – at least you couldn't about anything that *mattered*.

'She could feed us and clothe us and look after us materially, but she just didn't seem to have enough discipline to cope. She just couldn't handle us six kids. She worked too hard and she'd too much to do at home. She had it all to do herself and she had no control. She'd do owt for a quiet life.'

Much to everybody's surprise, Maureen's father didn't blow up when he found out that she was having a baby. In fact, he was surprisingly 'modern' about it all: she didn't have to get married, he assured her, unless she really wanted to; and when she said she really did, he did all he could to smooth the way.

John Sutcliffe had never sat down and discussed the facts of life with any of his children, but then his father never had with him. A joke that he used to sometimes like to tell summed up his whole approach: 'This little feller comes home and his dad says to 'im; "Now then, son, do you know anything about the facts of life?" And little lad turns round to his old man and says, "Yes, Dad, what do you want to know?"'

'Sex education', in other words, was another newfangled idea that 'those do-gooders' who believed that corporal punishment in schools was unnecessary and out of date had made their minds up to promote. 'I mean,' he'd say, 'it comes to everyone in their life. As you develop you find these things out. You hear all about it in the school playground and you sort the wheat from the chaff as you go along. It's the way that it's been done for hun-

dreds of years. Then suddenly these people in the higher eche-
lons of education are saying, "Well, if the parents aren't doing it,
we must do it in the schools." So fair enough, they're being
taught by people who are supposed to be able to explain it in
proper terms.'

In the case of his own children, however, the 'proper terms'
were not primarily addressed to the mechanics of sex but to the
ethics of it and came circumscribed by the attitudes of the Roman
Catholic Church: Peter and his brothers and sisters were taught
by the teachers at Cottingley Manor Secondary Modern that sex
should take place within marriage and in order to produce children, full stop. There could be no room for 'ifs' and 'buts'. How
the Sutcliffe girls resolved this dilemma was to declare themselves 'lapsed' as soon as they had left school. Only as adults
would they begin to recognise the truth of the saying that 'Learning in childhood is like engraving a stone.'

Mrs Sutcliffe certainly had difficulty curbing the energies of
Anne, her oldest daughter, who, at seventeen, had grown tall
and voluptuous-looking and enjoyed a reputation among Keith
Sugden and others of Peter's friends for being 'lively as a lop'.
Sugden was round at Cornwall Road at about 7.00 one evening
when Anne was shut up in her bedroom with a youth from up
the street: 'Her mother was screamin' and shoutin' at her to
oppen door, but she wouldn't an' in the end Peter just turned to
me an' said, "Oh c'mon, let's go." He left soup he'd been heatin'
up in pan.'

Mick, of course, in this as in all things, was a law unto himself. 'It were a bit awkward. You could never get the house on
your own or anything, because me mother never went out apart
from shopping and mebbe on her birthday when me father'd
tek her down for a drink. But I thought "Bugger 'em", like. I'd
just get a chair an' lock it under handle so they couldn't come in
while I were bullin', an' dive straight into bed.' On at least one
occasion, though, these precautions proved inadequate because
Carl, Mick's six-year-old brother, was already in the room, concealed on the top of the big old wardrobe with a pal. Things had

progressed too far for the boys to reveal themselves when they realised, as a result of Mick staggering over to the window to be sick, that his partner was the sister of Carl's friend.

It wasn't unheard of for Peter to be with a girl: Mick or Maureen would occasionally come across him in the kitchen or the coal-house 'snogging' with somebody off the estate. He always seemed more dutiful than driven in his courting, however, and never had a 'steady' girlfriend.

One night, a few months before his twenty-first birthday, though, Peter came home in a particularly exuberant mood. He'd met a 'right buer', he enthused to Mick in their bedroom, and went on to describe his elaborate method of picking her up: he'd spilled half a pint down her skirt deliberately and then insisted on taking her home on his motorbike to change. She'd then gone back into Bradford with him to the Royal Standard and had promised to see him again at the end of the week . . .

The word 'buer', though, which he'd never heard before, is what Mick's mind stuck on, and how unnatural it sounded falling from his brother's lips. He was like a sponge, always picking expressions up from other people, was Mick's last thought, as he grabbed his share of the bed-clothes, turned over and went to sleep.

9

It had always been a matter of pride to Eric and Laurie and their regular crowd at the Royal Standard that they were considered out-of-step with the times. But by 1967, in their greased quiffs and 'beetle-crushers' and Edwardian-style, velvet-trimmed coats, they were starting to look like the relics of an age that a growing number of drinkers in the pubs around Bradford knew only by reputation.

It was in retaliation to the 'psychedelic' fashions and the increasingly 'progressive' music that was so offensive to their ears, therefore, that 'the gravediggers' decided to organise rock'n'roll revival evenings of their own. The landlord of the New Miller's Dam made a room available and they booked in only those local groups with a solid, Gene Vincent–Little Richard–Jerry Lee Lewis-based repertoire.

Although it occurred to Laurie that Peter didn't 'over-enjoy' this kind of primitive noise, preferring 'softer', more melodic music, he was happy as usual to tag along: he tapped his feet appreciatively, cultivated more or less the right 'look' and took the money on the door when it was his turn. What he did seem to like was being able to say he knew Dave Lee of the Dave Lee Sound, a Shipley boy to whom he helped deliver a battered piano on the back of a coal wagon once, and members of the various other semi-professional outfits who turned up to play.

But his main qualification for inclusion continued to be his knowledge of, and enthusiasm for, motorcars and bikes, and a genuine rocker's addiction to speed. Given the choice between a pub and a bikers' 'caff', he'd invariably choose somewhere like the Tomato Dip where the conversation could be relied on to follow reassuringly predictable lines. Peter and Eric, who was his usual companion on these jaunts, could talk effortlessly, and endlessly, about revs and cylinders and cams, in an environment heavy with the smell of cooking-fat and exhaust fumes, whereas social encounters in general tended to make them clam up. Small-talk was not their forte, as anybody attempting to engage them in it quickly found out. Peter would lurch from taciturnity to over-excitement, sweating heavily and tripping over his words, while Eric expressed himself in a broad and soporific Yorkshire drawl.

Occasionally, and always on the strength of half a dozen pints of bitter, Eric would saunter up and ask the barmaid to 'Gimme a Luger-an'-lime', wild-West fashion. And on one occasion, having deviated from their normal route, he persuaded Peter to join him in 'taking off a couple of Yanks': they stood at the bar talking in heavily affected American accents which, Peter led Eric to believe, had the whole pub taken in.

Taking a rise out of 'Robbo' which, especially in mixed company, is something Peter frequently did, didn't mean, however, that he didn't like him; on the contrary, he found him undemanding company and a good foil, as the letters which he wrote to him in prison showed. It was when Eric was away serving one of his periodic sentences that Peter's dependence on him always became most pronounced.

Eric spent the first part of 1967 in Armley jail, which meant that, on weekends at the Royal Standard, Peter was left to fend for himself. What made it worse was that, by this point, most of his acquaintances were courting, and that included Laurie Ashton. For some months, Laurie had been going out with a girl called Cath, always known as 'Lupin' because of her slight build, and Cath had taken her place in 'Gravediggers' Corner' along with Christine, her friend. The difficulty was that, although Christine was attractive and unattached and theoretically 'available', she resisted all attempts to pair her off with Peter.

In fact, shortly after Laurie and Cath had taken up with each other, Christine had accepted a few drinks from Laurie's shy friend, but she'd caught the last bus home with Cath to Heckmondwike, and Cath had drawn her own conclusions from that:

whenever Christine found somebody she 'fancied', she tended to spend the night in some old rolling stock in a siding not far from the Standard, even though this inevitably brought her parents down to the pub searching for her the following night.

The truth was that there was something about Peter that Christine found eerie; she couldn't put her finger on it, but there was something about him that seemed to her not quite right. And, unfortunately, Cath agreed. He had never done or said anything to make her dislike him, but she always took care to make sure that the 'buffet' she was sitting on wasn't next to his.

From a distance, Peter struck most women as an attractive proposition; and many men were openly envious of his dark and broody good looks. Close to, however, as Cath discovered she wasn't alone in noticing, the collective features became most overpowering and, as they competed with each other for attention, seemed to assume independent existences of their own. The eye had difficulty reconciling them into a single picture and so tended to concentrate on them individually instead.

Cath knew from Laurie how long Peter spent in the bathroom before coming out at night, and both his hair and his beard were testimony to this obsessive preening: piled up in 'right knitty little curls like a Jamaican's', his hair looked strangely square-shaped, like a dense black hedge on his head; while the black beard that was sometimes strapped to the sideburns and sometimes not was always 'trimmed up like a masterpiece', regardless.

His teeth were even and spade-shaped but failed to meet at the front where there was a fleshy gap that he plugged with his tongue. And his eyes, which were the first thing everybody noticed, were bulbous and bloodshot and 'near-on-black'. Trying to keep track of their movements when conducting a conversation with him could make you dizzy, because they darted about so much, sneaking glances at everything in the room except your face.

Cath tried explaining all of this to Laurie, but he couldn't see it and it seemed to her you had to be a woman to understand. It also irritated her the way Peter was so polite and over-solicitous and even blushed on her behalf. The fact of the matter was that, as a mill-girl with twelve brothers and sisters, she wasn't unused to blue humour and salty language and was perfectly capable of – quite enjoyed, in fact – giving as good as she got. In this she was as typical of the girls who went to the Royal Standard as the girl who Peter appeared with out of the blue one night was not.

It was clear from the minute they saw her that Sonia didn't – and, more importantly, had no wish to – fit in. At sixteen, she was below the legal minimum age for drinking, but she certainly wasn't alone in that; what made her different was the way she hadn't gone to town with lipstick and mascara and chalky eyeshadow to disguise the fact that she was still at school. Every aspect of her appearance, in fact, suggested a girl who had been brought up in the Czechoslovakia that her parents had fled twenty years earlier, rather than one who had grown up just a few bus-stops away from the pub.

Her clothes, compared to the rather daring minis and stilettos that all the girls in Peter's crowd were wearing, looked lumpy and old-fashioned in a way that suggested that they were probably home-made. She was short and quite tubby and wore her hair 'in a sort of longish Afro' that, unlike Cath's and the other girls' elaborate beehives, didn't demand regular repair; the way she refused to stand and gossip in front of the mirror in the Ladies' at the Standard didn't win Sonia many friends, but then making friends of the regulars in 'Gravediggers' Corner' didn't seem to be one of her priorities.

She was as unamused by their conversation as by the tricks they got up to, such as igniting lighter-fuel on their breath and filing half-penny pieces down into 'shillings' to keep the jukebox fed. Like Peter, she was a curious combination of shyness and hauteur and very quickly succeeded in opening up a physical distance between him and his erstwhile friends. They started perching together on the platform that supported the juke-box rather than at the tables with the rest and, by the time Eric was released from Armley, they had taken to sitting off in a far corner by themselves.

They would be among the first in when the doors of the Standard were opened in the evening, and were cosily ensconced in the near-total darkness by the time the others arrived. The bond between them was now fortified by the barrier that they'd erected and both seemed to suggest that Peter and Sonia had found 'the real thing'. On at least one occasion the manager of the Standard felt obliged to remind them they were in public when all the signs were that they were getting carried away.

'You don't get a courtship like that, kissing and cuddling all the time,' Eric Robinson says. 'We just used to come in an' say, "'Ey up, they're at it again" and it seemed to go on all night long. They seemed to feel they were on their own.'

To Cath, soon to become Mrs Laurie Ashton, the Royal Standard represented the best days of her life; she was conscious, even as she lived it, that her time would never be so much her own again. For Sonia, though, it was merely an interlude, and all the good times lay ahead. 'The girlfriend will end up getting a right good job when she comes out of college,' Peter would say to Laurie. 'She's going to end up with a *real* job.' But Laurie wasn't in the least envious. It seemed to him that Peter could be getting in 'above his head'.

Sonia Szurma was born three years after her parents arrived in Britain from Czechoslovakia in 1947. Christened 'Oksana', she was officially renamed as she approached school age and her parents started to readjust – or resign themselves to – their new life.

Bohdan Szurma, who described himself on his daughter's birth certificate as 'woolcomb box minder', one of the dreariest, poorest-paid jobs in the mill, was a former physical education teacher who claimed descent from an aristocratic Ukrainian family. It was a descent, however, which Sonia's future father-in-law, for one, would always remain loudly sceptical about.

'He's supposed to be able to speak seven languages fluently. Well all I can say is, one of them isn't English. But you know what these communist countries are like,' John Sutcliffe would tell his friends. 'They give themselves a degree or some other fancy title if they think they deserve it. All I know is that he's never held a job down so long as I've known him. He came over here and saw what you could get and jumped on the bandwagon of the Welfare State.'

Although Mr Szurma upgraded his occupation to 'yarn tester' in later life, he never went out to work after the late 1950s because of ill health. His wife's job as a nursing auxiliary in a local private hospital was the family's main source of income, and he concentrated all his energies into helping Sonia and her older sister, Marianne, make their way in the world.

The council house in Clayton, a quiet, semi-rural suburb in the south of Bradford to which the Szurmas moved from the transit camp near York which had been their first home, became a small monument to Bohdan Szurma's austere, almost ascetic approach to life. Literature, chess and classical music were offered as substitutes for television, which wasn't allowed in the house. Most meals were taken from the same pot of goulash which was made on Sundays and stood on the stove all week, while the stove itself, a spotless but ancient mottled enamel model, was for more than twenty years, and even in the coldest winters, the main source of heat.

The kitchen, although cramped and spartanly furnished, was where the family spent most of their evenings and where visitors (a rare occurrence) were entertained. It was where Peter's parents on their only visit drank home-made wine ('an instant job – nice colour to it, but it wouldn't make you turn a hair; make you go to the toilet, that's all') and sat elbow-to-elbow eating their pink 'chewy soup'. Sonia's father, meanwhile, paced restlessly backwards and forwards in an adjoining, equally spartan room.

The Szurmas were on friendly but formal terms with their neighbours, who were kept at a distance, and Mr Szurma lived virtually a recluse's life. He rarely ventured further than the local shops and the Ukrainian Association, and he expected his daughters, who were discouraged from bringing friends home, to do the same. Marianne and Sonia were sometimes seen playing tennis in front of Tanton Crescent with their father dressed rather formally in white shorts, but most nights found them, again under paternal supervision, poring over their books.

Marianne responded well to the pressure to succeed, sailed effortlessly through school and became a graduate of the Royal Academy of Music. Sonia, though, was by comparison an under-achiever and therefore a constant source of disappointment to her father. Although she did well enough in the 11-Plus to get to Grange, the girls' grammar school near Clayton, she consistently failed to make the top stream and felt she was condemned to struggle in her 'brilliant' sister's shadow all her life.

So frustrated was Mr Szurma by what he considered Sonia's poor performance that he regularly checked her attendance record with her teachers and always took particular care to confirm that she was where she said she was whenever there was a school trip. During the breakdown that she was to suffer some years later, Sonia became inseparable from an old pop music annual that seemed to have become for her the symbol of her insular and in many ways deprived early years: she had saved for weeks to buy the book out of her pocket-money, only to have it immediately confiscated by her father for being cheap and frivolous and unsuitable in every way.

By the time Sonia was sixteen the independent streak that he had probably always suspected had begun to surface. But a disco-theque at a pub in the centre of Bradford still isn't somewhere that Bohdan Szurma would have expected to find his youngest daughter on St Valentine's night, 1967, four months before she was due to take her CSE examinations. And it wouldn't be until the exams were over, and the six passes that she needed in order to progress to the technical college secured, that Sonia would take the bold step of introducing her father to the polite, dark-eyed young man with whom she was so clearly enthralled. Within just a few weeks of meeting her, however, Peter took Sonia back to Bingley to show her off.

For all Peter's timidity and sensitivity as a boy, his aversion to

83

sports and his close attachment to his mother, it never occurred to John Sutcliffe that Peter – or any son of his – could turn out to be less than 100-per-cent 'normal' (or a 'puff', 'bum boy' or 'bender' as homosexuals are invariably called in Bingley). 'All my boys are boys, and all my girls are girls, and there's nothing in between with any of them,' he says firmly. 'Peter was just a quiet little lad, that's all. He didn't have any sort of . . . *affectations*. None at all. He had no affectations whatsoever.'

Nevertheless, relief was one of the emotions that Mrs Sutcliffe at least experienced when, without any prior warning, Peter came in one Sunday afternoon and quite simply said, 'Mum, this is Sonia.' The 'Hello' that Sonia permitted herself on that occasion was virtually the only word she addressed to anybody other than Peter, and on future visits she was hardly more forthcoming. But they put it down to the strangeness of her surroundings, and to her youth, and took it for granted that time was all she needed to unbend.

'She's just a quiet, shy girl who probably doesn't like expressing herself in front of other people,' Peter's father reassured his mother, who kept an open house, like everybody in Cornwall Road, and was used to people just 'mucking in'. The fact that Sonia *was* capable of expressing herself – and he took it on trust that she must be able to if she was planning to become a teacher – seemed to John Sutcliffe a distinct improvement over most of those whom Peter had previously chosen to call his friends.

'Basically, I don't know where he found a lot of them, but they didn't seem to have achieved the same level of education as he had. He could talk much *better* than they could. He wasn't a speaker of BBC English or anything like that, but at least he had no difficulty in making himself understood. Eric Robinson and people like that, they had very great difficulty stringing two words together, never mind speaking an intelligent sentence.

'Peter had the mental capacity to do better than a lot of the stick-in-the-muds he was knocking about with, and he probably knew that. A lot of them would stick with what they were doing for the rest of their lives, and just *do* it. But he wasn't content. He had a goal in his mind. He was going to do better. There was never any doubt in Peter's mind that he was going to get on, but there's no disgrace in that. Everybody should think that way.'

As the father of six children who wouldn't be able to muster a 'paper' qualification between them, John Sutcliffe started off well disposed towards the girl who, if Peter's proprietary, slightly overweening attitude was anything to go by, was destined to become his daughter-in-law. But as the expected breakthrough with Sonia failed to happen, Peter's father, in common with the rest of the family, started to find his patience running out. 'How the devil is that girl going to make a school teacher? How is she going to do it?' he'd wonder in exasperation at the end of another day in which Sonia would have done nothing but sit and twiddle her thumbs. 'She just doesn't have any conversation.'

She didn't seem to want to talk, and when she did it was in a whisper, so that, half the time, you couldn't hear what she was saying. What they had been prepared to overlook as shyness after several months started to look like arrogance; the popular interpretation of the sullen reserve which Sonia so effortlessly maintained was that she was sitting in judgement on them.

After the discipline and quiet of her own home, 57 Cornwall Road must have seemed like a bazaar. Through back and front doors, and even windows, there flowed a constant traffic of children and animals and neighbours and noise that continued long after it was dark. But by 1967, the overcrowding was marginally less than it might have been because, after six months living at Cornwall Road with her new husband, Anne, Peter's oldest sister, had recently moved out into a place of her own. Jane, the youngest of the girls, was ten; and Maureen, the closest in age to Sonia, a precocious fourteen. When, within two years, Maureen had her first baby, it emphasized the gulf which existed between them.

Unlike Peter, who bombarded her with baby-talk and wet-nursed Rachel 'like a woman', Sonia made her lack of interest plain; persuaded to hold the baby on one occasion, she simply opened her arms and dropped it when it started to cry, letting it fall heavily into a pram, which hardly endeared her to its mother.

Twelve years later Maureen would still feel that she had never got to know Sonia – or, rather, that Sonia had 'never taken the trouble' to get to know her. 'When they stayed with me in Cambridge on the way to their honeymoon, she turned to me and said, "You've got a lovely home. You're a lovely cook," like she was right surprised or something. I think she had me written off as some kind of gad-about right from the start.'

Maureen's first impression of Sonia was of 'a right quiet prim little miss; ever so serious'. To Mick, though, she was simply 'a robber's dog'. That first night, when he'd come home full of talk about the 'buer' he'd picked up, Peter had gone to great lengths to emphasise the coup he'd pulled off by snatching Sonia from under the noses of his friends. 'They were all after chatting her up,' he'd said. But Mick found it hard to believe it could be the same girl sitting in their front room. Putting it crudely, he thought she 'looked like a fuckin' horse.'

Mick took an instant dislike to Sonia, who was exactly three weeks older than himself, and the feeling, it soon became clear, was entirely mutual. An incident that took place on one of her earliest visits helped set the seal on what was always to be an uneasy relationship, no matter how badly Peter wanted them to get on.

'She said to me mother one day, an' she'd only been in house on three or four visits then, she says: "Will you make me a cup of tea, without any sugar, please?" We all looked round, like. Is she talking to me? I thought, Bloody hell, what a pillock. Any other lass'd probably say, "D'you mind if I put the kettle on. I'm a bit dry?" But it was: "Will you get up and make me cup of tea?" Sort of, *Now*! She were *really* highly strung.'

At the heart of the problem – and it was a feeling that Mick shared to a greater or lesser extent with all the rest of his family – was that Sonia seemed to radiate disapproval. People tended to feel inhibited by her presence in a room. 'If I'd had a few

86

whiskies an' pints an' that an' started to tell a few jokes and act a *bit* silly, like you do, she couldn't fuckin' understand it, how I were like that. 'Cause she'd still be dead sober, an' our Peter wouldn't have had much. I don't think she liked people drinking alcohol. Unless she made it an' it were home-made wine or summat. Her father did, and she'd have a drop of that at home. But she certainly thought she was *well* above everybody else. That's what I couldn't stand.'

Although he toned down his behaviour slightly in the early days of their courtship to spare Peter's blushes, John Sutcliffe wasn't the type to let a visitor – certainly not a sixteen-year-old female one – cramp his style. Sunday, which is when Sonia was normally there, was the one day in the week that he liked to indulge himself. After working four thirteen-hour shifts on four consecutive nights, at the end of which he'd fall into bed and sleep for twenty-four hours, he felt he ought to be able to let his hair down. On Saturdays, he'd enjoy a game of football or cricket and eat very little in order to make the most of his 'big drink night'. Then on Sunday, after choir duty at St Wilfrid's and another couple of hours in the pub, he'd really 'set out a stall'.

'This should be enough to keep the Biafran army on the march for a month,' he'd say, attacking a small hillock of meat and vegetables and gravy with a fortress of Yorkshire pudding on the top that at the Szurmas' would have been made to serve four. What Sonia, and even Mrs Sutcliffe, who'd cooked it, didn't know, was that the 'beef' with 'such a lovely colour to it' was, more often than not, grade-A horsemeat that a friend of John's who bred Yorkshire terriers had got him from the pet shop.

'Never eat owt me dad gives you,' Carl would warn people, only half-jokingly, after seeing his father scoop a dead pigeon up off the road and drop it into the pot. But John was always eager to share the passion for 'esoteric' foods, mainly offal, that he had inherited from his grandfather. 'If you can drink water, you can eat tripe. It's only like solid water: it doesn't *taste* of anything,' are the words that would often accompany the pleasurable squelch of best 'honeycomb' being chewed. 'You've to put salt and vinegar on to mek it taste of owt, but then it tastes *beautiful*.'

It irked him that Kathleen wouldn't try it simply because she didn't like the way it looked, and that their sons had followed suit. 'I know Peter were never very fond. You couldn't sit him down to a plate of cow-heel or chicklins or owt. But the girls when they were young, they used to lean more towards me than lads did, so they'd have a bash. Lads used to cling to their mother a lot, and I think Peter led the way there, because he was a right mother's boy from the word go.'

As a young man, Peter had a natural refinement that his father's more rugged manners threw into sharp relief; he was obviously never going to drink tea out of a pint-pot the way his father habitually did, or keep a 'jerry' with a spot of Dettol in it under the bed to save making trips to the bathroom through the night.

If anything, he grew increasingly fastidious as he grew older, and was particularly sensitive about a sweaty foot problem that in later years would lead to him wearing clogs and 'Dr Scholl' sandals and washing his own socks. At home, he'd leave his socks tucked into his shoes outside on the window-sill when he went to bed, which was a habit that became so ingrained he even remembered to do it on his honeymoon: there was some puzzlement, and not a little amusement, among those who didn't know about the 'problem' when a pair of men's shoes appeared outside an upstairs window at Maureen's house in Cambridge where Peter and Sonia were staying en route to Paris. To Peter, though, who never gave up searching for ways to minimise the smell, it was too embarrassing to be a joke.

The irony was that he still monopolised the bathroom and continued to shut himself up in it even if he'd brought Sonia home. It wasn't unusual for him to install Sonia in the front room with his mother the minute they arrived, and then disappear upstairs for anything up to an hour. Being women, it was assumed they must have a lot in common but, even with Mrs Sutcliffe, who was well known all over the estate for her sympathetic ear and her warmth and, perhaps her most unusual quality in the midst of the prevailing chaos, her repose, Sonia never really opened up. 'I am not a gushing person,' she would later say in the sort of tart understatement for which she had become renowned.

Whether or not Peter left her downstairs for a cosy chat, though, depended to a great extent on the whereabouts of his father, whose blandishments Sonia had shown herself to be particularly immune to from day one. John Sutcliffe always had more to say for himself than the rest of the household put together, but was particularly voluble in the company of anybody who had 'had an education', quoting Shakespeare and Aeschylus and pieces of wisdom gleaned 'from a professor in *Reader's Digest*', like whispering into the hood over its beak being the best way to get a budgie to talk. Sonia was no more diverted by any of this than she was by his dramatic monologues or his harmonica playing; she was aware of his earlier theatrical ambitions and was in no doubt that he had missed his vocation. But it was physical contact that she was always most anxious to avoid.

John Sutcliffe made no secret of the fact that he liked women, and he missed no opportunity to get to grips with them, plain or pretty, young or old. On odd occasions there had been some slight unpleasantness when one of his daughters' friends or a girl that one of Peter's pals had brought back to Cornwall Road felt that he'd overstepped the mark – Shelia Norton, for instance, who lived next-door-but-one to the Sutcliffes, had objected to his attentions at the time she was going out with Laurie Ashton. But within the family it was regarded as more or less harmless, a peccadillo, even something of a joke.

'He's like that wi' girls. He *mauls* 'em,' Carl would still be able to say good-humouredly of his father fifteen years later. 'If he's in pub an' any woman comes anywhere near, he'll always grab hold an' touch them, pretending to be joking and messing around. Our Mick used to say you daren't leave your girlfriend in room with 'im. When I used to bring my girlfriend back and he used to touch her, I used to say, "Gerroff! Look, but don't touch!" He's a crazy guy.'

For these reasons, perhaps, Sonia never used to leave Peter's side while she was at 'Corny' Road. If they were in the living-room, the two of them would make a point of sitting with their chairs hard against the wall, well behind everybody else, and as far away from the fire as they could get, 'as if they were scared they would melt'. Usually though you would find them in what had been Grandma Coonan's and, more recently, Anne and her new husband's bedroom, now returned to its intended use as a 'dinette'. They would sit for hours locked in intense, but inaudible conversation there or in the kitchen, although Carl and Jane did walk in on them once undressing in the bedroom upstairs.

The search for privacy frequently took Sonia and Peter out of doors and up to the 'moor-top' directly above Ferncliffe Estate, where they spent hours strolling among the craggy black rocks bearded with heather that, many years earlier, had been quarried and reconstituted as the mills and chapels and handsome villas spread out vertiginously below. Seen from here, the newer buildings, mainly council-built, that encircle the old town like a soiled collar, look pale and insubstantial, as if the westerly wind that rushes down the valley might one day just pluck them and brush them away.

At the Szurmas' the problem wasn't the noise so much as the resounding lack of it that was daunting; their reaction neverthe-less was the same. They sought refuge in an old graveyard where Peter broke his ankle once pretending to be a 'ghost': he'd jumped over a wall where he was going to hide and leap out at Sonia and give her a fright, but instead of the four feet that he had been expecting, realised too late that it was at least a twenty-foot drop.

Arnside, with its picturesqueness and health and crafts shops and boarding houses full of ladies reading Jean Plaidy and Anya Seton novels, was somewhere else that, even after they were married, they used to go to often. They also became regular callers on a couple who in those early days filled most of the requirements for what, it seemed to those who didn't fill the bill, they were coming to think of as 'their' kind of people.

Arthur Bisby, his wife Anne and their two daughters lived in a neat semi-detached house in a tree-lined street in Crossflatts. He was an ex-turner who had done well for himself as an 'insurance man' – he'd had Mrs Sutcliffe on his books for years and started insuring Peter after he learned to drive; she did the choreography for Bingley Amateur Operatic Society and was the leading light in an 'action' group campaigning against environmental pollution in the area around where they lived.

The Bisbys were among the few people who didn't find Peter at all tense; on the contrary, he'd arrive around teatime on a Sunday, make himself comfortable and sometimes would still be there at midnight, long after his hosts had run out of things to say. He was particularly fond of the children, with whom he seemed 'on the same wave-length' although, as far as Sonia was concerned, they might as well not have been there. She was difficult and reserved but seemed devoted to Peter with whom, it was as obvious to the Bisbys as to everybody else who knew them, she clearly saw a comfortable future stretching out many years ahead.

By summer 1969, they had been going out with each other for two years and Sonia was just coming to the end of her A-level course at Bradford Tech. Soon she would embark on the teacher training that her father had had earmarked for her since she was a child, and then when she had qualified they could be married and set up house on their own. That was always the plan. With no prior warning, however, and with few people other than themselves conscious of the fact, their relationship was suddenly on the rocks.

Mick Sutcliffe was working in a trench with a pickaxe one day that year, widening the main road on the southern perimeter of Bingley, when a white sportscar with a flamboyant young couple in it caught his eye. 'There were a scarf blowin' off of bird in passenger seat, a sort of silk job blowin' over top, an' I just fuckin' realised who it were when she got level. It were her.'

'I don't like sayin' owt,' he said to Peter as soon as he got in, grinning from ear to ear, 'but I don't like her anyway so I'm goin' to tell you: Sonia were in a fuckin' sportscar with a feller this afternoon, coming down Cottingley Bridge. Likely they'd been to Morecambe for the day.' He continued in this vein for some time, 'niggling' his brother, until something about the look on Peter's face told him he had better stop. It was an episode that was never mentioned again.

10

I remember Miss Brontë telling me it was a saying
round about Haworth, 'Keep a stone in thy pocket
seven year; turn it and keep it seven years longer, that
it may be ever ready to thine hand when thine enemy
draws near.'

Mrs Gaskell, *The Life of Charlotte Brontë*

A darkening of the eye, in which the iris became drained of any
hint of colour, was the only sight that Peter was upset or angry.
He rarely lost his temper with anybody, ever: he never betrayed
his feelings about anything. At work the morning after Mick had
dealt him what had actually been a devastating blow, nobody
detected any change in his always affable self. The only way in
which he deviated from his regular pattern at the Water Board,
where he had been working as a general labourer since his dis-
missal at Bingley cemetery, was that he packed up early, leaving
one of the other men to 'cover' for him.

The image of Sonia riding in a car with somebody else had
started to obsess Peter; each detail, as Mick had described it, had
instantly become etched in his mind. The time couldn't come fast
enough for him to discover for himself whether it was true or
not. It seemed inconceivable to him that it could be. And yet as
soon as he saw her he knew that it was.

He was waiting for Sonia when she came out of the technical
college, and was in a position to see the shocked expression on
her face. She immediately turned away, instead of walking
towards him, but he was at her shoulder in seconds and they
argued all the way to her home.

What Peter was desperate to know was if Sonia was sleeping
with the owner of the sportscar, who, she had admitted, was an
Italian. And in the course of the row he had sneeringly suggested

going to a chemist and buying some Durex to make it easier for her. In the end he simply walked off in what he would later describe as 'an angry and resentful frame of mind'. He started driving back to Bradford.

That there were prostitutes plying their trade in Bradford, and that their favourite 'patch' was barely half a mile away from the Royal Standard, was hardly news to somebody who had grown to be on such intimate terms with the Manningham–Lumb Lane area as Peter: in his regular forays away from the pubs in which Eric and Laurie were drinking up their courage, he had been able to acquaint himself with the derelict properties, dingy corners and narrow, litter-strewn 'ginnels' where the girls conducted their business, as well as with their working methods. By and large, these had remained unchanged for generations.

'Bradford's Great Curse – the monster evil which is a dark and ugly blot on our social and moral life . . . this seething whirlpool of immorality' was something which had much exercised pamphleteers at the turn of the century, when it was estimated that there were sixty brothels and 170 'notorious' prostitutes operating in the city. While, in the 1930s, a contemporary observer noted the irony of the fact that, in Bradford, 'the process of turning oneself into a street-walker should still be called "going gay", for anything less gay, anything more monotonous, dull, dreary, senseless, sordid, than the whole way of life, the surroundings, habits, manners, outlook of these women . . . can hardly be imagined. They nearly always look what they are – gross, greedy and stupid.'

Throughout the second half of the last century and the first quarter of this, Manningham enjoyed a reputation for being the most fashionable area in the city. Manningham Lane, the main route to the North, was a sedate thoroughfare flanked by golden, classically proportioned terraces that housed the managers, accountants and other white-collar workers attached to the mills whose massive black chimneys dominated the landscape. By the late 1960s, when 'the Lane' became the haunt of Peter Sutcliffe and his gravedigging friends, vestiges of that earlier elegance remained, but evidence of the squalor that the fine terraces now served to conceal was increasingly seeping through their façades.

Junk shops, 'private' (that is, sex) shops, betting offices, mini-cab and take-away curry places, drinking clubs and cobbled-together 'caffs' were the public face of what, even then, was starting to be recognised as one of the worst inner-city slums in the country. Lumb Lane runs parallel with Manningham Lane for just over a mile from the city centre, and the streets between and beyond them along that short stretch have accommodated succeeding waves of immigrants: the Irish up to the beginning of World War II; Eastern Europeans after it; and Asians (and, to a lesser extent, West Indians) from the mid-1950s on.

By the late sixties, slum clearance had demolished half the Lumb Lane area, but the demolition was taking place in such an apparently random, haphazard fashion that single shops and houses, or maybe small clusters of buildings, would inexplicably be left standing, like old teeth in a gaping mouth. Customers following the 'Toilet' signs in the Lahore (always pronounced 'La-whooer') restaurant, for example, would find themselves stumbling across a piece of waste ground where half a dozen cats were fighting each other over a hen's head. At the corner, two or three prostitutes would stand silhouetted in the dark, indifferent to the fact that the building which had once afforded them a degree of discretion and shelter was now gone.

Up to the end of the 1950s, most industrial towns in the West Riding had been able to boast small 'prostitute' populations of their own, made up almost entirely of mill-girls, earning a bit of much needed extra money on the side. In Bingley, the King's Head was their regular haunt, although Treaclecock Alley, a damp, permanently blacked-out culvert running under the rail-way, was where most transactions took place. Twenty years later, a woman of indeterminate age known as 'Mucky Mary' would be the sole survivor of her breed, and Mick Sutcliffe would be rumoured to be 'the only man brave enough to take her on'.

At weekends, the always steady traffic of serious 'punters' kerb-crawling along Lumb Lane would be swelled by carloads of boozy youths from the surrounding suburbs and small towns like Bingley who were in equal measure fascinated and repelled by what they saw, but only ever admitted to being there for one reason: 'the laugh'.

Peter, imbued with a religion which associated women with the dangers and degradations of the flesh, had, on odd occasions, been a party to the catcalls and abuse. But he had never approached a woman while he was on his own. And then, the night of the row over the Italian with Sonia, he found himself 'attracted' to a girl soliciting on Manningham Lane.

The idea, as he was to explain it some years later, was to 'level the score' with Sonia, whose relationship with the man whose existence he had been unaware of only twenty-four hours earlier was, so he now believed, more intimate than her relationship with him. He reached over and opened the front nearside door of the Morris 1000 and, having confirmed that she was 'doing business', invited the woman in.

'I thought I would have intercourse with the prostitute, but I changed my mind when it got to the stage where we had got to do it,' he later claimed. 'We were on the way to her place and were talking and I realised what a coarse and vulgar person she was. We were practically there and I realised I didn't want anything to do with her.

'Before getting out of the car I was trying to wriggle out of the situation, but I felt stupid as well. We went into the house and when she got into the bedroom she started taking her clothes off. She had told me it was five pound and I had earlier given her a ten-pound note. She had told me that when we got to her place she was going to change it. She didn't want to call it off and said we could get the note changed at the garage where I had picked her up.

'We went back to the garage by car and she went inside and there were two chaps in there. I don't know whether she did this regularly, but she wouldn't come back out. One of the men came banging on the car roof when I refused to go away, and the other one escorted her away. There wasn't much I could do about it, but I was a bit annoyed and drove off.'

His 'annoyance' at being 'duped and cheated' soon flared up into something more intense. 'It wasn't just the money. It was the fact that I felt annoyed because I wanted to resolve the situation with Sonia and hadn't done. It made me feel worse than ever . . . even more depressed . . . I felt outraged and humiliated and embarrassed. I felt a hatred for (the prostitute) and her kind.'

His depression deepened next morning when he finally reported for work: during his absence the previous afternoon there had been a 'disaster', in the course of which several of his workmates had almost drowned. Hauled before the director of the water works later in the day, he was left in no doubt that the accident was seen to be his fault, and he was summarily demoted for leaving his post. It was a setback that he contrived to keep secret from his family, who were to notice no difference in his behaviour over the coming difficult months.

He saw Sonia as usual the following Sunday, only to learn that she was still seeing the other man – was seeing him two or three times a week, in fact, whereas she was only seeing him once. Inevitably, they spent the whole time arguing, which is all they seemed to do whenever they saw each other for a long time.

Shortly after the ten-pound-note affair, Peter recognised the woman who had 'duped' him drinking with another 'obvious' prostitute in one of Lumb Lane's many well-known prostitutes' pubs. 'I went and approached the one I had been with three weeks previously and told her that I hadn't forgotten about the incident and that she could put things right so that there would be no hard feelings. I was giving her the opportunity to put things right and give back the payment I had made to her. She thought this was a huge joke and, as luck would have it, she knew everybody else in the place and went round telling them . . . Before I knew what was happening, most of the people were having a good laugh.'

After this, he said, his mind was 'in a turmoil': he developed 'a general loathing for any prostitute'. He felt himself being pushed 'over the brink'.

Peter was twenty-three in 1969; Eric and Laurie were two or three years older and engagements and marriages were beginning to break 'Gravediggers' Corner' up. On his 'nights off' from Sonia – that is, any night except Saturday – Peter still sometimes put in an appearance at the discos at the Royal Standard but, unknown to his old crowd, he had lately taken to hanging around other pubs where music wasn't the main attraction, usually with a new friend in tow.

Trevor Birdsall was so self-effacing and shy as to make Peter seem socially adept. If people noticed anything at all about Trevor it was usually his hair, and if they didn't notice, Peter would grab the first opportunity to point out to them that Trevor was wearing a wig. 'It turns red in the summer and goes frizzy,' he'd add quickly, laughing his fluting laugh, before Trevor got back from the bar.

Trevor also had a heart condition, as a result of which he'd led a rather sheltered life and, even as an adult, still tended to be rather fussed over by his mother. Being to a greater or lesser extent 'mother's boys', in fact, is something that Keith Sugden would retrospectively identify as the characteristic linking most of Peter's friends, not excluding himself. 'Trevor Birdsall, Eric Robinson Richard Varley, Patrick Slater, me an' Pete – we were all more or less dominated by our mothers. It seems as if he were drawn to people with something missing in their make-up like that.'

Trevor, though, seemed particularly 'cissified'. He played guitar, and Keith 'jammed' with him a couple of times in a room above the Hornby Dublo shop that Mr Birdsall ran in Lumb Lane, but their association didn't survive beyond the first weeks. 'I don't like weak character. Weak people. I don't like people who let other people walk all over them. An' Trevor were weak. Peter, though, wasn't weak at all. If anything, just the opposite. He'd play daft, but you felt he was laughing inwardly all the time.'

After his youngest brother was viciously beaten about the head with a stick coming out of a nightclub in the mid-1970s, Peter was to offer him some fraternal advice: 'Always carry a sock in your pocket,' he told Carl, 'and all you need is a stone or some other solid object to turn it into an effective weapon.'

A spare sock is something that Peter, in his usual fastidious fashion, always made sure he had on him after he decided he had been made to look a 'laughing-stock' for the second time by the prostitute whose features he was now always on the look-out for in his apparently aimless excursions around Bradford's 'red-light' area.

Sometime between a week and a month after approaching the woman in the pub and asking for his money back, he was sitting with Trevor in Trevor's mini-van in St Paul's Road, near Manningham Park. They had completed what was becoming their regular circuit of the Lumb Lane pubs and were 'parked up', eating fish and chips out of the paper when Peter suddenly disappeared. When he came back ten minutes later he was agitated and out of breath and abruptly instructed Trevor to drive off.

Once they were headed in the direction of Bingley Peter confessed that he had followed an 'old cow' along St Paul's Road to a house, where he had hit her on the back of the head with a stone. He produced a sock from his pocket and dropped the piece of brick that was in it out of the window. He also mumbled something about some money which Trevor didn't understand.

Next day Peter received a visit from the police. The injured woman, who bore no resemblance to the prostitute against whom he believed he had a grievance, had noted the number of Trevor's van. He admitted striking her, but only with his hand, and got off with 'a lecture'; for her own reasons she had decided not to press charges. 'I explained everything, and everything's all right,' he reassured Trevor, who was soon back in Lumb Lane with him, listening to his boasts about 'shagging' prostitutes and not paying, meekly following his instructions to look at a passing woman's 'big knockers'.

On the night of 29 September 1969, however, a further month

later, Peter went out alone and was arrested in the garden of a house in the Manningham area after his car had been spotted by a policeman with its lights on and the engine turning over. He was discovered hunched behind a privet hedge with a hammer and later charged with 'going equipped for theft', an offence which eventually brought a fine of £25.

Although, given what his motive had actually been, he was pleased to plead guilty to such a comparatively minor charge in court, at home he continued to protest his innocence. His father knew he had trouble with one of the hubcaps on his Morris because, driving through Harrogate with him just a few weeks earlier, it had flown off and had had to be tapped back on again with the hammer that Peter always carried in the car for that purpose. That was what had happened on the night of the arrest: the hubcap had come off; he was walking round the car with the hammer still in his hand after reseating it, and as he was opening the door on the driver's side this policeman had walked across the road and wanted to know what he was doing, he explained earnestly, and neither of his parents saw any reason to disbelieve him. Besides which, Peter had got very good at dissembling. He was, in Mick's words, 'a right genuine sort of a liar'.

'You can usually tell if somebody's lying, but he could tell me summat, our lad, an' it'd go straight in. He wouldn't let his face slip at all. Nothing. You wouldn't think owt about it.'

11

The influence of women in the Sutcliffe household was pronounced. As well as Anne, Maureen and Jane, who all appeared uncomplicated, assertive and noticeably well-adjusted compared to the boys, there was their mother and their mother's mother, who had moved in with them at Manor Road when Peter was six and continued to live with them at Cornwall Road until her death in 1964, twelve years later.

Gran'ma Coonan's sister, Reenee, lived in one of the old people's 'bungalows' further along Cornwall Road and was always popping in; and her only daughter, Mary, who had settled in Rotherham with her family, was a regular visitor. The Sutcliffes, on the other hand – John's parents, his two brothers and a sister – although all still living in the area, rarely darkened the door.

It was an estrangement that most people traced back to Ivy Sutcliffe, an unpopular woman who, in her later years, took a grim satisfaction in deliberately alienating everybody who might have been close – husband, children and grandchildren alike: John Sutcliffe would only learn of his mother's death, in a Bingley old people's home in 1982, several days after the funeral. 'Gra'ma Sutcliffe was a beast,' was Jane's epitaph. 'Some people are born sour. She were born sour.'

Lottie Coonan, though, earned a permanent place in the affections of the grandchildren whom she had helped to bring up, and was genuinely mourned. Carl, who was just four at the time, sneaked one of the neighbour's children in to have a look at his grandmother laid out in the front room in her open coffin; and Mick, who was then fourteen, served as altar boy at the Requiem Mass, which helped his father to see him in a new light. 'He was a dabhand at it. He really looked the part. I'm not a Catholic myself, but I was quite proud of him, the way he carried it off.

The seriousness of the job . . . I've seen all my lads do the incense-swinging bit and there's nothing any of them have got to learn about religion. Any one of them could walk into any Catholic cathedral in the world and follow the service.'

Eighty when she died, Mrs Coonan had been receiving communion at home every week for many years, and Kathleen usually took the sacraments with her. Although the demands of bringing up six children and running a house meant that she never got to church more than three or four times a year, Kathleen had never faltered in her faith and, with her mother, was seen as a perfect example of what the 'good' Catholic woman should be: 'big-hearted', 'hardworking', 'uncomplaining' and 'loving', she would be remembered by her neighbours as a 'devoted' wife and mother, the single criticism being that she was always 'too soft' with her children. His mother was certainly Mick's chief ally, both against the police and against his father, who was kept in the dark much of the time about what was going on. 'She were a right sort of an honest person, me mother. Right gullible. You could tell her owt an' she'd believe you without wanting to delve into what were goin' on. Like, police were allus coming round wi' one thing an' another, even when I hadn't done owt. If they were lookin' for somebody for summat, they'd come an' see me. An' she were one of them, she'd stick up for you, me mother, even though she might call you a bloody fool after they'd gone.'

Kathleen had a particularly close relationship with her sons. It was Kathleen whom John Sutcliffe had always blamed, of course, for Peter growing up the way he did, 'tied to his mother's apron strings'. But then he saw the process being repeated with Carl.

Although, unlike his oldest brother, Carl wasn't physically weak – he would, in fact, reach six feet by the time he was twelve – he was as shy and sensitive and as attached to his mother as Peter had been fifteen years before.

John Sutcliffe spent almost the whole of the 1960s, the decade when Carl was growing up, working nights. Carl, meanwhile, spent most of that time watching television from his mother's lap and resented being sent to bed early by his father when he was around at the weekends. Like the rest of the family (although Maureen, possibly his favourite, would only admit to holding him 'in awe'), Carl was afraid of his father, whose moods could be unpredictable, and for many years would even admit to 'hating' him.

'We were all frightened to death of me dad. He were like a monster. He were never in house, but when he was he ruled the roost. When he came in drunk we'd all sit there in fear; you didn't move. Whatever was on television, no matter how many were watching, was straight off and switched over to what he wanted to see, which were usually sport. If cricket come on, that were it. He used to sort of edge up to telly and sit right in front of it. Nobody dare say owt.

'Oh Christ, he had a foul temper. I seen Maureen get a beating off him when she was about fifteen, an' he once beat me black and blue when I were a kid. I threw an orange pip at Pete an' missed an' he just got up and beat hell out of me. I used to get up in a morning and go out to avoid him. I wouldn't go near him. I used to dread him *completely*.

'Me an' Jane, when we were right little, we used to bath together, an' he'd just put this chrome towel-rail on wall – he didn't do right many jobs in house, but one of them he had done was that. Anyway, as Jane were getting out of bath she slipped an' grabbed hold of it to save herself and pulled it off. And we were that terrified, we wouldn't come out of bathroom, even though it were an accident. An' he went berserk.

'I hated him. I really did. I even considered killing him. I were goin' to tek nuts off his push-bike wheels once. I unscrewed them all one night an' med everything loose. I thought, He'll go down that hill to work tonight an' . . . crash!'

One aspect of his father's behaviour that used to leave Carl feeling particularly confused was the different, conflicting personalities he seemed to assume: it was as though he kept one face for use in the house and another, much pleasanter one, for when he went out.

'One thing he did used to do, he used to put a bar of chocolate in us pockets before we went to school. He'd put a Milky Way in all the duffle-coat pockets hanging on the hooks when he came in in the morning. What I really hated about him, though, were fact that he were really good to other kids in street – he were always right nice to neighbours' kids; he'd give them money for sweets or owt. Whereas I can never remember him buying me a present in all me life when I were little. He bought me an Action Man when I were about eight, but that were the only present he ever bought. Me mum had to buy everything we got.'

Money had always been scarce at Cornwall Road and, after half a lifetime's practice, Kathleen had become expert at making a little go a long way. There was a limit, however, even to her ingenuity, and on one occasion she was discovered scratching about in a coalhouse belonging to one of her neighbours. The neighbour, who realised that she must have been desperate, said nothing. Other times she would live in fear of the Electricity Board coming to cut them off before she had had time to scrape together whatever was owing, although Mick once or twice paid the bill without saying anything and then encouraged his mother to spend the money on herself.

It wasn't something she was used to doing, and she never acquired the habit. A visit to the hairdresser every other Thursday was Kathleen's only indulgence, even after she started going out of the house to work. Mrs Coonan was housebound for the last years of her life, so Kathleen had her mother to look after as well as the younger children. But, from the mid-1960s onwards, she had a series of domestic and office cleaning jobs which, although poorly paid, helped to lift the financial burden. For a number of years she was employed at Bingley Teachers Training College, where the work, pushing heavy industrial equipment, was arduous and the hours anti-social – 5.00 p.m.–8.00 p.m. on week-nights, 7.00 a.m.–12.00 noon on Saturdays and Sundays. But, even though she was ailing much of this time, none of the women she worked with ever saw her looking less than pleasant, or heard her complain. The consensus was that she had plenty to complain about.

John Sutcliffe was almost as much a stranger to his wife as he was to his children, who would grow up feeling that they didn't know him any better than they would have known a lodger. The two of them were occasionally spotted together on Saturday nights, but Kathleen was never a drinker, and got bored sitting in pubs. Their paths mainly crossed at the breakfast- and dinner-tables where, having cooked the meal, she would serve him up and then clear away his food, and bring him his tea in the pint-pot that nobody else was allowed near.

When he wasn't working John was invariably following one of the sporting or recreational pursuits on which his reputation in Bingley rested. He played football for the town well into his forties, was in demand as a cricketer well into his fifties, and cut no less of a figure in middle age than he had as a young man. His tastes ran to hounds-tooth checks and paisley cravats and frothing handkerchiefs in his breast pockets, and to well-cut, formal suits on the occasions when he was singing with the Musical Union or out dancing. He loved dancing, which was another of his talents, and was invariably well-mannered and 'gallant' in a rather old-fashioned, self-conscious and (to some) self-congratulatory way.

He was considered merely self-centred and conceited by at least one woman who remained unimpressed by his somewhat theatrical 'Sir Galahad' manner. 'He obviously thought of him-self as charming and dashing and all the rest of it, but in fact he was too vain, too wrapped up in himself to really be.'

It was a criticism that was also often made of his father, in whose footsteps John seemed to be faithfully following. Retire-ment had done nothing to dull Arthur Sutcliffe's appetite for get-ting out and enjoying himself, and his patent pumps were a familiar feature of dances at Bingley Co-op and Ambulance Halls, and in the ballrooms at Morecambe. He was a 'very smart-looking young old feller' according to his son, who felt indirectly flattered when he heard people say that there wasn't a man in the area fitter-looking for his age than Arthur. But John was also said to take after his father in ways which were less flattering.

'Ladies' man' was a description that members of Arthur Sutcliffe's own family did not dispute. By the time their children had grown up and left home, Arthur's relationship with his wife had deteriorated to the point where, although they continued living under the same roof, they ate and slept separately and opened their mouths only to berate each other. In these circumstances their oldest son was not alone in feeling that his father was justified in seeking comfort elsewhere.

The caravan on New Barns Farm at Arnside was where Arthur Sutcliffe conducted most of his affairs, as Mick, who was almost as fond of the resort as Peter, discovered for himself. On one or two occasions Mick knocked on the door of what was known as his grandfather's 'passion wagon' to ask if he could let him have some dinner, and found him with a woman. But by no means all his involvements were carried on at such a discreet distance from home. He was regularly seen around Bingley in the company of various 'lady friends', but one particular liaison caused more eyebrows to be raised than most.

Arthur Sutcliffe had been friendly for some time with a woman who lived in one of the 'big houses' up on Crownest Road. But, gradually, he started to be seen around with the daughter of the house more than with the mother. Annie Rhodes had had a deformed spine since she was a girl and, because she was a cripple, had never been allowed to do anything for herself. Suddenly, though, she was seen at St John's Ambulance Brigade dances with Arthur Sutcliffe who, after her mother died, encouraged her to take driving lessons and buy herself a car, and generally 'brought her on'. After a while, John Sutcliffe, too, started to take an interest in Annie, and father and son both became regular – if separate – callers at the house, usually, it was noted, after dark. John would occasionally borrow Annie's car if he needed it, and the two of them were sometimes seen out in it together. The fact that Kathleen occasionally joined them for a ride into the country did nothing to kill the rumours.

Throughout his childhood Carl constantly overheard the neighbours talking about things to do with his father that they assumed he was too young to understand. Peter and Mick, however, got it straight from the horse's mouth. To Mick it was a sign of growing up, being able to talk about sex and women with his father and his brother, standing at a bar. 'Go on, get her into bed, lad,' his father would say, eyeing a courting couple. 'I couldn't wait.' And sometimes he'd produce something that he'd picked up at work, like a line drawing of a butterfly on greaseproof paper whose 'markings', when the paper was unfolded, turned out to be a column of bodies, coupled back and front. Occasionally, though, he'd go further and confide in his sons that he'd been with a 'right cracker' last night.

To Mick, whose philosophy could be summed up as 'What they don't know can't harm them', this seemed reasonable, even understandable, behaviour, and Peter didn't demur. Of one thing Mick was quite certain: his mother didn't suspect a thing. 'She were used to him being out at cricket do's an' all after; they used to have a booze-up till three and four in mornin'. Then there were Musical Union an' all sorts of stuff. She were right innocent about them kinds of things, so he could get away with it like that. She never used to ask about owt.'

By the age of eighteen, Maureen was already coming up to her first divorce. Within a year of Rachel being born in March 1969, Maureen had split up from the father and was back living with her family at Cornwall Road.

Kathleen looked after the baby during the day so that Maureen could go out to work, and then went out to work herself in the evenings, cleaning at the College and afterwards, on her way home, cleaning offices in the centre of the town. One night, around her fiftieth birthday in January 1970, she stopped dusting to answer the phone.

'I was calling to tell her I wouldn't be knocking off at the usual time because they'd asked me to work over on account of some patterns they wanted making,' John Sutcliffe would later claim.

'This was probably the first time I'd ever spoken to her on the telephone, plus I'd had all me teeth out a couple of months previously and she didn't seem to recognise the voice.

'"Who's that?" she says. So I said, "Who d'you think it is?" really just joking. And she named another feller altogether. She gave me another feller's name. "Oh," she said, "is it Albert?" Well, it shook me to me toenails.

'"Oh," she says. "Albert," she says. "When can I see you again?" So I went along with it. "Well," I said, "when would you like to see me again?" And by this time I were bloody trembling, trying to carry this conversation on. In the end I said: "I shall have to leave you now. I can't talk to you any more, there's some people just come in. I'll call you again tomorrow."' Which he did, still pretending to be the other man. And the next day. And the day after. By which time he had hatched a plan.

The Bankfield Hotel is a Victorian pile in a sylvan setting that most Bingleyites only ever see the inside of at retirement parties and silver weddings, and Maureen was intrigued to know why her father wanted her to meet him there at 7.30 p.m. on a Saturday, but he wouldn't tell her. All she could get out of him was: 'Just do it.'

The first person she saw when she stepped through the heavy swing doors at the Bankfield was Peter. Hovering in the background was Sonia. Peter, it turned out, didn't know what he was doing there either, which prompted Maureen to remark that it was like This-Is-Your-bloody-Life.

Their father arrived shortly before the appointed time but still didn't offer any explanation, even though Maureen kept at him about being late already and having to get to a 'do'. Peter told her he'd give her a lift when whatever they were there for was over, and his father bought a round of drinks. He kept looking behind him towards the entrance from where they were sitting, until Maureen saw her mother pacing up and down nervously outside. This surprised her because Kathleen had definitely told her she was going out for a meal and a drink with some of the women from work. The next thing she knew her father was tapping her mother on the shoulder and leading her triumphantly in the direction of the three familiar, if bewildered, faces in the bar.

It was 'typical' of her father, Maureen would say when the whole story had been unspun, pretending to be somebody else for three nights running on the phone, and then going home and behaving as if nothing was wrong: he was 'right deep, really secretive, like all the lads.' There was something in all of them that, even when they didn't need to, made them evade telling the truth. They all always kept everything in.

It had been on the third night of impersonating 'Albert' that John Sutcliffe had finally asked Kathleen to meet him that weekend at the Bankfield Hotel. He said he'd arrange for a meal and book a room for the night, adding, as if it was an afterthought, that she should bring 'something comfortable to slip into; something nice to wear in bed'.

On the Saturday afternoon he had gone upstairs and found a brand new nightdress, still in the bag it had come in from Marks & Spencer, in the top drawer of the tallboy in their bedroom where he knew his wife kept her things. And, having sat her at the table with Peter and Sonia and Maureen, it was this that he now produced with a flourish from the handbag that Kathleen mutely surrendered, like a conjuror drawing a rabbit from a hat. She didn't remonstrate with him, or cry, or do anything dramatic, but Maureen thought she had never seen anybody look so embarrassed in her life. Her mother seemed numb; all the blood had drained from her; she seemed stunned.

The first person to speak was Maureen's father, who thrust some money at Peter and told him to go and get them all another drink. And then, as if to soften the blow, or so at least it seemed to Maureen, he told Kathleen that there wasn't another woman in Bingley like her; that she was a special person, but that he'd been hurt.

Unusually, this seemed to strike a chord in Peter, who, although his family didn't know it, after months of turmoil had only recently got his relationship with Sonia back on the rails. 'I know how it feels, Dad,' he tried to say, but his father shrugged his sympathy aside. 'You can't,' he said dismissively. 'You're not married.'

But something about the way Peter had spoken, an unaccustomed directness in his tone, made Maureen feel that he did. 'He'd been hurt really bad. He'd taken it really hard. I didn't know when or how then, but you could just tell.'

Carl, at ten, and Jane, at thirteen, were too young to be told what was going on; they would pick up bits and pieces of the story in the course of the years to come. On the night when the rest of the family were down at the Bankfield, Jane sat at home on her own feeling disgruntled, convinced that everybody was out having a good time.

Mick, almost on principle, had turned a deaf ear to his father's instruction to turn up at 7.30 and, when he finally rolled home that Saturday, was made to pay the price. 'Because I hadn't tekken part, in me father's eyes I'd let him down. He said, "You're not my son any more," an' shut the door in me face an' locked it. He said, "You're finished, you." So I walked back on to me mate's an' slept there.'

When it was eventually explained to Mick what had 'gone off', all he felt was anger at 'such a fuckin' lousy trick'. It seemed to him his mother had been 'set up' for no reason. Mick had known Albert for years, and liked him, which was strange, because Albert was a police sergeant who only lived two streets away. But he was a 'decent bloke' who shared Mick's interest in guns, and the two of them had occasionally gone out ratting together.

Mick had a Bedlington terrier at the time that his mother liked to walk at nights on the field that dipped down to the canal from the bottom of Cornwall Road. And, because Albert also had a dog, the two of them would often meet. 'Albert used to walk his dog on past our house. He'd even knock at door sometimes and the pair of them would go for a walk on road an' back. I mean, me an' our Peter watched them out of bedroom window one night. "Look at the silly old sods," he said. "They think we haven't seen 'em sneakin' down path."

'You could see right to end where they went, then turned round an' walked back wi' dogs. They'd have a talk at bottom, then she'd come back in. But he never did owt. There were nowt sexual involved. It were more company than owt, because me father were never in to bloody talk to 'er. If he did come in he'd be washed and straight back out, an' when he came back at night he'd be popped.'

Maureen, too, thought it was unlikely that her mother would have slept with the policeman. For one thing, she didn't know where she would have found the time. 'She were an honest, ordinary, *motherly* type of person who, all she ever did all her bloody married life, was work and bring up kids. She didn't have any pleasure or any hobbies or anything because she had too much to do. She probably just wanted somebody to appreciate her. Somebody to tell her she was still an attractive woman which, at that point, she was. Because she had a miserable bloody existence. She'd had a *hell* of a miserable life. She just put up with anything. She kept it all to herself.'

For Maureen's father, however, the nightdress in Kathleen's handbag, which she'd brought only because he'd asked her to bring it, had been sufficient evidence. And he couldn't rest until he'd wrung a full and detailed 'confession' from his wife. 'Good God,' he'd boom at her, 'the woman I married, the mother of my children, the woman I'd loved and trusted all my life having an affair with another feller under my nose and you wonder why I'm making such a fuss?' In the end, she gave in to his demands to be put in touch with Albert, who, he had established, she'd known for 'near-on three year'.

'She kept trying to convince me that there'd been no sort of . . . sexual connotations in this relationship. So, after a couple of days, I said, "Well, I want to see this feller," who, it turned out, had a wife and a family and his own police house and everything. His wife had a good job at a big store in Bradford; a supervisor-type of woman. I said, "I want to have a word with him."

'And it all came out then. She told me *everything*. All about going to his house and spending the afternoon in bed, and going out in his car and parking it at the top of Harden, and sometimes just down the road by the cricket-field in a little cul-de-sac, and having sex . . . It all came out. She didn't hold anything back.

'So I had him come to my house then and we thrashed it all out. I told him, I said, "Look, this thing stops and it stops dead. Otherwise your wife is going to have to get to know. Plus I shall go to your superior officers and I shall report your conduct to them." I said, "We are members of the public who are supposed to be protected *by* people like you. And it comes to a pretty pass when we need protecting *from* people like you." I said, "I'm quite prepared to forget all about it, provided you give me your solemn word that the affair is over."

'"Oh," he said, "I can promise you that. That's it. It's finished." Then I found out that the following Friday night, straight after, they'd met again. So I had to have him back then and let him know I knew. She was there as well. And this time I said, "Now, what are we going to do? Am I going to go down and see your superintendent? Or are you really going to wrap it up?"

'"Oh," he said. "Oh my goodness, yes. I've only got another year to do and then I get my retirement pension. Please don't go and say owt down there." And that was it. That was the end. There was going to be no more.'

'The seeds of mistrust,' however, as John Sutcliffe liked to put it, 'had been sown.' He found himself sidling down Dubb Lane at nights, past the offices where Kathleen was hard at work. And he started checking up that she was where she said she was on the rare occasions when she went out for a drink with the 'girls' from work. One night he opened the door of the Queen's Head and saw his wife in conversation with a man at the bar. He went home 'and waited and waited' until she came in. When she did he hit her with the back of his hand across the face. He broke the face of his watch at the same time against the frame of the door.

Thinking back to the Saturday at the Bankfield Hotel, Peter would say that he believed he could see his mother start to die from that day.

12

Peter had always said that he intended to wait until he was at least thirty before he got married, and he was constantly lecturing Mick on how wise he would be to do the same. Mick, however, ignored all his brother's good advice and took the plunge some months before his twenty-first birthday, in 1971.

'He told me when I got wed, he said, "You're a fool." He says, "It won't fuckin' last the way you go suppin'." He says, "You can't go suppin', you know, when you get wed, because you won't have any money. At home, you're giving your mother a fiver-a-week, which means you can go out on booze every night an' still have summat left and run a little car as well. But once you get wed, you'll be ploggin' – giving it all over, handing all money over to wife. You'll have to get shot of motor."

'"It's the best time of your life," he says. "You ought to be enjoying yourself up to thirty, then, if you want to settle down, get wed then." Which is right, like, 'cause it only lasted about three or four years.'

It surprised nobody that Mick was the first of John Sutcliffe's sons to make a move; the fact that his oldest brother wasn't Mick's best man was the only thing that drew any comment. But if this, as was widely believed, was because Sonia didn't want Peter to be put in the position where he might feel obliged to return the compliment when it was his turn, she had been vindicated before the ceremony was over: as Mick knelt before the altar with his new bride, the trousers of the suit which he had had tailor-made for the occasion split from crotch to mid-calf on an inside seam, leaving the groom to hobble out of the church as though he was wearing leg-irons. Sonia, wrapped in grey fur for the group shots afterwards, failed to see the humour of the situation.

Her affair with the Italian had dragged on throughout the

whole of the second half of 1969, until, at the end of six months, Peter finally succeeded in wrenching a promise from Sonia that she wouldn't see the other man again. It signalled, as those who knew them couldn't help noticing, a change in the balance of their relationship.

Sonia, previously mute on her visits to Cornwall Road, started to make her presence felt, albeit indirectly. 'Come out here a moment,' she'd say to Peter, ordering him out of the living-room and into the kitchen, where she could be heard 'quietly upbraiding' him for something that he had said or done which didn't meet with her approval. Sometimes, though, she'd just slap him down without bothering to extricate him from the family, which left his father open-mouthed in disbelief.

'If he had a funny situation to relate or a funny story to tell, he used to get so wrapped up in the *telling* of it that I don't think he really cared whether we enjoyed listening to it or not. He used to get so excited and laugh at his own jokes. *All* the time. He'd have to stop and have a really good laugh, and he perhaps lost his way a little bit now and again so that it would take him twenty minutes to tell a tale it would take anybody else mebbe five minutes to tell.

'To us, that was *him*. But she'd just look at him when he was getting over-excited and say "Peter!" And he'd immediately calm down. She could bring him down just like that. Just by the way she'd look at him. Just like a schoolteacher telling a naughty boy in the class to behave by saying his name out loud in front of everybody. She could do that with him, quite effectively.'

Peter didn't drop his old friends entirely after he started 'going serious' with Sonia. He still went out for a 'run' on the bike occasionally with Eric, or down to Bingley Working Men's Club where a group played in the concert room on Wednesdays, his 'night off'. The back room of the Granby on Sunday nights was another regular haunt of Eric and Laurie and some of the old crowd, and sometimes Sonia would even put in an appearance with him. She tolerated the Cuban-heel boots and 'Wyatt Earp' ribbon-ties that he wore, much as she tolerated the company, but she drew the line at the green finger-tip 'drape' coat that Peter had had made to measure without her consultation, and forbade him to appear in it in public. In the end he gave it away.

Slowly, she began to re-educate him in his tastes, weaning him away from taproom rock'n'roll and on to the light classics. They went to see Marianne, Sonia's sister, give platform recitals at the piano, and took in the occasional opera and ballet. If his family generally were nonplussed by this 'going up in the world', Mick was openly disgusted. 'You mean you go an' sit for hours listening to her playin' fuckin' concertos an' stuff like that?' he'd ask, incredulous. 'To me, it'd send me crackers, like.'

Painting was going to be Sonia's main subject at the Rachel MacMillan Teachers' Training College in Deptford in southeast London, and her clothes, in the few months before she was due to embark on the three-year course, became – at least as far as Jane and Maureen were concerned – definitely 'arty': she was wearing long 'traipsing' skirts and thick-knit patterned tights long before they were 'in' in Bingley. In London, though, like everything Sonia said or attempted, they were considered unremarkable. She abandoned painting in favour of pottery within a few weeks of arriving at the college in the autumn of 1970, but the impressions that she made academically and extramurally were equally negligible.

Virtually her only social contacts were with her sister and with Peter, who conscientiously drove down to see her every weekend: as soon as he finished work on a Friday, he was into his car and away, arriving home again early on Monday morning, a few hours before he was due to clock in at the start of another week. Because Sonia was in a hall of residence with a strict curfew on male visitors, he slept in the car or in a tent pitched in the grounds for the first few months and then, at the age of twenty-five, made the major decision to strike out on his own for the first time.

He installed himself in a bedsit in the Deptford area and was able to survive on what he earned from doing bits of motorcar maintenance and joinery, but in the end he wasn't away from home long enough for his absence to be noticed: within just a few weeks he was back living at 'Corny' Road, retailing his experiences of living in 'the smoke' and working on the production line at Baird's TV in Bradford, alongside his old friend Trevor Birdsall.

In March 1972, Andrea, Trevor's three-year-old sister, went into a Leeds hospital for a 'hole in the heart' operation. It was a rare enough case with sufficient 'human interest' for it to be featured prominently in the local press and on television, and, while she was recuperating, Peter was one of her more frequent and attentive visitors. It was a role that he was increasingly being called on to play with Sonia, whose physical and emotional isolation in London had started to manifest itself in progressively confused and erratic behaviour. Although still detached and uncommunicative in class, in private she had become prone to unprovoked outbursts of rage and agitation that would eventually be identified as symptoms of her schizophrenia. Peter, on occasion, was forced to contain her physically by pinning her arms to her sides, but, as well as being unpredictable and violent, she also seemed to be wasting away.

In the interval between two of his visits, in the middle of her second year at the college, she shed around a stone and, the following week, back in Bingley, he received a telegram from Sonia which said simply: 'Meet me at King's Cross station', day and time unspecified. Believing that she was 'still her father's responsibility', he took the telegram round to Mr Szurma, who made a dash for the next train.

Convinced that 'all the machinery was stopping and the world was coming to an end,' Sonia had wandered out into the street at night in her pyjamas, where she had been apprehended and later admitted to a Bexley hospital. The next time Peter saw her was after her transfer to the Linfield Mount psychiatric hospital in Bradford, and he was dismayed.

He thought she looked grey and 'terrible'; she thought he was an aeroplane. Among her other delusions was that she was 'the second Christ' – she could 'see' the stigmata on her hands. She was also restless and shrill and insistent that she wanted 'a bigger teddy-bear'. Her parents suggested that, once she was discharged and back living at home with them, it would be best if he didn't see her for a while.

He didn't see her for several weeks, and when he eventually did it didn't strike him that progress was being made. Far from being emaciated, Sonia had now taken on a bland and bloated look from 'the tablets' that she had been prescribed. She was lethargic and almost devoid of personality, it seemed to him. He felt he hardly knew her any more.

His determination to get reacquainted, however, combined with an unusual gentleness and patience, impressed the Szurmas, who up to then had proved politely resistant to their would-be son-in-law's shy and occasionally queasy charm.

He was determined to 'pull her through', he told Mr and Mrs Szurma, as he had told members of his own family, who only knew that Sonia had suffered some sort of breakdown brought on by 'over-studying'.

She was well enough to go to Trevor Birdsall's wedding with Peter later in 1972, and they would occasionally go out drinking in pubs in Bradford or Halifax with Trevor and Melissa, who also worked at Baird's TV. But a few months after coming out of hospital, Sonia suffered a relapse: this time, part of the pattern of her generally disturbed and frenetic behaviour included tearing her clothes off in public or at odd times at home, such as in the middle of a meal. By the time she reappeared at Cornwall Road her condition had improved, but her rehabilitation was still far from complete.

She had become inseparable from the pop music annual that her father had taken away from her when she was younger. And one night, Jane Sutcliffe, who was still only fifteen and nervous of Sonia's unpredictable behaviour, was given a glimpse of the, to her, incomprehensible chaos of her mind. 'One night she came round and Pete went straight off to the bathroom as usual and left her with me. I were just sitting quiet, reading, when Sonia stood up an' did a little twirl in front of the settee. "Guess who I am today?" she said. She were just wearing a little summer cotton frock, a shawl an' these silver sandals. "Cinderella," she said. I thought, "Oh, bloody hell . . .'"

Nothing was ever said to Peter, though. Nobody at Cornwall Road ever broached the subject, or enquired into the details of what Jane's father called Sonia's 'queer do'. Peter, as always, kept his own counsel.

13

The atmosphere at Cornwall Road in the wake of the Bankfield Hotel affair was inevitably strained. John Sutcliffe was subject to abrupt changes of mood, and the family tended to keep out of his way as far as possible. Maureen was courting the soldier whom she would soon marry; Carl and Jane were growing up and making their own friends; and Peter spent most of his time when he was in the house 'playing' with his Bullworker upstairs in the bedroom.

They had never known their parents to show each other affection and it was embarrassing now to see their father reach for their mother's hand or slip an arm around her shoulder while watching television. It wasn't 'natural', and Kathleen seemed to share their discomfort, aware that at any minute he was likely to return to the subject of her 'unfaithfulness' to him; to Jane, her mother always looked 'dead embarrassed'.

John had been unable to stop himself brooding on the supposed infidelity, and repeatedly found himself raking over the recent past for 'clues' that should have alerted him. There was the evening, for instance, when he had left for work a couple of hours later than usual in order to watch a Buster Crabbe film on television, only to have it interrupted by a caller who turned out to be Albert, the policeman. In retrospect, he had seemed confused and had 'snapped together a quick excuse' that was never convincing, about coming to see Mick about some gun . . . Kathleen, he now believed, had looked despondent when he told her he was moving to the new late shift after working constant nights for six years, when he could have expected her to look pleased . . .

It got so that, whenever she wasn't in the house, he was suspicious about what she was doing. 'Did your mother meet any men?' he wanted to know when Carl came home after being away with her for a week in Arnside. And the more she pleaded with him to forget the whole thing, that he was blowing it up out of all proportion, the more inconsolable he became.

'I were so up-tight and upset about it all I couldn't even be me normal self. She just kept saying, "Oh don't let it worry you so much; when all's said and done it's nothing." Nothing! My wife having an affair with another feller for three years without my knowing . . . So I had to do something to persuade her that it was something. It had got to the point where I simply couldn't stand the sight of her any more. There had to be a break.'

The houses on the north side of Cornwall Road backed directly on to the houses on The Oval, so that their inhabitants lived under conditions of enforced intimacy with each other: the fences between gardens had for the most part disappeared, and the gardens' individual identities with them – they had disintegrated into a single greasy patch littered with the husks of gas cookers and refrigerators and the skeletons of prams.

The Sutcliffes' nearest neighbour on The Oval was a woman who hadn't let the fact that she was deaf and dumb preclude her from building up a firm friendship with Kathleen: they communicated in a kind of improvised sign language which, as often as not, consisted of Mrs Broughton indicating that she would like to borrow something of which she had 'run short'. The mother of four children, Wendy was not a 'good manager': this was reflected both in her own appearance and in her house, which was never a candidate for the compliment, much prized locally, that it was so clean you could eat your dinner off the floor.

It was only in 1972, though, after her husband left her to go and live with another woman in Bradford, that John Sutcliffe started 'bothering with' Wendy Broughton. He wanted, he told her, 'to do the same to Kath as she had done to him'. Ironically, it was Kathleen, he later claimed, who was responsible for bringing them together.

'I took the wife down to the Fisherman one night and Wendy

was in, and it were the wife who more or less introduced me to her. Her husband had just blown and she were at a bit of a loose end, I think, so she asked her to come and sit at our table. But there was something on the television at that time that wife were watching which started about nine o'clock, so after we'd been there about an hour she went home to watch this programme, leaving me an' Wendy just sat there.

'That was the first time I'd really spoken to her, and I was at a complete loss. But we sat and we gesticulated at each other as best we could. I sort of made meself agreeable to her. And then suddenly, after that night, I found that she started to come into the pub regularly, and if I was there by meself she used to make a beeline for me. I used to sort of get landed with her.'

He was experiencing similar 'difficulties' with Annie Rhodes, the woman with the crooked spine whom his father had befriended, but in whose company he was frequently seen. It was Wendy though who staked the greater claim to his attentions and who precipitated the break-up with his wife.

Maureen had married for the second time in 1973 and moved with her new husband to Cambridge where his regiment, the Royal Engineers, was stationed. Returning home later that year on a visit, she witnessed a scene that left her dumbfounded.

'I were just on me way up to bed when me mother, who was usually the most placid person, came out of the kitchen screaming and shouting and belled me dad one. She pinned him up against piano and belled him. I were just speechless. I didn't know what to think. And our Jane said, "It's him," she said. "He's been up to Wendy Broughton's."

'I just laughed. I said, "Don't be so *stupid*." And Jane said, "It's true. It's been going on for months." But nobody had told me. They never told me anything, because we tend in our family to, not exactly sweep things under the carpet, but to believe that: just ignore it and it'll go away. It just seemed so ridiculous, the whole thing. It were pathetic.'

Maureen was in the advanced stages of pregnancy at the time. Before the baby had been born, her father had moved out of

Cornwall Road and in with Mrs Broughton, who, by early 1974, was living a quarter of a mile away in a council maisonette on the edge of Ferncliffe Estate. To Carl, it seemed a real cause for celebration. 'I thought it were brilliant when he went. I nearly got flags out. I were right happy. It were only me mum that were miserable.'

Peter, however, as perhaps only Mick realised, was miserable, too. 'He got a bit sick when me father was knockin' Wendy Broughton off. He used to play hell about that to me. It were too near doorstep, that was the trouble. It were impossible for me mother not to know what was going off, an' our lad didn't like seeing her get upset over it.'

Peter went round to Mrs Broughton's and made representations on behalf of his mother, but without much effect. His father told him that he was only 'getting my own back', which is what he also told Jane on the day in April 1974 when she called to let him know that Maureen had given birth to Damien, his first grandson. The result was a stand-up row, in the course of which Jane said she thought that if that was the case then he'd taken a bloody long time about it – four years, to be precise.

The sniping continued back and forth for eleven weeks, at the end of which the main parties involved agreed to sit down and talk. It was decided, largely because of the financial mess Kathleen had got herself into in his absence, that he would return home, John would later claim.

'Although I were paying her money every week, she was getting into so much debt in one way or another during that traumatic time that it was obvious to me she'd been taught her lesson. So I went back and all her financial difficulties were straightened up within a fortnight.'

The neighbours, whose confusion was already considerable, eventually gave up trying to disentangle the web of relationships that, even after this episode, continued to exist between the two households. When Wendy and her children were temporarily forced out of their home by fire in 1976, many people living on Cornwall Road were astonished to see Johnny, one of the three

Broughton boys, being taken in by Kathleen. 'He wasn't getting fed properly. His mother never cooked him a decent meal, so he's living with us for a few weeks,' she blithely explained.

It seemed to support John Sutcliffe's contention that the separation had served to clear the air. 'We were able to put the past behind us then and live quite happily together. It eased my feelings towards her because I pretty well knew that she was on the level after that. I knew that she would *never* do it again.'

The day her father moved back home, though, Jane moved out. Mick's wife had left him, and Jane and her boyfriend moved in with Mick on Queensway until they were married in October 1974, two months after Peter and Sonia. Carl, the youngest, and Peter, the oldest of Kathleen's six children, were the last ones to go.

Sonia was in and out of circulation throughout 1972 and '73, depending on her 'nerves', which meant that Peter was left to his own devices much of the time. His unhappy experiences involving the £10 note and subsequent brush with the law had done nothing to dent his curiosity about Bradford's red-light district and its inhabitants; if anything, his fascination with 'the Lane' seemed intensified as a result.

No night out with Trevor was now complete without the *frisson* of a special detour to take in the barely lit, pitted streets around Manningham. 'What about two pound?' he'd say when the woman his car had been tailing quoted him £3 as her price for 'doing business'. 'Is that all you're worth?' he'd shoot back when she accepted his offer, and drive home with a grin on his face.

This pastime came to an end, however, when he started work as a furnace operator at Anderton Circlips Ltd, on the canal in Bingley, in April 1973. Working nights, as he would for the next two years, had several distinct advantages for a dedicated saver and 'planner', the most important being that he made more money and had less opportunity to spend it. In the process, though, Peter became an even shadowier presence within his family, going to bed when they were getting up, leaving the house as they were arriving home, and spending most weekends with Sonia.

Naturally reserved and cautious though they were, the Szurmas had had any doubts they may have harboured about Peter irresistibly eroded by his unselfish, and obviously sincere, commitment to nursing their daughter back to health. His readiness to forgo the livelier pleasures of the pub and 'disco' in order to sit indoors playing chess for hours with Sonia's father, or go for long quiet walks on the moors, convinced them of the seriousness of his intentions, and established beyond any doubt in their minds that he was 'steady'.

Mrs Szurma was especially taken with his earnest, endearingly awkward manner, and by his willingness to 'do anything' for her. He would drop everything and drive her to the nursing home where she worked; he was prepared to stand outside in all weathers tinkering with the small car that she ran. He was as happy to fetch and carry for her as he had always been for his own mother. She only had to say the word.

Sonia's recovery was a slow process, demanding a great deal in perseverance and patience from the people closest to her. Not until May 1976, exactly four years after her initial breakdown, would her doctor be able to issue a clean bill of health and recommend that she be allowed to resume full-time teachers' training. But she was intermittently well enough to tackle some student-teaching; and, with the proviso that she went on living under their supervision at Tanton Crescent, her parents agreed that Peter and Sonia should be married on 10 August 1974, Sonia's twenty-fourth birthday.

Peter had had religion 'pumped into' him all his life at school but, unlike Mick, had never resisted or particularly seemed to resent it. Mick was constantly being singled out by Father O-Sullivan on his Monday visits to Cottingley Manor Secondary Modern for having failed to turn up at Sunday Mass, and was always getting into hot water for daring to answer back. 'I mean,' he'd say, unable to resist the impulse to show off in front of the class, 'I were baptised an' brought up as a Catholic from when I were six months old. I had no say in it. I don't think owt about it. I'd rather be rabbiting.'

He submitted to wearing 'all them bloody white dresses an' stuff' when his turn came around, but limited his appearance at the Sacred Heart to once a year – Christmas Eve – as soon as he left school. Peter, on the other hand, had continued as an altar-server up to the summer when his grandmother Coonan had died, and the priest stopped coming to the house, around the time of his eighteenth birthday. After that he seemed to turn his back on the Church and struck Carl, then still in the throes of a Catholic education, as 'a complete atheist – anti-religious completely'.

The choice of Clayton Baptist Chapel for the wedding was Sonia's: built of local stone and picturesquely situated at the heart of the old Clayton village, only a quarter of a mile from where she had been brought up, the church offered the perfect backdrop for the kind of traditional, romantic, white wedding that she was envisaging. Peter, though, was deputed to go and see the Reverend William Nelson alone. He explained that Sonia was too shy to come and talk about the marriage herself, but Reverend Nelson told him that, because they were strangers to the church, he needed to see them both. When he did, the only reason he could get out of Sonia for wanting to marry at the Baptist's was that she had been to a friend's wedding there and she liked the service and the building. They seemed a nice, intelligent young couple and he could see no reason to turn them away.

A cold buffet lunch for forty was ordered at the Quarry Arms, a homely pub backed on to a field halfway between Tanton Crescent and the church; and John Sutcliffe, as his contribution, started work on a three-tiered iced cake topped with a silver heart. The only part of the arrangement that foundered was Peter's search for a best man. Mick was out for obvious reasons, and would have refused even if he had been asked, he let it be known, 'because of what he's marrying'. Trevor and Eric and everybody else who might have been considered were too daunted by the thought of wrestling with the etiquette involved, especially standing up to make a speech.

Just in time, however, a mild-mannered former classmate from Cottingley Manor called Ronnie Wilson was recruited and even inveigled into wearing the same two-toned, platform-soled shoes for the occasion as the groom. But on the ritual stag night pub crawl around Manningham, Ronnie fell down on the first of his duties: he let Peter get hopelessly drunk.

Mick, in fact, had decided in advance that this was how the evening was going to end and had been slipping large measures of Pernod into his brother's glasses of Guinness. When he realised, too late, what had been happening, Peter attempted to butt Mick with his head and, as a result, was married with a bruised lower lip. This, together with the red roses and the silver wedding dress that Maureen would remember as the most beautiful she had ever seen, was faithfully captured in colour by the cameraman hired to record the proceedings on cine-film.

When they returned from a short honeymoon in Paris, the new Mr and Mrs Sutcliffe started their married life in the back bedroom at Tanton Crescent that had been prepared for them. Almost from the beginning, though, things proved difficult. Peter's relationship with his in-laws was cordial enough, and they adapted to each other easily. But Sonia could still be temperamental and erratic, and the atmosphere around her was frequently explosive. Sonia was often the subject of rows between her mother and father, whom she rowed with herself independently, and neighbours would occasionally hear her raised voice at nights through the bedroom window. Her relations with her father before she left Tanton Crescent would eventually deteriorate to the point where they only communicated in writing or through a third party; but Mrs Szurma was insistent that they went on living there until they could afford the deposit on a house of their own, even if, as it did, this took a number of years.

For the first six months after they were married, Peter went on working on the night shift at Anderton's in Bingley, only a short walk from Cornwall Road. He was a regular caller at the house on his own on weekdays, and at weekends with Sonia. On these visits he took to elaborating on a habit so familiar that Mick, in common with the rest of the family, had stopped commenting on it years earlier.

'Me mother used to keep his dinner in oven till he came in from work, then it were straight on to table. It'd be cold and back on to table again, though, by the time he came down to get it. I don't know what he were up to, but he'd come in door and go straight up steps an' she'd be shouting of him to come down for his dinner for long enough or it'd be ruined.

'He wouldn't have changed or had a wash or owt. He'd come down same as he were. But you could hear him in one bedroom, then another an' sort of going right round house. You could hear doors opening an' shutting an' that, so you could tell he were rootin'.

'Even after he got married he were same. Even when he weren't living at home, he used to come in an' sneak about. If he came wi' Sonia he'd stick her in living-room or kitchen an' slope off.'

As with his other idiosyncracies, this had come to seem so routine that nobody in his family bothered to bring it up with Peter. Carl though, as he entered his teens, became curious about what his brother got up to upstairs, and from time to time attempted to find out.

'It's just a thing we'd got used to, because he'd done it for years and years. He were always rooting. We used to look on it as a bit of a joke. We used to say, "Oh, he's at it, creepin' about again. We'll just ignore him."

'Every time he'd come, he'd pop his head round door and say, "I'll not be a minute, I'll just go to toilet." And you'd hear him upstairs, moving about from room to room. Many a time I've crept up and caught him at it. I used to do it a lot on purpose, creep up, then say, "Hello, Pete!" He'd be stood in bedroom looking in drawers, wardrobes, all over the place; under beds. "Oh, I'm just looking for a screwdriver," he'd say, trying to look all relaxed. He liked to know what we all had.

'Other times, I used to walk up steps an' hear him *run* from bedroom into toilet and shut door. He used to do it all the time.'

A shirt, though, is the only possession of his that Carl ever noticed had actually gone missing. 'He had a really funny taste in clothes. Loadsa colours. He liked really jazzy ties an' things. An' I remember getting this shirt new, about two years earlier, an' Pete mekkin a right fuss about colour. He thought it were fuckin' superb.

'Anyway, one day about a month after he'd been round rooting he appeared in this shirt, which were fucked by then: all collar were frayed, 'cause I just used to wear it for working in. So I says to him, "Hey, that's my shirt," which seemed to right surprise him. "It's a real colour, isn't it?" he said. An' that were all.'

Peter's father, less aware than the rest of the family of the extent of the 'rooting' ritual, had a rational explanation. 'A lot of times he'd come down and, if he wanted to do a job on his car and he didn't have the equipment to do it, he'd go up and have a look at what I had in my drawer upstairs. I had a big bottom drawer that I kept a collection of various tools and things in . . . I remember a time when I had three pairs of pliers and eventually I finished up not having any at all.'

John Sutcliffe was more bemused by Peter's habit of isolating himself in the bathroom or the toilet for hours, which showed no signs of diminishing even as a married man. Carl observed him once through the hole made by an airgun pellet in the bathroom door: 'He were stood wi' scissors, trimming his beard, then he'd stop and look at it for ages and comb it. Then he'd sort of snip in thin air, not touching owt. Then he'd cut right neat little patterns on it. He were up there ages.'

The pleasure that Peter seemed to derive from being on his own in a confined space for long periods suggested, to a few of those who knew him, that he would be perfectly suited to earning his living driving a car or a 'wagon'. Although he had only got round to equipping himself with a full licence in his early twenties, he had never been without 'wheels' from the age of seventeen and was generally considered to be a 'brilliant' driver. By the time he got married the 'bangers' of his youth had given way to a wide-wheeled, lime-green K-registration Ford Capri GT, and he was constantly on the lookout for cheap motors to do up and sell at a small profit. Friends, even friends of friends, only had to mention that they were having engine trouble for him to be immediately under the bonnet.

To Mick, his tinkering at times seemed to verge on the obsessive: 'If they were all right he'd have to tek 'em to bits. He were never satisfied. If he'd have got a brand spanking new 'un out of a shop and it hadn't even done one mile, he'd still have been probin' about, tekkin summat off it.'

He often seemed to live not only for, but *in*, his cars, and sometimes owned two or three at once. They afforded a degree of privacy which, until he had his own house, it was impossible to find anywhere else. So when, in February 1975, Anderton's asked for voluntary redundancies, Peter leaped at the opportunity as a way of realising what by then had become an ambition. He invested half the £400 pay-off money in a course of HGV driving lessons at the APEX School of Driving (giving 'Cornwall Road' as his address, rather than Tanton Crescent). And, two days after his twenty-ninth birthday, in June that year, he passed his Heavy Goods Vehicle test at Steeton, earning himself a class-1 licence.

To get to Steeton, it is necessary to skirt the centre of Keighley which, by the summer of 1975, had been Anna Rogulskyj's home for more than a dozen years. Despite her name, Mrs Rogulskyj was originally from a rural part of southern Ireland, which was largely thought to account for her open, warm, almost childlike manner. In a tall, attractive ash-blonde in her early thirties, however, a divorcee and therefore frequently seen around town alone, her friendliness was felt to invite misinterpretation, and she was often accosted by men unaccustomed to seeing women leading happy, independent lives of their own.

She didn't pay much attention, therefore, when she was approached in the Town Hall square one day by a dark-haired man with a springy black beard who wanted to know if he could come home with her for a cup of tea. She was slightly more perturbed when he started following her up Highfield Lane to where she lived, but she eventually managed to throw him off.

A few weeks later the same man followed her into Wild's coffee bar in the town centre where she used to work and, sitting across the table from her, offered to buy her a drink. This time she was aware of his large, 'racing' eyes and his 'dainty' hands. When it became obvious she was about to make a fuss, he disappeared, only to re-enter her life after a gap of a further few weeks.

On the evening of Friday, 4 July 1975, Anna Rogulskyj had a row with the Welshman who was her current boyfriend. It ended with him hiding every pair of shoes that she owned to stop her going out that night, which was the sort of behaviour she was coming to expect from Geoff: shortly after she had met him, he had grabbed her head and plunged it into a full bucket of water, in the house in the centre of Keighley where he lived. She later learned that he had been a long-term patient in a mental hospital and, on release, had been advised 'to keep away from women for five years'.

But Geoff had bought her a colour television that week, and Anna was 'made up' with it. She eventually discovered where he'd hidden her shoes – on the seats of chairs pushed under the kitchen table – and couldn't resist calling on him on her way to the bus station to let him know that she'd 'escaped'.

The television apart, though, she was becoming frightened of Geoff, and that Friday night was feeling 'a bit tearful'. She took the bus to her sister's in Heaton and, finding her out, went on to the bar at the Victoria Hotel near Bradford's bus and rail 'Interchange', which enjoyed a reputation for being 'select' compared to the many other 'places of low renown' in the vicinity.

After last orders she was given a lift home to Keighley by a taxi-driver friend who dropped her at her front door. It was a warm, pleasant night, and she found herself playing Elvis Presley's 'Crying in the Chapel' over and over while she brought some sheets in that had been drying and folded them in the kitchen. It was then that she noticed that 'Dum-dum', her deaf kitten, was missing, and she convinced herself for some reason that Geoff had been and taken him.

It was now after 1.00 a.m., but where Geoff lived was no more than a five-minute walk away and she set off purposefully, walking downhill in the direction of the Town Hall and the police station.

She had left the police station behind her and was approaching the largely vacated and boarded up North Queen Street when she heard a man's voice in a darkened doorway asking whether she 'fancied it?' 'Not on your life,' she said, and hurried on to Geoff's house where even her knocking and pounding, however, couldn't raise him. Turning on her heels, having first put one of the downstairs windows in with her shoe in a fit of pique, she heard the same man asking the same question and again she rebuffed him.

Unable to find anybody to go with him, Peter Sutcliffe had been out doing the rounds of the pubs alone all night. He allowed Mrs Rogulskyj to walk a few paces further before levelling three blows at her head with the balled end of a ball-pein hammer. He had raised her blouse and made exploratory slashes and was about to plunge a knife into her stomach when a man living in Lord Street, calling out to ask what was happening, panicked him and he fled.

Anna Rogulskyj wasn't discovered for an hour, and after being admitted to Leeds General Infirmary was given the last rites. A twelve-hour operation, in the course of which splinters of bone were tweezered out of her brain, saved her life. But the description of her attacker, whom she had in fact encountered twice before, was effectively erased.

Living in Clayton, Peter had once again become a near neighbour of his old friend Trevor Birdsall and, after a two-year lull while he was working constant nights, they had resumed their late night tours of the red-light district. By 1975, though, they were starting to broaden their horizons and had added Huddersfield and Leeds, as well as smaller towns like Skipton and Halifax with no known prostitute populations, to their itinerary.

On the night of Friday, 15 August 1975, five weeks after the attempted murder of Anna Rogulskyj in Keighley, and the week of Peter's first wedding anniversary, they went drinking together in Halifax where, in the Royal Oak, their path crossed that of Olive Smelt. Mrs Smelt, a forty-six-year-old office cleaner, looked forward to her Friday nights on the town with a woman friend as both a break from the tedium of work and the occasional turbulence of her family life, and she was a familiar figure around the pubs.

Peter, however, singled her out immediately as a 'prostitute'. 'I bet she's on the game,' he said to Trevor, and he said much the same straight to Mrs Smelt's face when he passed her on his way to the toilet. Mrs Smelt was capable of giving as good as she got, though, and emerged the clear winner of this exchange.

Later, less than a mile into the ten-mile drive back to Bradford, Sutcliffe pulled his car sharply over. 'That's the old bag who was in the pub,' he said, indicating Olive Smelt, who had just turned into an alleyway two or three hundred yards from her home. Slipping out of the car, he quickly caught up with her and mumbled a pleasantry about the weather before striking her twice on the back of the head with a hammer. He had had time to drag a hacksaw blade once or twice across the small of her back when approaching headlights disturbed him. Back in the safety of his own car, he appeared 'unusually quiet' to Birdsall; when asked what had taken him so long he replied that he had been 'talking to that woman'.

Next day, reading about the apparently motiveless attack on Olive Smelt in his local paper – she 'had not been sexually assaulted'; nothing had been stolen – Birdsall had little doubt that it was the same woman. But misplaced loyalty prevented him from doing anything about it. Violence aimed at women was, in any case, a commonplace in the circles in which he moved, both in Allerton, where he lived, and around the Manningham area where his face was becoming increasingly familiar in the pubs and between-hours 'dives', and in the cafes where the 'pot-dogs' sat in the windows touting for business.

Violence could, and regularly did, flare up in a matter of seconds in all these places, and women – prostitutes who had 'crossed' their pimps, girlfriends turning up late, wives 'caught' looking at another man – were not infrequently on the receiving end. The fact that Melissa, Trevor Birdsall's wife of three years, had lost a leg in a road accident as a child, did not guarantee her

133

any immunity: she was constantly complaining to neighbours in Allerton that Trevor had been 'braying' her again, and had the bruises to prove it.

Late in the summer of 1975, Peter and Sonia joined Mr and Mrs Szurma on a holiday visit to some of their relatives in Czechoslovakia, stopping in Rome on the way. Sonia not only had a grandmother who was still alive but also great-grandparents who were both aged around a hundred and still growing their own tobacco and brewing their own beer in the countryside near Prague.

On their return at the end of September, Peter joined the Common Road Tyre Company in Bradford as a driver. The work involved short- and medium-distance hauls all over the North and the Midlands, and he used the experience to familiarise himself with the network of motorways and trunk-roads linking his destinations to each other and to West Yorkshire. He also became an authority on the best access routes to many town and city centres, to some of which he was already less than a stranger.

The rivalry between Leeds and Bradford, two cities whose western and eastern suburbs have long been hopelessly entangled, is so ancient and so fierce as to preclude either place surrendering its identity to the other. Both prospered from worsted and woollen manufacturing throughout the nineteenth century, and vied with each other to erect the grand houses and prestigious civic monuments that, even a hundred and fifty years later, still loaned them the same air of unshakeable Victorian solidity.

Although geographically less compact than Bradford's Manningham area, by the mid-1970s Chapeltown in Leeds presented the same picture of 'inner-city' dereliction and decay. The red brick villas once occupied by prosperous mercantile families had gone over to multi-occupation; former Methodist chapels had become mosques, and synagogues had been converted for use as drinking clubs and permanently twilight 'shebeens', where drugs, jewellery and sexual favours were indiscriminately bartered, wrangled over, sometimes even bought and sold.

The Chapeltown ethos had taken root in several city-centre pubs such as the Regent, the White Swan, the Scotsman and Bar-Barella's in Vicar Lane where bar-maids with denim hot-pants gnawing into chapped thighs took orders for 'the Barbarella Legspreader', and the disc-jockey, between records, did commercials for amphetamines: 'Worried that your willie's two inches too short? Buy a bottle of poppers from behind the bar! Only twelve pound! You won't know what you're doing, but it'll feel like a snake!'

It was in this milieu that Wilma McCann, after moving to Leeds from Scotland with her husband and four small children in 1970, felt most at home. By 1975, though, Gerry McCann had left her and Wilma was bringing up her children, then aged from five to nine, on what she could earn on the street. Most nights she turned her back on the dirty dishes and unmade beds in the council house where she lived on the edge of Chapeltown and began her tour of the clubs and pubs, leaving Sonje, the oldest, to take care of things until she returned home.

On the night of Wednesday, 29 October 1975, Wilma, wearing white flared trousers, a blue bolero jacket and a pink blouse, was spotted drinking whiskies in the Regent, the Scotsman and the Royal Oak.

On her way home she called at the 'Room and the Top', a drinking club in Sheepscar, and emerged shortly before 1.00 a.m. carrying a container of curry and chips.

It was only a short walk back to Scott Hall Avenue but, as often happened, Wilma staggered around recklessly in front of the traffic on Meanwood road in the hope of 'commandeering' a lift. A lorry heading towards the M62 did stop, but the driver declined to pick her up. And then Peter Sutcliffe's green Ford Capri pulled over.

'I was driving through Leeds at night. I had been having a couple of pints and I saw this woman thumbing a lift,' he would later claim. 'I stopped and asked her how far she was going, and she said, "Not far. Thanks for stopping," and jumped in. I was in quite a good mood and, just before we set off, she said, Did I want business? I asked what she meant and, to me, a scornful tone came into her voice. She said: "Bloody hell, do I have to spell it out?"'

A few minutes later they parked near the Prince Philip playing fields, only a hundred yards from Wilma McCann's back door. 'Before we started she said it cost a fiver. I was a bit surprised. I was expecting to be a bit romantic. I couldn't have intercourse at a split-second. I had to be aroused. But all of a sudden she said: "I'm going. It's going to take you all fuckin' day. You're fuckin' useless." I felt myself seething with rage. I wanted to hit her.'

He asked her to 'hang on a minute' and not to 'go off like that'. 'She said, "Oh, you can manage it now, can you?" It sounded as though she was taunting me. I said: "Can we do it on the grass?" . . . and she stormed off up the field.' Taking a hammer out of his tool-box in the car, he followed her and spread his coat on the damp ground. 'She sat down on the coat and unfastened her trousers and said, "Come on, get it over with." I said, "Don't worry, I will." I then hit her with the hammer on top of the head. She made a lot of noise and kept on making noise, so I hit her again.'

In a 'numb panic', he sat in his car watching Wilma McCann's arm jerking up and down. He returned to his tool-box and this time removed a knife, with which he approached her still moving body.

He 'shot off' home once he was quite sure she was dead, and checked his clothes for blood before quietly letting himself into his mother-in-law's house. Once inside he went straight to the bathroom, washed his hands and climbed quickly into bed.

Wilma McCann's body was discovered by a milkman on the Prince Philip playing fields at 7.41 the following morning. She was lying on her back with her trousers around her knees and her brassiere lifted to expose her breasts. She had been stabbed nine times in the lower abdomen and five times in the chest, as the police photographs and the pathologist's report would testify. But because of the nature of her wounds, the lacerations and dark brown holes perverting her pale body, by the time she was found she was already starting to look like merely the remnant of a person, like an impersonal bundle or a crumpled mannequin; or like something out of what Michael Sutcliffe would come to think of as 'Peter's room'.

PART TWO

Room

15

There is a direct rail link between Bingley and the sea. The journey to Morecambe, on the Lancashire coast, takes just under ninety minutes and Bingley people, usually travelling en masse, have been making it for years.

Smaller, slower and less brash than Blackpool, which lies thirty miles to the south, Morecambe – or 'Bradford-on-Sea' as it was known before the mill-hands who used to swarm over the Pennines in their hundreds of thousands discovered Corfu and the Costa Brava – has remained cheerfully, almost resolutely, set in its ways. Few attempts have been made to cater to 'the younger stream', and in fact the Mods who took to descending on the town on Bank Holiday weekends were strenuously discouraged.

Even the illuminations, the traditional destination for generations of school and works outings, ritually acknowledging the fact that the nights have started to set in, have made few concessions to the times; extraterrestrials and characters from the Muppets have failed to oust Gilbert and Sullivan and Silent Comedy Classics as popular tableau themes.

'Health Abounds, Beauty Surrounds' is a slogan that has sustained many Bingley couples throughout their working lives. And many a coach-clock presented with due ceremony at the Bankfield Hotel has eventually claimed pride of place on a mantelpiece in one of the neat, gaily painted terraced streets situated within gentle strolling distance of Morecambe front.

Anne Sutcliffe's parents-in-law, the Stookys, moved to Morecambe from Bingley shortly after they retired, and Anne and Trevor followed them a few years later. Because she was the closest in age to Peter, Anne grew up understanding him better than her sisters. She had acted as his 'protector' at school, defending him against the bullies and, later, in their early teens, Peter had insisted on returning the favour, escorting her to dances and parties 'to make sure she was all right'.

After her marriage to Trevor Stooky, a general labourer, in 1966, Anne went on living in Bingley for a number of years. But as work became more and more scarce in the area, and because Trevor was constantly getting into scrapes, usually after being out drinking with his brother, they decided to take his parents up on a generous offer of self-contained accommodation in their house. Their move to Morecambe in the mid-1970s happened to coincide with the storm that was then raging around one of the longest established tourist attractions on the promenade.

The old Whitehall Theatre at the west end of the town had stood empty and wind-lashed for many years when Mr George Nicholson, late of Tussaud's, Blackpool, purchased the freehold and converted it into a waxworks 'in the Tussaud family tradition', just in time for the beginning of the summer season, 1956.

Mr Nicholson started off modestly at first, with only twenty-eight models. The exhibition was comprised mainly of historical figures – Abraham Lincoln, Florence Nightingale, William Shakespeare, Disraeli – and leading sporting, political and entertainment personalities of the day. Stanley Matthews, Gilbert Harding, Norman Wisdom, Sir Anthony Eden and Sabrina were among those who took their places in the room-sized cabinets that stood where the front-stalls once had and therefore inclined gently with the floor.

Business, however, didn't exactly boom. 'The bodies,' as Mr Nicholson, a clipper little man with a toothbrush moustache, would say, 'aren't coming in to seè the bodies.' But, instead of concentrating on increasing the verisimilitude of his dummies, whose heads were disproportionately large for their uniformly foreshortened trunks, making them look like the victims of some unpleasant stunting disease, the proprietor's solution was to expand upstairs, into what had once been the dress-circle.

The glass cabinets and wall-eyed models were duly manufactured and installed, but still the expected crowds failed to flock in. This was largely thought to be because Mr Nicholson had not achieved the vital balance between the 'respectable' and the macabre that, a century earlier, had made the original Madame Tussaud a household name. That the scales were tipped heavily in favour of the latter it was possible to sense without even crossing the threshold of Nicholson's wax museum. The theatrically over-made-up old woman in the ticket booth, the heavy, cast iron turnstile and the effigied 'commissionaire' generated an atmosphere all too reminiscent of the Edgar Lustgarten and Edgar Wallace 'chillers' that had played as second features at the Whitehall in the years immediately leading up to its demise.

Twenty years later very little had changed, except that quite unwittingly, in the 1970s, Mr Nicholson's wax museum had turned into a grotesque, if curiously compelling, period piece. The patterned wallpaper had faded, the ubiquitous black paintwork had grown scuffed and dulled, and the moths had feasted indiscriminately on everything from Pat Smythe's jodhpurs to Arthur Askey's shirt. 'Stalin' had been reduced to black wellington boots and a lady's astrakhan coat, and 'Princess Margaret' had been graced with a particularly ill-fitting, matted brown wig.

Upstairs, meanwhile, visitors had to be careful when walking round the Chamber of Horrors not to trip over one of several buckets put down to catch the rain seeping in in large drops through the roof. This was a real possibility in the almost palpable darkness which, together with the 'murderers' in their chicken-wire-and-boxwood cages – Dr Crippen, Ruth Ellis, Reginald Christie, Neville Heath – and lurid set-pieces – 'Murder in the Bath', 'The Blood Hook', 'Jack the Ripper' – was guaranteed to make even the hottest blood run cold.

Even at the height of the season the waxworks would remain deserted for long stretches, and rarely welcomed more than a dozen visitors at any one time. Once inside, the familiar smells of the seaside – frying onions, diesel oil, the sea itself – were instantly blocked out by the smell of floor-polish and dust; the rasp of bingo callers and squeals of riders on the Magic Meteor at the nearby funfair gave way to silence only occasionally punctuated by the sound of rubber soles on lino and the faint clack of the turnstile turning outside.

By the mid-1970s, a diversity of business interests meant that Mr Nicholson no longer depended on the waxworks for his living. But even as a hobby, which is what it had more or less become by then, he was determined that it should, at the very least, pay its way. To this end he commissioned a smattering of new figures – Billy Connolly, Terry Wogan, whose head, for reasons of economy, was mounted on the body of the 'fifties 'crooner' Johnny Ray. More controversially, however, he introduced a whole new room to the exhibition, the contents of which he had acquired from a friend and associate of many years, recently bowed out of the world of wax.

'The Museum of Anatomy' was discreetly situated on the upper floor of Mr Nicholson's sea-front premises, its entrance no more than a hole in the wall between two of the big display cabinets; it lay directly behind an 'African tableau' featuring a 'Giraffe Necked Woman', a 'Plate Lipped Negress', and a 'Witch Doctor' consisting almost entirely of an ancient black rubber mask and a flaccid pair of black rubber gloves. It was not discreet enough, however, for the local watch committee who tried, and finally failed, to have this 'obscene' display closed down.

An inevitable result of the controversy that raged for weeks in the local press and on television was that Mr Nicholson's takings reached an all-time high. This upturn in business, though, was shortlived and, within a very few months, the woman in the ticket kiosk could go back to reading her woman's magazines and paperback romances virtually undisturbed. She certainly never noticed the actually rather striking young man with the frizzy black hair and friendly, gap-toothed smile who was becoming a regular customer.

With Anne and Trevor and, more importantly, his two nieces living there, and his grandmother Coonan's sister, Reenee, living in an old people's home in Morecambe, Peter had all the excuses he needed to stop off and see any or all of them after the middle of 1975, when he was regularly driving a wagon to or from Wales or Scotland, along the M6. Morecambe is only a ten-minute drive from the motorway at Lancaster, and he would drop in on Anne and her family or, less frequently, old Reenee, a couple of times a month. It was a rare visit when he didn't also find time to call at 'Tussaud's', either on his own or with Mick or Carl, to see 'if there was owt fresh in'. There rarely was.

Entering, he would immediately head for the steep wooden staircase on his right. After climbing the stairs to the upper gallery, he would then turn sharp left under the unblinking gaze of a rag-bag of dishevelled dummies, and pass quickly under the sign warning that what lies beyond is not suitable for anybody under the age of sixteen.

'The Museum of Anatomy' is a grandiose title for the two rather small, dimly lighted and musty chambers that the title embraces. Negotiating the sort of frosted glass 'modesty' screen often erected at the entrance to public lavatories, the visitor finds himself standing in a room whose first assault is on the nostrils: being Victorian, and therefore much prized by the Museum's owner for their 'antique' value, the exhibits here are fashioned out of ordinary candle-wax. Deployed in such bulk, it imbues the atmosphere with the warm, slightly sweet smell of animal fat. Candle-wax is also more brittle than the commercial tallow used in modern modelling techniques, and so some of the items on display in the second of the two rooms which make up the 'Museum of Anatomy' are held together with Sellotape or merely cratered with irreparable holes and cracks.

The exhibits hanging in Room One are, by comparison, in excellent condition. The only holes in the chorus of identical fig-ures occupying three of the walls of what Mick would come to think of as 'the Macabre Torso Room' are intentional. The torsos are life-size, headless, legless and female. There are nine of them and the cross-sections cut from their lower abdomens betray their function, which was to illustrate 'The nine stages of pregnancy' to an audience of Victorian lay people. Time, however, has eroded definition and basted the developing foetuses and the glistening ropes of internal organs to a uniform ox-blood colour; the impression is of gaping wounds around the umbilicus, growing progressively bigger, gorier and more congealed. Their antiquity is highlighted by the paleness of the simulated flesh and the freshness of the butcher's muslin which provides a 'bed' for the bodies and is neatly tucked and trimmed to just above the bare breasts and just below the pubic area.

But 'the Macabre Torso Room' merely serves as an antechamber to the smaller, airless, tunnel-like and infinitely more macabre gallery which leads off it and which is the focus of the exhibition. It is here that Peter used to like to linger.

'In these models you see the awful results of men leading immoral lives before marriage,' a sign announces at the centre of a room whose walls are crowded with heavy glass-fronted cases of the kind usually associated with the Victorian taxidermist's art. Here, though, each case is an essay in the terrible frailty of the flesh, rather than a sentimental composition of brightly feathered songbirds or frolicking kittens: the chancred lips of a vagina ooze and fester beneath a grey cloud of pubic hair, which itself is surrounded by male sexual organs in varying degrees of rottenness and putrefaction, like half-eaten sausages, decorously framed in muslin. Four babies' faces are obliterated by the sort of green scabs and horrible running sores that are an insistent theme, filling the room with images of feculence and pus. A hand is thrust deep into a womb, its fingers closed around a deformed foetus. Diseased scrotums are shown in cross-section then billow and burst . . .

The centrepiece of this battered collection, however, is the bust of a woman, 'an allegorical sculpture in wax', originally inspired by one of the numerous pieces of religious statuary representing the Virgin suckling the infant Jesus. The head is inclined sweetly and enclosed in a muslin 'wimple', and the first and second fingers of the right hand gently offer the left nipple. The nipple, though, is discoloured and heavily encrusted, and the bare, waxen white breasts are covered in burning venereal sores and hives.

To this piece, as to all the others, is affixed a faded card on which a homily has been penned in a fussy, Gothic script. 'Vice is a monster of so hideous a mien/That to be hated needs but to be seen,' it says on the case illustrating 'French pox in the female'. 'Wise men see the evil and avoid it/But fools pass on and are punished,' it says above the four mutilated children's heads. 'His own iniquities shall take the wicked himself. And he shall be holden with the cords of his sins,' it says above the rotting penises. 'To thoughtless husbands, this case well deserves their attention. For how many there are who are good husbands and good fathers yet when in their cups fall into temptation and contract a complaint which destroys the happiness of the family' is the inscription pinned to the bust of the 'Madonna'.

Stepping out of the 'Museum of Anatomy', the visitor is confronted with a full-scale replica of Christ on the cross whose brightness, after the half-dark, and in the half-dark in which it is one of the main sources of illumination, seems almost blinding.

Peter Sutcliffe was to claim that he was suffering from venereal disease several times in his life. The first occasion was around the time of the Bankfield Hotel 'unmasking' of his mother, and his reconciliation with Sonia, when he was almost twenty-four.

Keith Sugden hadn't exchanged more than a few words with his former best friend for nearly two years, not since his engagement to Doreen Hawkes, when Peter sought him out in the Ferrands one night to ask his advice on something which seemed to be worrying him. 'I were stood at bar when he suddenly came over and asked me did I have a minute? I asked him what were up and he said, "I think I've got summat. I think I've got a dose. Anyway it don't look right nice."

'So I went to toilet with him and he showed me an' he were right, it didn't. I mean, he didn't get it all out; he just showed me offending part. An' it had all gone white at end, where he hadn't been circumcised. All end had gone bloody white an' flaky. So I told him, I says, "You better go up to 'ospital with it, to St Luke's in Bradford, and get job sorted out."'

'Off one of them mucky bitches' had been Peter's reply when asked where he thought he'd picked up the infection, which Keith took to mean off 'a good-time girl' like the two he'd turned up with the night he'd arranged to go out for a drink with Keith and Doreen in Shipley. 'So bugger must be getting it somewhere,' Keith told Doreen when he got home, concluding his account of the incident. 'I don't know where though.'

16

Mick Sutcliffe never made any secret of his philandering. He could sleep in a different bed every night in Bingley if he chose to, and he frequently did. In Carl's eyes, however, this achievement never amounted to much. 'There's a wrestler on telly who looks just like an ugly old slag who lives in Bingley, but our Mick's given her one. Our Mick's given everybody one. He'd fuck a pig in knickers. He fucks anything that moves.'

From time to time Mick had 'gone with' a prostitute on Lumb Lane, and he was no stranger to the Carlisle or any of the other pubs around Manningham. But, on two or three occasions in the years after he was married, Peter insisted on giving his brother a demonstration of his superior knowledge.

'He used to tek us round red-light districts in motor an' say, "This is best spot to get 'em." He thought he were showing me summat new, but I knew already. He'd say, "Look at these here." So I'd fuckin' look at them, and that's all I'd want to do. "Look at this old scraggly cunt," he'd say, "coming towards us." Then he'd wind window down and ask how much. "A fiver," she'd say. "Oh fuck off," he'd shout, and we'd just drive off.'

This behaviour bore no resemblance to the thoughtful, gentle, courteous Peter whom everybody knew at home, the Peter who was always especially conspicuous at Christmas. Kathleen had made it a tradition at Cornwall Road to hold 'open house' on Boxing Day for any old people in the family who lived alone. These included Grandma Coonan's sister, Reenee; Grandfather Sutcliffe's sister, Mabel; and an 'adopted' aunt, crippled with arthritis, called Josie London. And Peter had taken it upon himself to collect 'his' old ladies from their homes every year and run them back again in the evening. In fact, these were the parts of the day that some of them seemed to look forward to with the greatest sense of anticipation.

Even in the late 1970s, long after her own failing health had obliged his mother to withdraw her standing invitation, Peter continued to visit his elderly aunts during the Christmas period. Sometimes with Sonia, sometimes alone, he'd call with a card and a small present, staying long enough for a cup of tea and a chat.

Hand-delivering his Christmas cards and, in the process, reviving friendships that had perhaps been allowed to lie fallow became a regular habit with Peter after he moved away from Bingley. This was one of the ways in which he kept in touch with Arthur Bisby, the insurance agent in Crossflatts; and Christmas 1975 was no exception to this, nor was it in any way exceptional.

Less than four weeks after Peter's usual protracted visit, though, Arthur Bisby was shocked to read a report in the local paper on the death of the wife of an old school-friend of his. Emily Jackson's mutilated body had been found by a workman in a Leeds alleyway on a wet January morning. What disturbed Arthur Bisby almost as much as the fact that she had been so brutally murdered, however, was the fact that Sydney Jackson's wife should have turned out to be a prostitute.

It was a reaction he shared with all the Jacksons' neighbours in Churwell, a hillside village on the southwestern perimeter of Leeds, who only knew them as a hard-working, middle-aged couple with three children – a fourth, a boy, had died after falling from his bedroom window five years earlier – who seemed to enjoy life. He ran a one-man roofing business; she helped with the paperwork and drove the old Commer van from job to job for him.

Mrs Jackson also drove the van on their jaunts into Leeds which, since the death of their son, had become almost nightly. Having dropped her husband off at a large, cosmopolitan 'entertainments' pub on Roundhay Road called the Gaiety, it was her habit to cruise the streets of Chapeltown until closing time looking for 'business', although she would sometimes leave the van in the Gaiety car park and go off to have sex with clients in the comparative comfort of their own cars.

That is what Sydney Jackson thought had probably happened on the night of Wednesday, 21 January 1976, when he came out of the pub at around 10.45 to find the van parked in the quickly emptying car park but no trace of his wife. Philosophically, he set off to find himself a taxi. By then, however, Emily was already dead.

Mrs Jackson had been murdered within an hour of leaving the Gaiety. She had been picked up by Peter Sutcliffe some time before 7.00 and had driven half a mile with him in the direction of the city centre, where they parked away from the lights of the main road on a piece of derelict land. He contrived to get the woman, whose 'overwhelming smell of cheap perfume' he would later claim had nauseated him, to hold a torch while he raised the bonnet of his car to examine the engine. He had then taken 'a couple of steps back' and aimed two blows at her head with a hammer.

Once she was unconscious he had manoeuvred Mrs Jackson's body further into the shadows where, having pushed her sweater, cardigan and brassiere up to expose her breasts, he had stabbed her a total of fifty-two times, in the breasts, neck, back and lower abdomen, with a cross-ply Phillips screwdriver. He had also taken a piece of wood and thrust it between her legs in order, he said, 'to show her as disgusting as she was'.

Sutcliffe arrived at his mother-in-law's without a trace of blood on his clothes and suffused 'with a feeling of satisfaction and justification'.

He couldn't wake up next morning, the 22 January, and, as often happened, arrived late for work. It was his mother's birthday and, that night, he made a point of delivering her card personally to Cornwall Road.

The murders of Wilma McCann and Emily Jackson in Leeds were front-page news all over Yorkshire. But the murder of an old-age pensioner in Bingley, exactly three weeks before the Jackson killing, had stunned the community and was still the main talking-point in the town.

Bingley Main Street is always at its busiest between the hours of 8.00 and 11.30 on Friday and Saturday nights, when the pedestrian traffic between the pubs at the 'top of the town' – the Harvester, the Ferrands – and those at the 'bottom' – the Queen's Head, the Fleece, the White Horse and, across a stone bridge on the other side of the river, the Brown Cow – reaches its peak.

The restless to-ing and fro-ing generates an atmosphere of expectancy and rough vitality that is conspicuously missing during the rest of the week, and this had been the case with a vengeance on New Year's Eve, 1975. Most people, several Sutcliffes among them, asked to account for their movements that night, later experienced great difficulty recalling precisely where they had been, with whom and when.

But even though she lived virtually next door to the White Horse, Mrs Grace Adamson, an eighty-five-year-old widow, was oblivious to what was going on outside in the street. She was sitting in the small living-room of her terraced cottage opposite the church, knitting and watching television, when a teenager from Shipley, a student later identified as Mark Andrew Rowntree, spotted her through the window and knocked on her door.

When Mrs Adamson opened it, Rowntree lunged at her with a long-bladed, 'commando-type' knife and stabbed her a total of seven times. Afterwards, he buried the knife and went for a drink in a pub in Crossflatts, where he also washed the blood off his hands.

Two days later, Rowntree returned to the shop in Bradford where he had bought the original knife and purchased a second one. Packing it in a shoulder-bag, he set off by bus for Sutton-in-Craven where, in the Black Bull, he engaged the landlady on the subject of the Bingley killing. 'They might have let her live life out properly,' he said with some feeling, before strolling down to the village and casually stabbing a youth to death at a bus-stop.

On 7 January, a further five days later, Rowntree called at the home of a Leeds prostitute whom he had visited once before, for sex, after getting her address from a contact magazine. This time the knife was taped to his leg and he stabbed the woman with it eighteen times. He also stabbed to death her three-year-old son, who had witnessed the murder, then took the bus to Guiseley, where he again buried the evidence.

Returning to his lodgings in Shipley, however, Rowntree was met by Detective Superintendent Dick Holland, deputy head of Bradford CID, who was perplexed, and more than a little thrown, by his suspect's disdainful manner and 'posh' accent. 'I will just tell you a little story which may interest you. I did those two killings,' Rowntree remarked pleasantly and, after a sleep, volunteered a calm and detailed description of all four attacks.

At his trial five months later, Rowntree admitted that he had failed in his ambition to execute girls between the ages of fifteen and twenty, whom he despised, 'at bus-stops, chewing gum, smoking and who were shallow-minded'. He had been 'hurt and let down by girls'. This had motivated him to seek revenge on anybody or anything. He admitted experiencing 'high elation' after each death, and expressed 'excitement and regret in shocking the public and making the police work'.

Giving evidence, the senior medical officer at Armley jail told the court that the conclusion he had reached was that, at the material times, Rowntree was suffering from a mental illness, namely schizophrenia. 'There was a voice commanding and telling him to do it,' the doctor explained, adding that, in his opinion, the defendant was in need of urgent psychiatric treatment in hospital.

Details of the trial were accorded many hundreds of column-inches both in West Yorkshire and in the national press, with Peter Sutcliffe's regular morning paper, the *Daily Mail*, leading the field as usual in the comprehensiveness of its coverage of the case, which was heard throughout the first week of June 1976.

A month earlier, at around 4.00 a.m. on Sunday, 9 May, Sutcliffe had himself attacked another woman, a coloured prostitute called Marcella Claxton, on Soldiers Field, near Chapeltown in

Leeds, hitting her twice with a hammer and leaving her needing fifty stitches in the head.

Saturdays and Wednesdays were the nights when Sonia most often worked at the Sherrington Private Nursing Home with her mother. They were usually back at Tanton Crescent in time for an early breakfast, unaware that sometimes the reason Peter went on sleeping so soundly upstairs was because he had spent half the night prowling around the seamier areas of Bradford and Leeds.

Although, outwardly at least, he was his same, casual self, the fact that Marcella Claxton hadn't died had shaken him and, not for the first time, he spent a few weeks living in fear of the police knocking on the door. Marcella Claxton, however, was an educationally subnormal West Indian with an IQ of only 50 whom the police, privately, regarded as 'just this side of a gorilla'. They therefore treated her account of what had happened in the early hours of 9 May, and her description of the 'black and crinkly bearded' man who had attacked her, with scepticism, and didn't immediately link it with the other recent attacks on women in the area.

Sutcliffe stayed away from prostitutes and the red-light districts for the rest of 1976. On Saturday, 5 February 1977, though, he was back kerb-crawling in Chapeltown in the white Ford Corsair that he now ran in tandem with the green Capri. He had approached a number of women without success when, with the time coming up to midnight, he spotted the plump, long-haired figure of Irene Richardson dashing from the rooming house where she had managed to reserve a bed for the night to Tiffany's 'Supper Disco' in the centre of Leeds.

Like Wilma McCann, Irene was originally from Scotland; and, also like Wilma McCann, she had fallen on hard times. Separated from her husband, with her two daughters, aged four and five, fostered out, she had spent most of the previous ten days wandering about, homeless and practically penniless, in Chapeltown.

When the smart white car pulled up a few yards ahead of her

she jumped in without a word. 'I might not have wanted you,' Sutcliffe said once she was sitting beside him, but she told him not to worry, she'd give him a good time. They drove a mile along Roundhay Road past the big houses on the edge of the park to almost exactly the spot where he had attacked Wilma McCann on Soldiers Field. While she was crouching to urinate on the grass, Sutcliffe slipped a hammer from his pocket and hit Irene Richardson three times in the head.

Her body was discovered by a jogger soon after dawn the next morning, only a short distance from the disc-jockey Jimmy Savile's house.

She was lying face down, with her imitation suede coat that she had been wearing draped over her legs. Her skirt had been pushed up and her knee-length, zip-up boots had been positioned carefully over her thighs. She had been stabbed in the neck and throat, and her stomach had been slashed so violently with a Stanley knife that her intestines had spilled out.

Irene Richardson was the third victim of the man local papers began to call the 'Yorkshire Ripper'. Between looking at houses and tinkering with the engines of cars, Peter Sutcliffe was to attack five more women, killing three of them, before the end of 1977.

17

In October 1976, nine years after being sacked from Bingley cemetery and a full sixteen years after leaving school, Peter had at last found another job which seemed to suit him and which it looked like he might want to keep. Working for T. and W. H. Clark, a small engineering transport firm, took him all over the country and involved a lot of 'overnights' which, apart from the few weeks when he joined Sonia in London, represented the closest he had ever come to living alone.

Most of the drivers working out of Clark's yard on the Canal Road industrial estate between Bradford and Shipley slept in the bunk-beds built into the rear of their cabins in order to pocket the £9.50-a-night accommodation allowance. But it struck many of those who knew him that Peter, although never averse to saving a few shillings, would have preferred to do this anyway.

Having proven himself over several months in one of the firm's four- and six-ton 'big rigids', he had been assigned one of the two articulated lorries owned by Clark's and this had very quickly become the pride of his life. The Ford Transcontinental was at that time the most advanced truck of its kind on the road in Britain and Peter was like a child with a new toy at the wheel of his £250,000-worth of machinery.

It was something of a mystery to his workmates why he was quite so 'loopy' about his wagon. He'd kill the hours it took to load and unload the massive trailer cleaning and polishing, and the cabin in particular was always spotless. He always carried a few 'nuddy' books, but of the *Playboy* and *Penthouse* variety rather than 'the right mucky ones' that the other men tended to pore over, and the pictures always stayed inside their glossy covers rather than finding their way on to the cabin walls. Mick preferred his pin-ups 'with a few things on – knickers, stockin's an' that – better than when they're wearing nowt', and Peter seemed to share his tastes.

The Transcontinental had a physical presence that matched its price. The bed of the trailer was a good five feet off the ground and eye-level for the driver was five feet higher than that. This is what Jane remembered, after its 'immaculateness', when Peter gave her a lift home in it once. 'You could see for miles from that cabin. You were up above everything. It were real.'

The height, combined with the sense of mass and speed, seemed to invigorate Peter and fill him with the confidence he normally lacked. It was Peter who taught Carl to drive, and Carl, like Mick, would often go off with his brother on overnight runs. 'He were just like a normal lorry-driver wi' arm out window, shouting and hooting horn at birds.

'He used to feel right powerful in that truck, though. If any cars got in way of him, he'd get right close behind them going downhill and frighten them to death if they couldn't get a move on. He liked going fast. He used to go fast everywhere.'

Working at Clark's, Peter got into the habit of dropping in on his mother whenever his route took him along the Aire valley past Bingley, which was usually once or twice a week. Although for a long time her doctors couldn't find anything specifically wrong with Kathleen, her general health, in the years leading up to her fifty-ninth birthday, started to gradually deteriorate. Peter himself traced it back to the Bankfield Hotel confrontation orchestrated by his father, and saw it as part of his job to cheer his mother up during his brief visits. The way he attempted this was by making light of her various complaints, and it was a rare visit when he didn't leave her with at least the trace of a smile on her face.

Although things could never be the same between them after the break-up, John and Kathleen had settled back into an uneventful, if rather uneasy, domestic existence. They were seen slightly more often in each other's company, but John was reluctant to drop any of his outside interests and she seemed content to let him go his own way. John's crowd had never been

Kathleen's, and she was happier sitting at home with the television than struggling to keep her end up among people whom she considered her natural social and intellectual superiors.

The rigid class divisions, status rivalries and petty snobberies that characterised 'Warnley', the thinly disguised portrait of Bingley drawn by John Braine in his 1950s' novel *Room at the Top*, were still very much in evidence twenty years later, as Carl Sutcliffe could hardly help noticing. Socially, to say you were from Ferncliffe Estate was the kiss of death, and Carl therefore would never admit to it. 'The people up Gilstead and Eldwick really look down on the people from "the estate" as they call it. They're in another bracket. They always seemed totally different to us. They always seemed really posh. So we used to say we lived somewhere else.'

John Sutcliffe, however, not only chose to ignore the social barriers that had been erected but was pleased to call the bank managers and schoolteachers and other backbones of the amateur dramatic and operatic societies and the Musical Union – in other words, the very people singled out by Braine as the embodiment of small-town bourgeois values in his book – his friends.

'He likes to think of himself as a bit of a toff,' Carl would say. 'He's always like that: allus trying to prove summat. Everybody on estate thought he were a nutter. We used to build dens out of old wood in back garden an' he went in once an' liked it so much he slept in there two nights running. I were tempted to throw a match on it. I were always tellin' me mother I thought he were puddled.'

John celebrated his return to Cornwall Road by turning the downstairs dinette into a 'bar', complete with pub counter, piano and home-brewed wines and beer. Carl, by then the only one still living with his parents, used to live in dread of the Saturday nights when it was his father's turn to bring some of his 'cronies' home with him from the pub. The trouble he went to, baking sausage-rolls and pies and cutting sandwiches, was confirmation in Mick's eyes of him 'allus trying to mix a bit higher up than anybody else'.

There was no mistaking the pleasure it gave John to be able to say that he had entertained what, to him, were some of the pillars of the community, in his own house. 'One night I had a headmaster, a bank manager, the area manager from the telephone department, a chap who had a radio and television business, a detective-sergeant who got made up to an officer later, the theatre critic from the *Telegraph and Argus* and his wife . . .

'I always had a few friends that were capable of giving a nice entertainment on the piano and always a few who could sing a bit. And that particular night the Musical Union had had a concert somewhere in Bingley and I just threw an open invitation to anybody that wanted to come back. There was about twenty-odd of us in that room and we supped and we sang and we had a real do.'

The ladies, meanwhile, 'who couldn't quite bustle theirselves into hullabaloo', sat in the front room with Kathleen. This kind of overflow, however, wasn't often a problem because the usual Saturday crowd didn't normally exceed ten, including Peter, who, with Sonia at work, would regularly look in for a drink for half an hour. His arrival was always particularly welcomed by the wives of his father's friends to whom, unlike his brothers, he was unfailingly charming, and who, as a result, considered him 'a proper gentleman'.

The popular view of Mick and Carl as 'rough diamonds – you know, a bit scattish' was reinforced one Friday night just after Easter 1977 when they were both arrested following a 'riot' at the Granby. Carl, who was only seventeen at the time, was eventually acquitted after being remanded in custody for nearly a week. But Mick was fined £225 for hitting a police sergeant and, because he was already the subject of an eleven-month suspended sentence for burglary, ended up in Armley jail for three months.

The running battle, which it had eventually taken forty policemen to contain, was given extensive coverage in the next day's local papers. Nobody would be able to remember whether Peter looked in at Cornwall Road that Saturday night, 23 April 1977. But his car was travelling away from Bingley in the early hours of Sunday morning. As it passed Cottingley Bridge, a heavy object was thrown from the driver's window of the white Ford Corsair into the grounds of Harrison's Printers. It was the claw-hammer that had been used to beat Tina Atkinson to death, just over an hour earlier.

Patricia Atkinson had been given the name 'Tina' by the Asian immigrant whom she had married in Bradford in the early 1970s, and who had been awarded custody of their three daughters when the marriage broke up a few years later, because of Tina's unruly way of life.

The remarkable thing was that time hadn't been as unkind to Tina as it had to many of the other prostitutes whom she walked the streets with and drank with in the pubs on Lumb Lane. These were the women whom John Sutcliffe, now working for Stroud, Ridley, Drummond, owners of the huge mill whose black chimney and slab walls overshadowed everything else in the Lane, thought of as 'the old hags who'll do it for a packet of fags and a pint from the old black men, who live from hand to mouth'.

Tina's features hadn't become coarsened like most of theirs, nor her flesh slack, and her long, dark hair had kept its natural colour. Tina was also unusual in that she had somewhere to go with her 'punters' that wasn't open to the elements. She had a bedsit on the ground floor of a modern building only a few minutes' walk away, near the southern boundary of Manningham Park.

The death of Irene Richardson in February, the third prostitute murdered in Leeds in fifteen months, had had a dramatic effect on activity in the city's red-light area, at least in the short term: what prostitutes there were left on the streets had started to go about 'team-handed', working in twos and threes; but the real professionals had decamped to Manchester, the Midlands and London until such time as they felt it was safe to return.

Despite their geographical proximity, however, the mood of fear and suspicion gripping Chapeltown hadn't descended on Manningham by the spring of 1977. By 2.00 p.m. when the early shift at Drummonds mill let out, 'the girls' were already starting to appear on Lumb Lane; and by 4.30 they were out in sufficient numbers to provide a constant diversion for the commuters returning to the outlying towns and villages and to the western suburbs of Bradford.

Standing at one of the busiest intersections in the area, on a corner between an Asian second-hand clothes shop and a West Indian social club, the Perseverance is a natural meeting place and trading centre for people from all parts of the community. The persistent muzak reflects the cosmopolitan nature of the clientele: the tape of a northern comedian telling jokes that almost anywhere else in the country would be considered both tasteless ('So I says to the doctor, me dick's like a friggin' walnut-whip . . .') and racist ('I saved a Paki from drowning the other day. I took me foot off his head') is followed by high-decibel selections of soul music and reggae.

The Perseverance was full as usual on the night of Saturday, 23 April, and Tina Atkinson, as she usually was, was in the thick of it, shouting to make herself heard above the din. In the middle of the evening, though, wearing the short leather jacket, blue jeans and largely unbuttoned blue shirt that everybody in the area was used to seeing her in, she left the 'Persie' and tottered up Lumb Lane to another of her regular haunts, the Carlisle, in Carlisle Road. After three quarters of an hour, the manager there decided that she had had enough to drink and, around 10.30, she set off again in the direction of the International – 'the Nash' – a mainly black after-hours drinking club standing on its own in an acre of rubble back on the Lane.

It was en route to the International that she fell into the orbit of Peter Sutcliffe. He noticed her banging on the roof of an unoccupied car, obviously the worse for drink and using the sort of 'foul language no decent woman would have been using'. When he stopped, she jumped in beside him without any coaxing, and they drove the few hundred yards to Oak Lane where she lived.

He retrieved a claw-hammer from under his seat as he got out of the car and hung his coat up in Tina's flat with the hammer still in it. He waited until she was sitting on the bed with her back to him before he struck her, and the four blows knocked her to the floor. Having hoisted her back on to the bed and exposed her breasts and the lower part of her body, he continued hitting her with one end of the hammer and clawing her with the other and watched the marks appearing on the flesh.

When he stuck a knife in her stomach, the blood looked red to him for the first time rather than the dark colour it had always looked in the dark, and he threw the sheets over her before leaving, to conceal it. She was still making 'horrible gurgling noises' when he closed the door, but he was satisfied that she 'would not be in any state to tell anyone' what had happened.

Discovering it thirty-six hours after it had been thrown there from a passing car, the groundsman at Harrison's Printers in Cottingley Bridge happily appropriated the claw-hammer and used it for the next three years as he went about his business.

18

The Saturday following the murder of Tina Atkinson in Bradford, Peter had company on his rounds of the pubs which, that week, included one or two in Bingley.

The Barker family had been the Szurmas' next-door neighbours for as long as they had lived in Tanton Crescent. And, although she couldn't claim to have actually broken down their reserve, Mrs Barker had got to know the people on the other side of the wall well enough to buy a set of photographs of Sonia's wedding.

Ronald, Mrs Barker's younger son, had grown up alongside Sonia Szurma. But it was only after she became Mrs Sutcliffe, and her new husband moved into number 42, that 'Ronnie', an awkward, overweight young man with one overactive and one lazy eye, established any kind of significant social contact.

As at Cornwall Road, messing about with engines continued to be Peter's main source of recreation, and most evenings found him in the road in front of his father-in-law's fiercely well-tended garden: Mr Szurma never allowed so much as a leaf to settle in the guttering around his copperplate-shaped lawn, and the same vigilance was extended to the outside of the house – the door-knocker had received so many coats of shiny black paint that it only produced a soft, muffled thud.

Ronnie Barker earned his living as an insurance agent, and his social life centred around the church choir, of which he had been a member for some years, the local Liberals, and Bradford City football club. As a result of getting to know Peter, though, through a mutual friend who lived in the children's home directly opposite, he developed an interest in cars which his new neighbour was happy to encourage.

Ronnie's experiences at the wheel, however, were not happy

ones. His first car was a 'sported-up' Cortina with rally wheels, custom sprayed with streaks of lightning which Peter and his brother Mick had been happy to look over for him. The next time Mick saw Ronnie, though, in Bingley a week later, he had 'two right shiners and a bust nose and stitches and dark glasses on, which our lad thought were hilarious'. After a few lessons from Peter, Ronnie had ventured out on his own and smashed the car straight into a brick wall.

Ronnie's next purchase, in August 1977, was the white Corsair with the black roof that Peter had been running for the previous two years. Peter's reluctance to return what had been paid for it when it failed to go strained their relationship almost to breaking-point. But he relented when it was obvious that Ronnie intended to make a fuss, and the split that for a short time had seemed inevitable never happened.

As a consequence, though, both Barkers, Ronnie and his older brother, David, were happy to leave the driving to Peter on the pub crawls with which they whiled away Saturday nights throughout 1977. Their usual route took in the towns and pubs that Peter was used to visiting with Trevor, but occasionally he insisted on travelling further afield, beyond the boundaries of the old West Riding.

Manchester, thirty miles away on the M62, was one such destination, although Peter didn't seem to know which part he was looking for when they arrived, and they ended up wandering aimlessly around the deserted business area on foot. But wherever they got to, the likelihood was that Peter would decide to make a detour through the red-light districts of Leeds or Bradford on the way home.

Cruising in the dark, he would regale the Barkers with the stories, so familiar to Trevor, of how he went with prostitutes without paying and of the sort of things he got up to in the Corsair. 'Last night, two birds followed me back to the car. I had one of them in the back seat and the other over the bonnet,' he told them in the small hours of one Sunday in 1977.

On 28 May, exactly a month after the murder of Tina Atkinson,

Peter wanted to make a return visit to Manchester, but Ronnie persuaded him that it was too far and they eventually ended up in York. They called in at a handful of pubs but, tired of traipsing and of Peter's pointed jibes at Ronnie about it being time he fixed himself up with a girl, the Barkers gave each other a game of pool. It was only at closing time that they realised they hadn't seen Peter for nearly an hour. Later he told them that he'd 'followed a lass' out of the pub.

Ronnie fell asleep in the back seat, as he often did, in the course of the drive home to Bradford. The next thing he knew they were in Chapeltown and Peter had disappeared again. He didn't say where he'd been or what he had been doing in the twenty minutes or so that he was away from the car, but four Saturdays later, having shed the Barkers, he returned to Chapeltown alone.

By the summer of 1977, Wilma McCann, the first of the four women Peter Sutcliffe had murdered, had been dead for nearly two years. It was impossible to pass the house where she had lived with her four children, or the spot a few minutes' walk away where her body had been found, without recalling some of the details of her death. But the lives of her neighbours in and around Scott Hall Avenue on the western edge of Chapeltown were crowded with more pressing concerns.

Because of his asthma, Wilf MacDonald, a railway worker who lived within hailing distance of the McCanns, was often 'on the sick'. By the end of June, though, the money worries that were a constant preoccupation seemed to have receded slightly because Jayne, at sixteen the third of his five children, had been one of the lucky ones who had been able to walk out of school straight into a job.

A confident, attractive, sweet-natured girl, she had quickly become as popular with the staff at Grandways supermarket in Leeds, where she sold shoes, as she had always been in the streets around where she lived. The Birnbergs were particularly fond of her and, because they were on the phone, she knew she could rely on them to pass the message on to her parents if she was going to spend the night at a friend's house or get home particularly late.

This only ever happened on Saturdays, when Jayne went out roller skating or to the Merrion Centre, to a disco. On the night of Saturday, 25 June, though, she had decided to have a change. Wearing a blue flared gingham skirt, a blue-and-white halter-neck sun top, a waisted summer jacket and 'cloggy' platform-soled shoes, the outfit that had recently replaced her younger Bay City Rollers look, she was going to the Astoria ballroom and then on to a club on Roundhay Road, she told the Birnbergs when she looked in on them on her way past.

Earlier that Saturday, with no great enthusiasm, Peter had accompanied Sonia and her mother to view a house belonging to a barrister in Heaton, the residential area of Bradford north of Manningham Park. Sonia was at last on the point of qualifying as a teacher and was hoping to have moved out of Tanton Crescent before taking up her first post at the beginning of the autumn term, then only a matter of a few weeks in the future. That night, though, she was working at the Sherrington nursing home and, having collected the Barker brothers from next door, Peter dropped her off there on their way into town.

In fact, that night, they bypassed the city centre and made their first stop in Allerton, near to where Trevor Birdsall lived, at the Jack and Jill. From the Jack and Jill they drove to the Hare and Hounds in Heaton, which would be Peter's local if he bought the house he'd been to see earlier, and which Sonia had obviously set her heart on, in Garden Lane. From the Hare and Hounds it was a short hop to the Flying Dutchman, down towards the centre of Bradford on Lumb Lane. They finished the evening on Leeds Road, at 'a disco-place-cum-queers-pub' called the Dog in the Pound which Ronnie in particular reckoned to be 'a bit of a laugh': apart from the ordinary 'puffs', there was a big ex-sailor behind the bar who always wore drag.

The evening ended on a sour note, however, when Peter

refused to get another round in at last orders, even though it was his turn. They queued up for their fish-and-chips in near silence on the way back to Clayton. Then, although it was turned midnight, Peter dropped the two brothers at the end of the street, as he sometimes had in the past, before slipping back into the traffic on the main road.

Jayne MacDonald had changed her mind. Instead of going to the Astoria, she had met up with some friends and gone to the Hofbrauhaus, a German-style 'Bierkeller' near Leeds city centre. There, over the noise of singalongs and an oompah band, she had fallen into conversation with an eighteen-year-old called Mark Jones and had danced with him until it was time to leave. At 10.30, they had set off in the direction of Briggate, the main shopping street, as part of a crowd, and then Jayne had suggested going for some chips.

By the time they found somewhere that sold chips and had eaten them, Jayne had missed her last bus, so they sat on a bench outside C & A until about 12.00, when they started walking towards the estate near St James's hospital where Mark lived. If his sister was in, Mark told her, she'd run her home. But it was a warm night and Jayne gave the impression of not minding either way. When there was no car outside the house, they continued walking up Beckett Road in the general direction of Chapeltown, then lay down in a school field opposite 'Jimmies' until well after 1.00 a.m.

They parted outside the main gates of the hospital, having arranged to meet again in the middle of the week, and Jayne set off with the intention of calling a taxi from the taxi firm's own kiosk at the corner of Harehills Road. Receiving no reply, however, she turned left down one of the maze of streets that would bring her out near Grandways, the supermarket where she worked, and the Gaiety, the pub where Sydney Jackson had last seen his wife alive.

At 2.00 a.m., Peter Sutcliffe saw Jayne walking along Chapeltown

Road. He parked and got out of his car, equipping himself with a hammer and a kitchen knife. He followed her past Sharma and Son and the Latvian Welfare Fund, past the Hayfield, an enormous pub set well back from the road, and left into Reginald Terrace; and, although the distance between them wasn't very great, she never once looked round.

Thirty yards into Reginald Terrace he struck her from behind. Dragging her face-downwards into a playground that had been salvaged from the rubble, he was startled by the noise her shoes made scraping along the ground.

19

The murder of Jayne MacDonald, described by the police as the first 'innocent' victim of the man coming to be known throughout the North of England as the 'Ripper', devastated those who had known her or lived near her, and outraged the rest of Leeds.

Petitions demanding the return of capital punishment started to circulate independently in several parts of the city; 'Hang the Ripper' graffiti started appearing on Chapeltown walls; and an open letter in the *Evening Post*, pleading with the 'butcher' of five women to reveal his identity – 'How did you feel yesterday when you learned your bloodstained crusade had gone so horribly wrong? That your vengeful knife had found so innocent a target?' – was picked up by the Manchester offices of most Fleet Street morning papers.

By the time WPC Susan Phillips dressed up in the clothes resembling those Jayne had been wearing seven nights earlier to retrace her two-mile route from St James's hospital to Chapeltown Road, the 'Yorkshire Ripper' was becoming national – if still not headline – news.

In October 1975, when Wilma McCann's body had been found on a playing field in Leeds, there had been nothing to indicate that she was to be only the first of many women to die at the hands of a man believed by the police to have 'a pathological hatred of prostitutes', over the next five and a half years.

The head of Leeds CID had commandeered all the manpower at his disposal in an effort to make an early arrest. Daily press conferences were held for the first two weeks and local newspapers and television news programmes were encouraged to run pictures of the four McCann children in an attempt to elicit the sympathy and co-operation of the public.

News editors, though, and the majority of their readers, were inclined to regard Wilma McCann's as just another 'fish-and-chip murder', to be forgotten in the space of a week. The police's only hope was the reappearance of the white plastic purse with the word 'Mumiy' written on it that Wilma had been carrying when she left home for the last time.

The murder of Emily Jackson barely a mile away, three months later, had largely been deemed remarkable for the fact that she had lived in the same village with her husband and children for years without any of their neighbours suspecting that she was 'on the game'. The news that she had almost certainly been killed by the same man who killed Wilma McCann, and in the same manner, had sustained the public's interest for a further couple of weeks. But then, with no leads other than the heavily ribbed, size seven or eight wellington bootprints found near the dead woman's body and on her thigh, the case had quickly 'died'.

There was an interval of more than a year before Peter Sutcliffe murdered Irene Richardson. But Professor David Gee of Leeds University's Department of Forensic Science, who was to perform post-mortems on all the Yorkshire victims, immediately read in Richardson's injuries the 'signature' of the so-called 'Ripper'.

Multiple fractures of the skull, displaced clothing and mutilation of the lower abdomen and breasts with a knife or screwdriver gave 'a clear badge of identity' to the killings, although exact details were never released while the murderer was still at large, so afraid were the police of 'copy-cat' crimes and hoax 'confessions'; they also wanted to have something in reserve if and when an arrest was made.

The conduct of the enquiry was anyway dogged with problems so long as the women being murdered were 'vice-girls'. Not only were the general public less co-operative than they would have been if the victims had been 'decent' women, but the red-light areas of West Yorkshire, like ghettoes anywhere, were in many ways self-contained, self-regulating communities whose members instinctively closed ranks against the police.

Prostitutes and their pimps were no more likely to come forward with information than their customers, many of them married men with families, were to own up to being in Spencer Place or Leopold Street any night after dark.

Despite having 120 detectives working around the clock on the Richardson case, the feedback was so disappointing that Detective Chief Superintendent Jim Hobson, head of Leeds CID, took the drastic, and potentially dangerous, step of putting policewomen on the streets of Chapeltown disguised as call-girls. Their brief was to use short-wave radios to transmit details of any man who stopped and asked if they were 'doing business' to male colleagues parked some distance away in the shadows. As a tactic it proved no more effective than any of the others, and was quickly abandoned.

But if the gathering of information presented problems, they were nothing compared to the difficulties the police faced when it came to organising and retrieving what they had. A major stumbling-block was that the indexing and cross-referencing work on statements relating to previous murders usually hadn't been completed when a new set started to flow in. The shortcomings of a system which relied on teams of individuals to process volumes of material that would have kept a computer occupied twenty-four hours a day were especially apparent in the eighteen months from the spring of 1977, when seven women were murdered and another two left for dead.

Irene Richardson's murder was still being investigated when news came in, in April 1977, that the 'Ripper' had struck for the first time in Bradford. And a surveillance operation was just being set up in the Lumb Lane area as a result of Tina Atkinson's death when, four weeks later, the mutilated body of his fifth victim was discovered in Chapeltown.

Jayne MacDonald had been stabbed repeatedly through the same two openings in the front and back of her body. A broken bottle with the screw-top still attached was embedded in her chest. Police spokesmen, as usual, gave reassurances that everything possible was being done to catch the 'maniac' responsible. But the widespread public concern at this most recent abomination demanded a change in police tactics.

Up to June 1977, a different investigating officer had been appointed to each case, depending on the area. It had then been up to the 'Ripper Room' in Millgarth to establish some common link. Now, the Chief Constable of West Yorkshire, Ronald Gregory, called in his most senior and experienced detective and put him in overall control.

Invariably described as 'blunt' and 'ruddy-faced' and looking 'like a gentleman farmer' in his bold, Evelyn Waugh-style tweeds, George Oldfield publicly staked his reputation on the success of the investigation and, in typical fashion, showed that he meant business from day one. A mobile police post complete with radio mast and generator was set up only yards from where Jayne MacDonald had been killed, and detectives set about tracing the 400 individuals who had been seen in the area of the adventure playground on the night that she died.

Before the end of the first week George Oldfield was pleased to announce that, of the 400 people on his list, 380 had been tracked down and cleared. And more figures quickly followed: 152 women had been arrested and reported for prostitution in the Chapeltown area and a further sixty-eight cautioned. A total of 3,780 statements had been taken with regard to the MacDonald murder from 13,000 people. Convinced that a friend or a relative must know or suspect the identity of the Ripper, Leeds Freefone 5050 was open twenty-four hours a day to receive recorded messages, which poured in non-stop for a fortnight.

After a fortnight, though, as with the other enquiries, information began to dry up. 'The public have the power to decide what sort of society they want. If they want murder and violence they will keep quiet. If they want a law-abiding society, in which their womenfolk can move freely without fear of attack from the individual we are seeking, then they must give us their help,' Mr Oldfield was repeatedly quoted as saying, until some observers started to detect a hint of desperation in his daily appeals for information.

Two weeks after the murder of Jayne MacDonald, the newly formed Debating Society at John Sutcliffe's local in Bingley, the Ferrands, carried the motion that 'this house believes that women have always held a privileged position in society and that the women's liberation movement can only detract from this status', by a majority of more than two to one.

That Saturday, Peter was out drinking as usual with Ronnie and David Barker. 9 July 1977 saw them trailing round their usual haunts in Bradford. At the end of an uneventful evening Peter once again deposited them at the end of Tanton Crescent and drove off alone.

He spotted Maureen Long, a small woman with hair as black as her old-fashioned-looking, floor-length black evening dress, coming out of Tiffany's on Manningham Lane just after 2.00 a.m., and cruised slowly behind her as she tottered unsteadily towards Hustlergate. He waited until she had passed the long queue of people waiting for taxis before pulling over.

A well-known figure around the Manningham area, Mrs Long had spent the evening drinking heavily and dancing energetically and, no longer as young as she imagined – she was the mother, in fact, of one of the girls working the Lumb Lane beat – was grateful for the lift. She was living in Bowling, she explained, a rundown area among the railway yards just on the other side of the city centre, with an ex-boxer whom she described as 'a spoilsport'.

Reaching Rendle Street, she cautioned her driver not to stop immediately in front of her door. She asked him if he 'fancied' her and, when he said he did, she told him they could go inside the house if there was no one in. Within a couple of minutes though she was back and directing him towards some waste ground nearby.

He struck her with the hammer while she was crouching, urinating in the dark. Ripping her dress to the waist, he stabbed her repeatedly in the chest, stomach and back. He saw lights going on in a nearby caravan belonging to some gypsies, but he didn't stop.

He felt certain she was dead when he drove away from her body in the small hours of Sunday morning, and learning from Monday's papers that she wasn't gave him a 'nasty shock'.

'The investigation is beginning to bubble,' a buoyant George Oldfield told a press conference two days later. 'I feel we are getting nearer to the man I am looking for . . . I feel sure we will win.' But reading the description of the man Maureen Long believed was responsible for the attempt on her life – white, aged thirty-six or thirty-seven, over six foot tall, with puffy cheeks, noticeably large hands and collar-length wiry blond hair – Peter Sutcliffe started to relax.

The description of a car seen speeding away from the scene of the attack – a white Mark 2 Ford Cortina with a black roof – was the only thing that gave him any cause for worry. A month later he attempted to palm his white Ford Corsair off on Ronnie Barker and, when that didn't work, stripped the car down and redistributed the spare parts around the red Corsair that he bought as a replacement in September 1977.

At the end of the summer he drove his parents to Anne and Trevor's house just off the front at Morecambe, and returned a couple of days later to pick them up.

20

Although Peter had always seemed fond of children, and children of him, it was generally assumed by those who knew them that, given Sonia's marked indifference, they would be unlikely to have any family of their own.

So it had come as something of a surprise when Peter, during one of his regular visits to Cornwall Road, had explained that the reason Sonia wasn't with him was because she was at home in bed, recovering from a miscarriage. They had been married a little over a year at that point and so, although sad – and Peter had seemed genuinely upset – it was hardly a disaster. But Maureen got the strong impression that they were unlikely to try again. 'No, they just keep you poor, do kids,' was Sonia's response when her sister-in-law offered her her sympathies the next time they met.

In 1976, four years after her health had forced her to abandon the course she'd started in London, Sonia had resumed her studies, this time at the Margaret MacMillan Teachers Training College in Bradford. And a year later the chances of her ever having children seemed to become even more remote as she planned to mark the transition to full-time teaching by moving into a house of her own.

In August 1977, a week after their third wedding anniversary and just a month before Sonia was due to start work as a supply teacher at Holmfield First School, in Bradford, contracts were exchanged on the house in Heaton that she had fallen in love with two months earlier; by the end of September, Mrs Szurma-Sutcliffe, as she signed herself on the purchase documents, and her husband, were the new owners of No. 6 Garden Lane.

Heaton was the last place Peter's former friends in Bingley

would have expected him to end up living and, when news filtered through that he was buying a house there, it was final confirmation to Eric and the rest that he'd left them standing.

Although only ten minutes on foot from the 'foreign' aromas and cosmopolitan bustle of Manningham and Lumb Lane, there is little sign in Heaton of the kind of life being lived further down the hill. The outside paintwork on the houses, whose large, underheated rooms are furnished with large, dark pieces of furniture, is soberly wood-grained rather than rainbow-coloured, and the food in the shops, if not the Lautrec Bistro, is still 'traditional' English. At the heart of Heaton is St Bede's, the Catholic grammar school where his father had hoped Peter would finish his education; and the glowering formality of Lister Park, home of the Bradford city art gallery and museum.

The houses on the broad streets fanning out to the north and west of the park are in the style known as Bradford Baroque: stolid, detached stone buildings enlivened with monumental decorative detailing – and, in the 1970s, 'Rock Against Racism' and 'Friends of the Earth' posters and plants in macrame baskets, a sign of the Art College and University lecturers moving in.

Even by Heaton standards, though, Garden Lane was a backwater, which explained the number of elderly and retired people living there. Built much later than the surrounding stone villas, the houses were for the most part unprepossessing pebble-dashed semis of the type to be found in similar dormitory suburbs the length and breadth of the country. Garden Lane's one unique feature, which helped keep property values buoyant, was the tract of open land known as Salem Field, used by Bradford Salem rugby football club for their fixtures. The raised field occupied most of the north side of the street and guaranteed that those people living opposite could never be overlooked.

Only a few houses had been built adjacent to either end of the pitch, and No. 6 Garden Lane was one of them. No. 6, in fact, was the last house before the eastern perimeter, one of a handful which stood at the top of steep concrete drives, looking out over the neighbouring rooftops towards Bradford.

Tall, pale pink and pot-bellied, like a bow-fronted sentry box, it looked peculiarly out of proportion. 'It's just like a half a semi, really. It's like a semi that's never had the other one built on to it,' as John Sutcliffe wasn't slow to notice. To Peter, though, it was 'detached' and, what was more, the only detached house in the street.

Built in the 1930s, with most of the period fittings, including the leaded lights that cast a soft, ecclesiastical glow on to the hall and staircase, still intact, it had known just two previous owners. Mr Wilcox, the Bradford grocer who had lived there most of his life, first with his wife and then with a housekeeper, had sold it after thirty years to an Asian barrister, which had caused a number of eyebrows to be raised.

'Coloureds' were the last thing Mrs Bowman, who lived diagonally opposite at No. 15, had expected – and, if she was honest, *wanted* – to move in. But, much to her surprise, the Rahmans had turned out to be very nice people. She had been sorry to see them go when they decided to sell up and return to Pakistan, and was sorrier still when she saw what had taken their place.

The first time she saw him, wearing white wooden clogs with a pale green suit, Peter Sutcliffe startled her. Taken with his 'Pancho Villa' moustache and shock of coarse black hair, she thought he must be something to do with show business. Driving a lorry is one thing she never pictured him doing, because he looked too thin and insubstantial, 'almost unhealthy', apart from the fact that they had never had a lorry-driver living in the street.

In common with the rest of her neighbours, though, she soon found out that this was precisely what the new arrival did for a living. He had only been living at Garden Lane a few days when Peter brought his 32-ton Ford Transcontinental home with him, churning up the grass verge alongside the rugby field when he parked it. When it happened again the following night, the place was up in arms.

'This is residential. It's not one of these new estates,' Mrs Bowman complained to her husband. 'We're not paying high rates on here to have that thing parked on the street,' the man next door complained to her, and everybody told everybody else that something must be done. It was while the debate was still raging as to who was going to be their spokesman that one of the neighbours, without saying anything, took it upon herself to knock at the door of No. 6. To her surprise and relief, she found Mr Sutcliffe immediately contrite and understanding, and the wagon never appeared in Garden Lane again: whenever he brought it home in future, he always parked it in a layby around the corner in Leylands Road.

Living just across the street as she did, Mrs Bowman hadn't been able to resist watching while the Sutcliffes' belongings were unloaded and carried up the steep drive. And what she saw – a brand-new Dralon three-piece suite with apple-green and pink reversible cushions; a handsome upright piano, one of many nice old pieces; fitted carpets, a front-loading washer and separate spin-drier – made her wonder how, when the asking price had been more than £15,000 for the house, they could afford it. Her husband was a wool merchant and she worked part-time as a medical secretary and it was still a struggle to meet the payments on a £12,500 mortgage and bring three children up at the same time.

These were thoughts that she shared with her neighbours, who also joined her in speculation about the small black car that turned up outside No. 6 first thing most mornings. When it transpired that it belonged to Mrs Sutcliffe's mother, a nurse at the nearby Sherrington, the talk then turned to why she should be forever on the young couple's doorstep. Mrs Bowman volunteered the thought that maybe he had a history of beating his wife up and her mother had come round to make sure she was all right.

From her front lounge, Mrs Bowman also couldn't help noticing that Mrs Sutcliffe – it would be some time before she came to know her as 'Sonia' – retired to bed early with the portable television every night, whether her husband was at home or not.

This kind of inquisitiveness wasn't all one-way, however.

Peter still had a sharp eye for human foibles and, working on cars for hours on the sloping drive at the side of the house, he was able to casually observe his new neighbours. The people next door, whose kitchen window looked straight across a low dividing fence into his, inevitably came in for particularly close scrutiny. He had not only their daily routine but also their mannerisms off to perfection, as Carl discovered one Sunday morning when he was visiting Garden Lane.

Giggling, Peter called Carl over to the kitchen window. 'He says, "He hasn't come out yet, they've just got up. But watch him: he'll come out in a minute, he'll lock door, lock wife and daughter in behind him, an' he'll walk round his Volkswagen, have a look at it, rub roof wi' cuff, then he'll unlock kitchen door wi' key again, rub his hands an' shout: Brrrrrrr! It's cold this morning, mother! Then he'll be out later and do it again. Then, between eleven and half-past he'll be out and give it a right good polishing and waxing, after he's made sure he's locked all family in. I bet he does it." And he did. Exactly as our Pete said.

'Monday morning he said it would be: Brrrrrrr. Bloody hell. Work again, while he walked round car wi' wife locked in house. Then when he got home he'd shout: Another day over, mother! Four days left! An' the same every day until Friday, when he cheered up. Pete thought it were really hilarious, this chap.'

Peter had a natural talent for mimicry and, whenever the family were gathered together, he'd have them in stitches taking individual members off: the little habit his father had of dancing round the room when the *World of Sport* signature tune came on; Mick's forward-falling, stooped walk . . .

It was a facility that never failed to intrigue Carl. 'You only had to say, Do you remember so-and-so? who he probably hadn't seen for years, and he'd give you a twenty-minute running commentary on things that they did. Habits and how they walked and what they wore.

'He'd really tek piss out of everything. He'd turn owt anybody said into a joke. You'd just say summat an' he'd just bust out in *hysterical* laughter, really fuckin' loud, almost rollin' on floor. He might have been quiet with strangers, but wi' family he could be right silly. He'd get really excited.'

This was certainly the case on Sunday night, 9 October 1977. Peter had known Sonia for seven years before they were married; they had spent a further three years living with her parents, and now, for the first time, he was able to entertain his own family in a home of his own.

It was a small group who gathered for the house-warming 'party' at Garden Lane that Sunday: Jane and her husband, Ian; Mick and Susan, who would eventually become his second wife; John and Kathleen; and, of course, Peter and Sonia. Annie Rhodes, John's friend with the deformed spine from Bingley, was the only 'outsider'; she had insisted on giving Peter's mother and father a lift in her car to Heaton, and Peter had insisted that she stay.

The evening had started off with the men gravitating towards the drink in the kitchen and the women discussing the soft-furnishings and cream satin-look wallpaper in the sitting-room with Sonia. It was only when conversation turned to the most arresting aspect of the decor that both groups finally came together.

Examples of Sonia's pottery were on display all over the front room and, indeed, all over the house. Gazing at these twisted, abstract cylinders, many of them painted green, Mick didn't know what to think. He just remembered Peter warning him not to laugh.

'I hadn't a bloody clue, me. I'd more appreciate something right, somebody mekkin a dog or some wild-fowl or a fox or summat like that. Summat that looked perfect as it should do. I admire stuff more real, like, instead of that loada bunkum. Our Peter used to talk about them, what she could mek on them an' that. I couldn't imagine anybody paying owt for them at all, but I don't know anything about art.'

Mick had been at a loss for words when Sonia, perhaps mischievously, asked him his opinion of her work. His father, on the other hand, had not. He had volunteered the opinion that they were 'halfway between pottery and that bloke that does the sculpture with the holes – Henry Moore'.

'It was incredible to think that those sculptures came out of her. They could've looked right nice with a bit of floral art, but really they were individual works of art on their own. She could have been world successful, I reckon.'

More of Sonia's sculptures stood on top of the piano in the dining-room. And it was only when they sat down at last to the dinner that she had prepared, and the home-made elderflower wine that John had brought with him, that the awkwardness inhibiting everybody had finally disappeared.

Realising that Sonia had underestimated the appetites of the men in his family, Peter had thrown some potatoes into the oven shortly before they arrived. He hadn't given them long enough, however, and when Jane tried to stick a fork in hers, it was 'hard as nails'. Then Peter attacked one of the potatoes on his own plate and it skidded to the floor. What followed was two hours in which Jane thought she had never laughed so much in her life. Peter was quick to recognise the potential of the potato joke and, in his insistent, excitable fashion, wouldn't let it drop.

Sonia alone remained unamused, prompting her father-in-law's later remark that she would have made 'a beautiful Queen Victoria'. Such was the general hilarity, though, that not even disapproving looks from Sonia could bring them down to earth. It was a mood that continued through the group snaps that Jane took with her Instamatic and the short ride home. Annie took Mick and Susan in her car back to Bingley, and Peter took Jane and Ian and his mother and father in his. As usual, rather than just dropping them off, he made a point of walking up the path to the front door with his mother and waiting until both parents were safely in.

Instead of turning round and driving straight home to Heaton, though, although it was already past midnight, he pressed on through the centre of Bradford and out on to the Manchester Road. In less than an hour he was ripping the clothes off the body of the woman he had murdered eight days before.

21

Southern Cemetery serves Moss Side, Hulme and other districts in the southern part of Manchester. It is about a mile from the M63 link with the trans-Pennine motorway direct to Leeds and Bradford, and it is this route that Peter Sutcliffe had followed on the night of Saturday, 1 October, his first Saturday in his new home.

In the course of earlier visits to Manchester in the company of his friends Ronnie and David Barker, he had been able to familiarise himself with the geography of the city, and in particular the exact location of the red-light district; coming off the motorway on 1 October, he had headed straight for it.

Shortly after 9.00 he had stopped and asked a 'slim and not bad looking girl' if she wanted business. Jean Jordan, known to the other prostitutes in the Nile and Reno Clubs and the pubs of Moss Side as 'Scotch Jean', had been about to get into a car driven by one of the other 'kerbies' when she changed her mind and opted for the red Corsair with the smiling, personable young man at the wheel.

They had quickly agreed on the standard charge of £5, to be paid in advance, and she had directed him towards the spot to which she had directed many other drivers in the past. Beyond the gridded acreage of Southern Cemetery in Chorlton, adjacent to the municipal allotments on Princess Road, was a piece of wasteland overgrown with weeds and shielded from the traffic by high hawthorn hedges which had long been a favourite haunt of the prostitutes from Moss Side and local courting couples.

After he parked, Jean had led the way into the deeper darkness some yards from the car. The previous owner of No. 6 Garden Lane had left a hammer lying in the garage beside the house, and it was this that the new owner had weighed in his left hand before crashing it down on to Jean Jordan's skull. She had fallen, moaning loudly, as a result of the first blow, and he had hit her again and again – a total of eleven times – until the moaning stopped.

At this point the headlights of a nearby car had come on. The car had started up its engine, though, and he had realised that in seconds it would be pulling away. He had pulled her body nearer some bushes to hide, but no sooner had the first car gone than a second one drove up. Crouching behind the Corsair, he had watched the new arrival nose into the allotments and stop exactly where the first car had just been. The chances of him being spotted had now been very high, and his instincts had told him to run. He had scrambled into the driver's seat and made for the centre of Manchester and home.

He had been surprised when there was nothing in Monday's papers about the murder. And as the news that the 'Yorkshire Ripper' had struck in Manchester for the first time failed to break, he had grown increasingly perplexed. The reasons, however, were simple: he had hidden the body in the bushes by the cemetery's perimeter fence too well for it to be easily discovered, and nobody had reported Jean Jordan's disappearance to the police.

Arriving in Manchester from Motherwell when she was sixteen, five years earlier, Jean had been found wandering around the concourse of Piccadilly Station by a hotel worker called Allan Royle, whose common-law wife she had eventually become. The Royles, as they were known on the 'problem' estate in Moss Side where they had been given a flat, had two small sons, but theirs wasn't a conventional family life: he would occasionally go off on two- and three-day 'benders' with his friends, and she would take a bus to the motorway and hitch a lift back to Scotland for a week or two, just as the mood took her.

Jean also had a set of girlfriends whose existence Allan was aware of but whom he had never met. And when he returned from the pub on the night of 1 October to find the children asleep but their mother missing, he had assumed that she'd gone out looking for female company. When Monday arrived and there was still no sign of her, he had taken it for granted that she was in Glasgow. It had certainly never occurred to him to report her as missing to the police.

In his haste to escape undetected from the scene of Jean Jordan's murder, Peter Sutcliffe had not forgotten the hammer with which he had broken her skull like an egg. Driving along the M62 in the direction of Bradford, however, it had suddenly occurred to him that he had left a piece of evidence behind which was potentially every bit as damning. Before setting out for the Southern Cemetery, Jean Jordan had taken possession of the £5 that they'd agreed on as the price for 'straight' sex. Freshly minted and included in his Clark's wage packet only two days earlier, the note was now somewhere on or near Jordan's body. If found, he believed, it could lead the police straight to him.

There had been two alternatives: he could turn around immediately and go back to Manchester, which carried the obvious risk of being spotted; or he could sit it out. He had decided on the latter course, and had expected every morning to bring news of the killing. When there was still nothing after a week, he took this as confirmation that the body was lying where he had left it, undisturbed. He made up his mind to risk going back to retrieve the incriminating evidence, and the house-warming at Garden Lane on 9 October presented him with the perfect opportunity.

Being a Sunday, he made the outskirts of Manchester within three quarters of an hour of seeing his parents safely home. Within another quarter of an hour he was parking alongside the Princess Road allotments on the South Side of the city.

He remembered almost exactly where he had attacked Jean Jordan, and he dragged her rapidly decomposing body roughly out of the bushes. Frantically, he stripped her of everything she had been wearing and examined each garment closely before flinging it into the dark. He even pulled her boots off and searched them, but there was still no sign of the £5 note.

Convinced now that she must have been carrying a handbag, he started running wildly all over the allotments to see if he could find one. When he couldn't, he returned to the body and vented his frustration on it with a knife. Having stabbed her repeatedly in the breasts and chest, he snatched up a broken pane from a nearby greenhouse and opened a wound from her right knee to her left shoulder. The stench as her stomach blew open made him vomit but, by then, he had already hatched another plan.

He would remove the head and, with it, the hammer-blows characteristic of the 'Yorkshire Ripper', thereby making 'a big mystery of it'. He set about this with a hacksaw blade he had brought with him, and then with the ragged edge of the glass, but soon gave up. He aimed some heavy blows at the body with his feet before turning his back on it for the last time and, feeling thwarted, started driving home.

Once home he put his trousers, which he had worn to entertain his family in some hours earlier, into the small wood-frame garage at the top of the drive, to be burned with the garden rubbish later.

The mutilated remains of Jean Jordan were discovered by an allotment holder on Monday morning, 10 October. Her handbag, however, with the £5 note folded into an inside pocket, wasn't found for a further five days; and public confirmation that she was the sixth victim of the Yorkshire Ripper wasn't forthcoming until early 1978.

Within hours of visiting the Princess Road allotments, however, Det. Chief Supt. Jack Ridgeway, head of Manchester CID, had made contact with members of West Yorkshire police's 'Ripper Squad'; and within a very few days the officers of both forces were agreed that they were looking for the same man.

Where there was less unanimity, though, was on the significance to the enquiry of the £5 note which, after drying, had been found to be brand new. The Bank of England had quickly furnished the information that it was one of a large batch issued by a sub-branch of the Midland Bank at Shipley, just outside Bradford, four days before Jean Jordan's murder. The batch had been split up and paid out to various local factories and businesses in time to go into wage packets on Thursday and Friday, 29 and 30 September.

To Jack Ridgeway, this appeared to be an enormous break: the possibility of the note crossing the Pennines in such a short space of time in any way other than in the original payee's pocket to him seemed extremely remote. Find the man who handed the £5 note to Jean Jordan, he argued, and you had found the Ripper.

George Oldfield, characteristically, adopted a rather more phlegmatic approach: £5 notes, he kept on saying, were being passed around 'like ten-bob notes were a few years ago'; the one found in Jordan's bag could have been through two or three pairs of hands before reaching Manchester, and the assumption that it couldn't have travelled from Yorkshire to Lancashire so quickly was a weak one in his view.

Nevertheless, happy by this stage to try anything, he gave Ridgeway thirty men to work with the thirty he had brought with him from Manchester and set them up in a disused schoolroom in Baildon, on the moors above Shipley and Bingley.

At a press conference to launch the campaign to trace some of the other dozens of £5 notes in the same sequence as the one in their possession, Ridgeway was described as 'resolute and optimistic', although 'still uncommitted on the Ripper connection'. 'We are attaching great significance to this £5 note,' he told the assembled reporters. 'There is no way I will be going back to Manchester before we have traced its source, even if it means interviewing every person in the factories we have on our list.'

His list originally included the names of twenty-three firms, mostly in the engineering and textile industries, but it eventually grew to over thirty, who between them employed nearly 8,000 men. Undaunted, the Manchester team set about the task of interviewing them all.

Most men were seen at their place of work. But in the case of haulage firms like T. and W. H. Clark (Holdings) Ltd., of the Canal Road estate, their employees were usually visited at home. Working steadily through their roster, detective-constables Howard and Smith arrived at the home of Clark's driver Peter Sutcliffe on the evening of 2 November, a full month after Jean Jordan had been killed.

They knocked on the door of No. 6 Garden Lane at 7.45 p.m. and found both Mr and Mrs Sutcliffe at home. Relaxed and casual, he told them that on the night Miss Jordan had died he had been at home and had retired to bed at about 11.30. His wife confirmed this story.

Questioned about the second crucial date, eight days later, when the murderer had returned to the scene, Mr Sutcliffe said he had been having a house-warming party. The police officers found nothing to arouse their suspicions and subsequently filed a five-paragraph report saying so.

On the evening of 8 November, Mr and Mrs Sutcliffe were again seen, by two different policemen, at home at No. 6 Garden Lane and he was again questioned about the £5 note. Both he and his wife gave the same stories and agreed to the house being searched. Nothing was found.

When police later called on Mrs Kathleen Sutcliffe at 57 Cornwall Road, she confirmed that she had been present at a house-warming party at her son's home on Sunday night, 9 October, and that afterwards he had run her and her husband back to Bingley.

As a result of the spate of murders in Chapeltown, Marilyn Moore didn't go with just anybody any more, as Peter Sutcliffe realised on the night of 14 December, when he saw her refuse to get into a car in Leopold Street, in the heart of the red-light district. Thinking quickly, though, he parked and jumped out of his and shouted, 'Bye now, see you later, take care!' at a nearby building, to reassure her he was 'all right'. As a result, when he asked her if she was doing business, she climbed quite happily into the front of the Corsair.

She was further reassured by 'Dave's' chatty manner, and by

the way he obviously knew his way around. They drove from the centre of Chapeltown to the quiet of Scott Hall Street, and when he suggested that they 'do it' in the back seat, she readily agreed.

It was as she got out of the car that he took a swing at her with a hammer, but he lost his balance in the mud and only caught her a glancing blow. He hit her again, and then again a third time, but she was still screaming when he saw some people about forty yards away. He gunned the engine, producing 'a lot of wheel-spin', and drove straight home.

In February 1978, as he prepared to vacate his schoolroom head-quarters at Baildon and return to Manchester, Det. Chief Supt. Jack Ridgeway would tell the press: 'We have just about exhausted the enquiry. It has drawn a blank.'

'I personally don't believe that we have yet met the killer in our multitude of interviews. When we do I am positive we will realise and nail him,' Mr Ridgeway's assistant said.

22

John and Kathleen made a point of always waiting until they were asked before visiting Garden Lane, and Peter asked them over with other members of the family during Christmas week, 1977. It was less than three months since the house-warming which had gone off so successfully but, while this second evening faithfully followed the pattern of the first – drinks, a meal, drinks and chocolates in front of the television – a distinct pall hung over the proceedings.

Sonia had lavished all her energies on the house in the short time that they had been in it. 'Oh Sonia's been pulling an old fire-place out,' Peter would say, explaining their late arrival for Sunday tea at his mother's (and they could always be relied on to be at least an hour and a half late); or 'Sonia's papering the attic,' he would say, rather shamefacedly, apologising for her non-appearance. They were 'excuses' that John Sutcliffe took with a pinch of salt. But he had to admit that you could see the amount of work that had gone into the house that first Christmas.

The only trouble was that it was underheated. With the exception of Sonia and her mother, who were wearing layers of cardigans and jumpers and knitted 'leggins', everybody was freezing. Kathleen was particularly susceptible to the cold because of the poor state of her health, and John was forced to bend down and switch on the electric fire in the living-room himself when neither Peter nor Sonia volunteered. Within quarter of an hour, though, Kathleen, who had drawn her chair close to the only source of heat, was shivering again: the fire was off and they could only assume the reason it refused to relight was because the power had been turned off at the mains.

Kathleen spent what was left of the evening sitting huddled in her winter coat, and this time even Peter's customary 'daftness' couldn't rescue the situation. When she got home that night, his mother swore she would never set foot in Garden Lane again, and she never did.

1977, in fact, was the last Christmas that Kathleen was to spend in her own house on Cornwall Road. From the mid-1970s on, everybody who knew her had noticed that she was starting to age very fast. Never a woman to complain, despite the fact that she still had to go out cleaning every night at the Teachers Training College, she had put on weight, she seemed less cheery than she had always been, and she sometimes had difficulty drawing breath. By the beginning of 1978, she was starting to look considerably older than her fifty-eight years, and nobody was able to come up with a satisfactory explanation as to why.

'It's supposed to be angina, but she's had all sorts of exploratory treatments and cardiac jobs done on her, and they can't find anything seriously wrong,' John would say whenever friends enquired after Kathleen's health. 'The doctor's told her it won't kill her, that it's just something you've got to live with, but she does let it get her down'

Although two years was all that separated them, John Sutcliffe in late middle age looked many years younger than his wife. His hair was still dark and thick, his body was still lithe and he still turned out every Saturday during the summer for Gilstead and Eldwick second eleven: in the team photograph published in the Bingley *Guardian* at the beginning of the 1977 season he was to be seen, arms folded across his chest, immaculate in his 'whites', conceding at least thirty years to every other player in the picture. That didn't stop him being his team's top scorer week after week, though; and if anybody ever had to strip off to retrieve the ball from the stream running along the boundary, it would almost invariably be him.

Dancing is another thing John retained a youthful enthusiasm for and, with Kathleen more or less immobilised by her illness, he started escorting a local widow to dances in Bradford and the surrounding district. He had known Mrs Dean when he worked in the mill alongside both her and her husband. And, because she also knew Kathleen, Marion had refused when John first looked into the mini-cab office where she took calls and asked her to go out with him. But after reassurances that his wife was an invalid she had relented, and they had embarked on what was to become a longstanding relationship.

If Kathleen knew, she never gave Marion any indication of it whenever they bumped into each other in town, her only conversation being her family and, in particular, Peter and how he'd 'got on'.

The huge Clark's wagon had become a common sight in Cornwall Road. Peter had started going out of his way to drop in on his mother, even if it was only for ten minutes; and by the end of 1977, it had become as apparent to him as to the rest of the family that she couldn't go on living on Ferncliffe Estate very much longer because of the climb: carrying shopping from the new covered 'precinct' in the centre of Bingley up a succession of hills to Cornwall Road was now out of the question.

Details of Kathleen's predicament had been communicated to the Town Hall and, early in 1978, she was offered a two-bedroomed maisonette on the first floor of a post-war council block closer to the centre of town. Rutland House stood across the street from both Mornington Road Methodist Church, known as the 'Cathedral of the North' because of its bulk, and the school which John had attended as a boy, and was surrounded by the sort of tightly packed, black stone terraces that had been pulled down to make way for it.

The previous tenants of No. 8 were no strangers to John and Kathleen, being former neighbours from 'the estate'; nor, as John would occasionally point out to visitors, were they entirely unknown to regular readers of the *News of the World*: the husband had attempted to strangle the wife after catching her with another man many years earlier and, after being charged with rape, their fifteen-year-old son had gone out and committed suicide by putting his neck on the railway line.

All the new key-holders saw, though, was a suite of small,

easily maintained rooms on two levels, and they arranged to move into Rutland House on Sunday, 22 January 1978, Kathleen's fifty-ninth birthday.

After eighteen years on 'Corny' Road, there was plenty to get rid of; the ledger of Top Twenty hits that Peter had so laboriously compiled and the green toboggan that he had crashed into a set of railings in, seriously bruising his head, in the course of his 'delayed' adolescence, were just two of the pile of objects thrown out as rubbish on the Saturday of the move.

Most members of the family turned up at some point during the day to lend a hand, but it was Peter himself who took charge. Unfortunately, being a Saturday, he almost left it too late to hire the van that they needed to transport his parents' modest belongings down to the flat in. By the time they drove over to Bramhall's, on the far side of Bradford, they were closed and, with Mick and his father as passengers, Peter drove for miles trying to find a van-hire firm that was still open. It confirmed everything John had always said about Peter leaving everything he did to the last minute, but finally, around 4.30, they were able to get hold of a box-van from a place in Keighley.

Mick drove Peter's red Corsair back to Cornwall Road, with Peter following, and they at least managed to get the carpets down in Rutland House by Saturday night. When they were finished, Mick agitated to be allowed to keep the keys to the box-van until the next day, but Peter knew his brother too well. The keys were in his pocket when he climbed into his car and drove away saying he'd see them to finish the work the following morning.

Mick and his father both assumed it was because he had to get home to Sonia that Peter wouldn't stay for a drink. But, driving towards Bradford from Bingley, he bypassed Heaton, and by nine o'clock was in the familiar territory of Lumb Lane. Cruising slowly, he was able to narrowly avoid an accident when another car backed out of a side street in front of him without any warning. But he was obliged to brake and, when he did, a smart, blonde-haired woman in a black sweater and black slacks tapped on the front passenger window and then opened the door.

Yvonne Pearson had two convictions for soliciting and was due to appear before Bradford magistrates again five days later on a third charge. He asked her where she had sprung from so suddenly and she said, 'Just good timing. You can put it down to fate.' She told him it was £5 for 'a good time' and £10 for 'more than a good time' and asked him how much he could afford. Not £10, was the answer, but she got in anyway and accompanied him to a piece of waste ground at the back of Drummond's, the mill where his father worked.

As soon as she stepped out of the car he beat Yvonne Pearson several times over the head with a heavy walling-hammer that had been under his seat. At that precise moment, though, he was alarmed to see another car pull in alongside his and, 'to keep her quiet', he grabbed handfuls of horsehair from an old settee lying nearby 'and stuffed it into her mouth and down her throat'.

He knelt behind the settee 'for what seemed like an hour' and 'kept holding her nose so that she couldn't scream out'. He let go after a while 'to see if she was still making a noise' and, when she was, grabbed her nose again and held it until the other car was gone.

Alone again, he dragged her trousers down and bared her breasts and started kicking her relentlessly about the head and body. He came down on her chest with the weight of both feet and, before leaving, hid Yvonne Pearson under the upturned settee and scattered clods of earth, which is where she was to lie, undiscovered, for the next two months.

The next morning, a Sunday, he took his mother a small present for her birthday and helped his father and brothers complete the move in to Rutland House which they had started the day before. They were able to do it in just two trips with an hour off in the middle for a lunchtime drink. By bedtime that night, with the curtains hung and the small light glowing on top of the television, it already seemed to John Sutcliffe as if they'd lived there years and years.

He soon made himself known to the young people who had turned the front room of a small terraced house opposite into a health-food shop called 'Fodder': 'I like a touch of garlic in my stews,' he'd tell them. But he refused to patronise the late-night general dealers two streets away which had been taken over by an Asian family.

Although there was a flight of stone steps to climb from the streets to the first-floor landing, and she still had to climb stairs to the bathroom and the bedroom, the new flat, being closer to the floor of the valley, was less demanding on Kathleen's health. They had only been living there a few weeks, though, when she turned to her husband and told him: 'I don't think I'm going to be here much longer.' He did what he could to reassure her that she was still a comparatively young woman but, at her insistence, arranged for the priest from the Sacred Heart to start coming in to give Kathleen communion every other week.

23

Loneliness is to live in a world
Where people do not care.
Loneliness is to go outside,
To find no one is there, and
You fall down in despair,
Falling on your knees in prayer.
Asking God to rescue you,
From this cruel snare,
But no one comes
No voice is heard . . .

Unloved is to miss the love
That all parents should give.
Yet they cast you aside
Put you out of their minds.
They put you in care.
There is no love there.
Yet the staff really care
Or they wouldn't be there.
Yet I know I shall die,
As my years drag by,
Oh, why was it me, Lord?
Why?

As the result of a series on fostering and foster children published in the *Yorkshire Post* in May 1974, two fifteen-year-old twin sisters living in a children's home in North Yorkshire had sat down and composed a poem and posted it off to the newspaper with an accompanying letter.

'Dear Sir/Madam,' the letter began. 'If my twin sister and I got fostered out together it would be like winning £1,000 on the football pools . . . To get fostered out together means to us a place of love and care and it is then that you feel wanted, because someone somewhere realises what love really is and to get fostered out is part of love itself. We can only wait, hope and pray to get fostered out together, but some day I hope we will.'

In 1974, Rita and Elena Rytka, who preferred to be called 'Helen', had been in St Theresa's, a Catholic hostel in Knaresborough, for five years. St Theresa's, though, was just the latest in the long list of institutions the sisters had known since their Italian mother split up with their West Indian father when they were children.

A few years in a rundown house in Leopold Street in Chapeltown was the only 'home' life they had previously known. But, within a few days of their letter and poem appearing in the paper, they had been offered a home by a civil servant and his wife in Dewsbury. Helen and Rita had been happy living with their foster-parents in the comfort of their large house for two years but, in September 1976, they had moved in with their brother and sister, Tony and Angela, who were also twins and lived in a tower block close to the centre of Bradford.

After leaving school, Rita had won a place at Batley Art College and Helen had gone to work as a £20-a-week packer at a confectionery factory in Heckmondwike. Helen's real ambition, though, was to be a singer, and she went out dancing most nights of the week at clubs in Bradford and Leeds. One of her friends during this period was a girl who happened to be related to Peter Sutcliffe's neighbour, Ronnie Barker, and Helen was a frequent visitor to Tanton Crescent in the years when the Szurmas had their son-in-law living with them: she was a guest next door at the Barkers' on at least one occasion.

Shortly before Christmas, 1977, however, Rita Rytka had dropped out of her art-school course, left the flat where she was living with her sisters and her brother, and gone to live in a shabby bedsit ten miles away in one of the poorer districts of Huddersfield without offering any explanation.

Elmwood Avenue is in the Highfields area, on a shelf overlooking both the M62 Leeds–Manchester motorway and the town centre, and Highfields is where Helen eventually tracked Rita down after a two-month separation. It was the longest they had ever lived apart and it was immediately understood that Helen would move in and share her sister's double bed in the damp downstairs room. Inevitably, she also joined her under the viaduct on Great Northern Street in Huddersfield, working the 'car-trade' in the hope of one day making enough money to break into the music business.

Although the 'Yorkshire Ripper', so far as anybody knew, had never struck in Huddersfield, the posters – in Punjabi and Urdu as well as English – appealing for information, the almost daily stories in the press and on television, and the endlessly circulating, increasingly gruesome rumours had had the effect, by the beginning of 1978, of creating an atmosphere of watchfulness and caution.

In their few weeks of walking the streets together, the Rytka twins had evolved a way of working which, although hardly foolproof, was at least designed to frustrate the efforts of any man who might want to harm them: they would accept clients at the same time; they would each give them a precise twenty minutes; and afterwards they would each attempt to rendezvous in the same place – a block of public lavatories, well-known as a homosexuals' 'cottage', at the market end of Great Northern Street.

The prostitutes of Lumb Lane and Chapeltown, many of whom had also started to work in pairs, had taken these precautions a significant step further: one woman would conspicuously take down the number of the car her 'partner' was about to go off in and then tear the number up in front of the driver when her friend returned.

To Helen and Rita, though, the looser arrangement seemed to offer sufficient cover and, shortly after 8.30 on 31 January 1978, a wet Tuesday night with snow threatening, they set off on what was becoming their regular 'beat'.

Aged eighteen, dark-skinned and slim, with unforced smiles and flawless complexions, the Rytkas were, by any standards, strikingly good-looking. Great Northern Street, however, with its railway arches and its abattoir and its general air of rankness and dereliction, was not the best showcase for their youthful attractions. Collars up against the cold, they started patrolling the street, with the motor traffic between them, watching their step on the uneven pavements.

At ten minutes past nine Rita saw a dark-coloured car draw up alongside Helen on the other side of the street and watched her sister get in it. A short time later she was herself picked up in a Datsun by another 'punter' and, unaware that they were being followed by a peeping-Tom in a van, drove off to have sex in one of the quiet streets away from the town centre.

When Rita returned after twenty minutes to find no sign of Helen, she was puzzled. She hung around, squinting through the sleet until it became obvious that Helen wasn't coming, then turned around and trudged back up to Highfields to see if she could find her.

It was ten days since Peter Sutcliffe had murdered Yvonne Pearson, whose body still lay under an old settee half a mile from the centre of Bradford. He spotted Helen Rytka waiting for her sister outside the public toilets near Huddersfield market, and convinced her there was time for a 'quickie' over in the timber yard whose piles of wood seemed to shore up the streaming walls of the railway arches which towered above them.

Once inside the yard, he had planned to strike Helen with a hammer while she was getting into the back seat of the Corsair. As soon as he turned the engine off, though, she undid her trousers and indicated that she was ready for him to have inter-course with her straight away. Unusually, and despite himself, he realised that he had achieved an erection, and he got out of the car with the excuse that he wanted to urinate. When he came back she too agreed to get out so that they could have sex in the back.

It was as she stood with her back to him, fumbling with the rear door, that he swung the hammer. The hammer, though, caught the roof of the car and only grazed Helen, who thought he had struck her with his hand.

'There's no need for that,' she said, and he immediately sensed her terror. 'You don't even have to pay.' But he hit her again with the hammer, and again, until he realised that what he was doing was in full view of two taxi drivers parked some little distance away. He grabbed her by the hair then and dragged her into a far corner of the yard. She had stopped moaning but she wasn't dead: her eyes were open, 'staring', and her hands were up in order to ward off further blows.

He told her not to make any more noise and she would be 'all right'. He had intercourse with her because she had 'aroused' him, but also 'to keep her quiet', then produced a sharp knife which he plunged 'five or six times' into her ribcage and her heart. He tore off what was left of her clothes and hurled her shoes seventy yards up an embankment. He forced her body into the narrow space between a stack of wood and a disused garage and covered it with a sheet of asbestos before leaving.

Back at Garden Lane he sponged off the blood which had spattered his shoes and put the knife back in the kitchen drawer where he had found it.

It was three days before Rita Rytka gathered up her courage and reported her sister missing to the police. It took a police dog ten minutes to locate Helen's battered body in one of the dim recesses of Garrard's timber yard. The morning after the murder, men working at the yard had noticed a blood-stained patch in the mud, and a lorry-driver had pinned the pair of black lace panties that he'd found to the door of a shed. Such early morning discoveries were nothing new at Garrard's, however, and tended to be shrugged off with a laugh.

On 9 February, six days after the discovery of what was believed to be the Ripper's seventh murder victim, George Oldfield appeared on Radio 2's popular early morning programme, the *Jimmy Young Show*, and urged the predominantly female audience to search their collective conscience and report any man of their acquaintance whom they suspected of behaving oddly. Husband, father, brother, son – it shouldn't matter: it was their duty, anonymously or otherwise, to let the police know. Mr Oldfield – 'George' to Jimmy Young and his several million listeners

– also reiterated his personal commitment to catching the man whose activities were causing increasing numbers of women in the North of England to live in fear.

Within days of the Assistant Chief Constable's unprecedented advance into the public arena, the *Yorkshire Post* and its sister evening paper announced a £5,000 reward for information leading to the arrest and conviction of the Ripper; and the West Yorkshire Police Authority, flying in the face of official Home Office disapproval, added a further £10,000 (later £20,000) of their own.

The discovery of Yvonne Pearson's body at the end of March, lying on the piece of waste ground where she had met her death two months earlier, contributed considerably to the gathering disquiet. And, in April, as proof of the hunt being stepped up, Det. Chief Supt. John Domaille was appointed special assistant to George Oldfield and put in charge of a team of twelve 'crack' detectives who were to make up a special 'Ripper Squad'.

At the same time, secret surveillance operations were mounted in Leeds, Bradford and the red-light districts of other towns in West Yorkshire; registration numbers were noted and fed into the central police computer at Hendon: the driver of any car spotted repeatedly in Chapeltown or Manningham, or in more than one of the surveillance areas, was – eventually – contacted and questioned.

By August 1978, the red Corsair belonging to Peter Sutcliffe had been seen in Lumb Lane a total of seven times and, on 23 August, Detective-Constable Peter Smith called at No. 6 Garden Lane to interview the owner. Mr Sutcliffe was in his overalls decorating the kitchen at the time, but he didn't seem to mind in the least being interrupted. He explained that he had to travel through the Manningham area every day to get to work, and dismissed as preposterous the suggestion that he used prostitutes. Mrs Sutcliffe confirmed his story, and told the officer that her husband rarely went out at night: when he did, she usually went with him. As confirmation of this, she said that he had taken her to Rockafella's, a discotheque in Leeds, on the night of one of the murders.

Peter Smith was not the same Constable Smith who had had cause to interview Peter Sutcliffe on a previous occasion; and because that earlier report was still part of the huge backlog of paperwork waiting to be processed at Leeds police headquarters, he didn't know that Peter Sutcliffe had been seen ten months earlier in connection with the £5 note enquiry. There was also nothing about the interviewee's behaviour to lead Detective-Constable Smith to suspect that a little more than three months earlier he had gone out and murdered for the ninth time.

On the night of Tuesday, 16 May 1978, two days after buying a grey, H-registration Sunbeam Rapier, Peter Sutcliffe had returned to the same part of southern Manchester in which he had picked up Jean Jordan. Vera Millward's body was found in a sitting position, slumped against a fence in the car park of Manchester Royal Infirmary in the early hours of 17 May. When her coat was removed, it could be seen that her stomach had been mutilated so badly that her intestines had spilled on to the ground.

There were to be no more attacks in 1978. And as the severe winter of 1978–9 receded and there were still no fresh reports, the men leading the hunt for the Yorkshire Ripper would find themselves weighing the possibility that the man they were looking for was no longer in circulation: he could be in a mental hospital or a prison; he could be serving with the army in Northern Ireland or with the navy abroad or, like his Victorian namesake, he could have committed suicide: he could be dead.

On the other hand, the drives that had led him to murder nine women in less than three years could simply have played themselves out: he could have settled down and married and might never kill again. This was the theory advanced by Dr Stephen Shaw, a lecturer at Wakefield police training college, in November 1978, in an interview with the *Yorkshire Evening Post*: 'I have never felt this was a married man, but it may be that since the murder of Vera Millward he has found a woman and settled down . . . Someone he can pamper and at whose feet he can worship. Someone who is in his eyes a paragon of virtue.'

Many of the prostitutes of Chapeltown and Manningham had started carrying long-bladed scissors and hat-pins and knives but, reassured by the hiatus in the killings, they had returned to the streets in force. 'If I thought about the Ripper every time I was on the street, I'd run home and lock the door. I stop myself thinking about him by thinking about *money*. It always works,' a twenty-two-year-old called 'Skip' was reported as saying in the Halifax *Courier*.

The differences that had been apparent between Mick and Peter in adolescence had become reinforced as they'd grown older. Peter's evident need for stability and approval bore no relation to the kind of life his brother led, in which nothing was fixed, least of all an address.

For his part, Mick admired Peter's determination to 'mek summat of hissen', but knew it wasn't for him. He was happy living day to day and, not infrequently, hand to mouth, scratching a living from Dowley Gap tip and the fields, only turning to legitimate – and not-so-legitimate – forms of employment when things were desperate.

Most of his friends had seen the inside of Armley jail at some point in their lives, and Mick was well known for dealing in small firearms, with no questions asked. It was livestock, though, which provided him with a basic income, mainly pigeons and goats, in addition to what he was able to poach. The goats he bought at auction, for selling on to Asian restaurants in Bradford, although he would occasionally slaughter one himself and keep it for feeding to his lurcher; for a short period he sold the same pigeons to the same stall-holder in Bradford market every Saturday, in the firm knowledge that they would be his – and the stall-holder's – to sell again within hours of being released.

After a shortlived marriage, Mick had been reluctant to commit himself to any one person and had stayed constantly on the move. But in mid-1978 he found himself homeless with a girl-friend and a new baby and was obliged to ask his mother and father to take them in.

John had made little attempt to hide his disappointment in the aimlessness of Mick's existence, and over the years had subtly dissociated himself from his 'waster' son. But Susan was a nice girl – her father was the weakling-turned-wrestler who had once been held up as an example to Peter – and, even if her husband had had the heart for it, Kathleen would never have allowed him to turn them away.

They lived at Rutland House until the early autumn, when they were allocated a house on the far side of the valley, in Cottingley, close to where Mick had spent his early years. It was one of the council's more run-down properties: the coal fire in the living-room was no match for the draughts sweeping in around the windows and the doors, and the place was infested with mice: Mick would lie on the settee with an air-gun in the evenings, shooting them as they crept out from under the skirting. But it was a roof, and they were out from under his mother's feet, and they were prepared to put up with it until something better came along.

The move to Rutland House at the beginning of the year had witnessed no dramatic improvement in Kathleen's condition. She had been forced to give up her job and now rarely got out. On 5 November 1978, though, she wrapped up well and made a special trip over to Cottingley to be with her new granddaughter on her first Guy Fawkes night. It was almost as if she'd had a premonition, Susan would say, because, three days later, Kathleen was dead.

Kathleen was noted for the guileless way she'd believe anything anybody told her, and Carl, like his two brothers before him, enjoyed stringing his mother along. 'Why don't you ever bring girls home?' she'd asked him, and Carl would tell her it was because he didn't like girls. 'You're not one of them, are you?' she'd want to know anxiously, and he would solemnly tell her that he was.

It was this kind of game Carl started off playing on the morning of 8 November, as his mother attempted to push a vacuum cleaner around the maisonette in Rutland House. But it became clear very quickly that she wasn't up to his usual teasing; she was in obvious pain and gasping for breath and Maureen told her brother that he had better bloody well cut it out.

After three years as an army wife in Germany, Maureen had returned to Bingley in the summer and was living in a council house a few minutes' walk away, at the end of Mornington Road. She had taken Rachel and Damien to school that morning and then looked in to check that her mother was all right.

Kathleen, in fact, was to see several members of her family that Wednesday, given that it wasn't one of the Wednesdays when Father Roncetti from the Sacred Heart was due to pay a visit. Mick, with a baby to feed and bills to pay, had swallowed his dislike of working indoors and had gone labouring at Wilkinson's mill on the canal. And, rather then traipsing back up to Cottingley, he went round to his mother's for his lunch.

His father was just about leaving when Mick arrived, because he was on the late shift, two to ten, so they only had time for a quick hello. Kathleen hadn't said much in front of John but, as soon as he was gone, she started complaining to Mick about the pains in her chest. 'I says, "Well, do you want me to stop off work, like? I'll stop in with you this afternoon instead of going back." She said, "No, don't lose your job; stick to it. I'll be all right." She took a pill then, for angina.

'I said, "I'm not going back if you're not really all right." She said, "Oh, I'll be all right; get back." So I went back to work, and it was only five minutes from where she lived, so all they had to do was ring up an' I'd have come straight over an' gone on.'

It was when Maureen looked in again around 4.00 p.m., after picking the children up from school, that she found her mother collapsed on the bed. The handful of tablets that she had been trying to take had dissolved in her mouth, leaving a white residue caked on her lips. Kathleen was conscious by the time the doctor arrived, but he immediately called for an ambulance.

Maureen telephoned her father at Drummond's to tell him that her mother had been rushed into Airedale General, and he telephoned the hospital himself straight away, only to be told that, although his wife was in intensive care, he would be of more use staying where he was. When he called again at 5.30, however, he was advised to get there as quickly as possible.

While he was on his way to Steeton, Kathleen died.

Peter broke the news to Maureen, who had got in touch with him earlier at home. 'She's dead, Mo,' he said when she opened the door, and kept repeating it as if that would make it real. But being 'more used to death, working in a cemetery an' that', as Maureen later reasoned, he quickly collected himself and drove straight to the hospital, to be there when his father arrived.

Hurrying through the dusk towards the modern glass buildings, John was relieved to see Peter standing in a doorway under a lamp. 'He was the only one there, but he hadn't been there long. He'd only been there about quarter of an hour before me. And he said, "Well, Dad," he said, "sit down." And I thought, Oh my God, what's up? Then he reached out and put his hand on my shoulder and said, "She's gone."

'He'd probably had time to get over the shock by the time I got there. And I think he was probably more concerned for me, so he put a very brave face on at the time. I went into the hospital and they let me go in and see her. They had her all laid out, and he came in with me. He was all right. He took my arm and sort of led me out.'

On their return to Bingley, his father got in touch with the police to ask for somebody to be sent around to Anne's house in Morecambe, and Peter pressed on to Shipley where Jane had been living since the break-up of her marriage earlier in the year. Mick didn't find out that his mother was dead until nearly midnight, and a rift developed between him and the rest of the family for some weeks as a result.

He had gone straight into the Granby after finishing work at 5.30 and stayed there until the pub closed, when he had taken a taxi home. Maureen and Robin had been the ones to break the news, and then Peter had knocked at the door just after they'd gone. Mick's grief took the form of anger at being the last to be told, but then a curious thing happened which made them realise how upset they all really were. Mick was eating the dinner that Susan had been keeping warm for him for hours when Peter arrived. The dinner was on a low table in front of the settee and, as he leaned forward to load his fork during an uneasy silence, the plate appeared to move: all three present in the room that night would later swear that it rose of its own volition and hovered five or six inches in the air.

The next day, Thursday, Peter went off on an overnight run to the North. As he passed Airedale General he turned to Carl, who was travelling with him, and said: 'It's funny to think of her lying dead in there, isn't it?'

On the return journey, they made a detour to visit Anne and her family in Morecambe, but Anne had already travelled to Bingley to be with her sisters, and so the two of them went for a walk along the seafront. The walk eventually took them to the west end of the promenade where Tussaud's was situated, but, being a week past the switching off of the illuminations, marking the official end of the season, they found the turnstile to the waxworks locked.

It was only recently, however, that they had visited the exhibition together. On that occasion, Peter had seemed particularly drawn to the central tableau in Hall Three, at the entrance to the Museum of Anatomy. As his contribution to the campaign alerting drivers to the danger of drink, Mr Nicholson, the waxworks proprietor, had staged a car crash in the room's biggest showcase, and in appropriately horrific detail: two figures were slumped over the bonnet of a Mini, disfigured in a way that suggested they had just been hurled through the windscreen, while other bodies, dramatically mutilated and bloodied, authenticated the scene.

Carl hadn't been able to understand what Peter found so fascinating, or amusing, and at one point had thought he would never be able to drag him away.

Kathleen's body was received into the Church of the Sacred Heart in Bingley at 7.30 p.m. on Sunday, 12 November 1978. A Requiem Mass was said for her at ten o'clock on Monday morning, and her remains were then taken to Nab Wood cemetery to be cremated.

25

Reading the 'Deaths' and 'In Memoriams' and attending funerals was a popular pastime among the older generation in Bingley. But even so, Kathleen's popularity among her friends and neighbours was accurately reflected in the numbers who turned out for her funeral. Afterwards, Peter made it his business to go round and thank some of those known to him personally.

It was many years since he had 'gone best mates' with Eric Robinson, but Eric's mother and his had remained friendly, and Mrs Robinson was gratified to open the door and find Peter standing there on the evening of the funeral. Peter had always struck her as being 'of a nervous disposition' – when called on to speak, his temperature would go up, his eyes would blink and he'd stammer the words. And so, although it was a mature adult and not a youth she saw standing on her doorstep, it didn't surprise her to see large tears rolling down his cheeks and into his beard.

Unlike Peter, Eric had never married. He was a window-cleaner and still living at home, but that night, as most nights, he was out at the Working Men's Club. She told Peter that if he wanted to see Eric, this is where he would certainly find him, but he preferred to leave his telephone number and, it seemed to her, the rather forlorn message, 'He could come and see me.'

The last time the two former friends had met was by chance in the Star in Bingley, when Eric's reminiscences of the good times they had known in their 'Gravediggers' Corner' days at the Royal Standard hadn't gone down too well with Sonia.

To see Peter and Sonia together in one of the local pubs at all after they were married was considered something of an event. It wasn't unknown for her to sit outside in the car while he had a drink with one or other of his family, or for Sonia to come and get him if she felt she had been kept waiting too long. 'A boring woman' was her brother-in-law Robin Holland's conclusion, after an hour or two spent in her company one night at the Fisherman. Robin and Maureen had gone out with Peter and Sonia as a foursome shortly after his demob from the army in 1978. Robin, however, had soon 'called it a draw' because it was 'dead'. 'She's got no conversation,' he complained later, 'and she whispers all the time when she does speak. She talks to you like you were a kid.'

But if Peter's relations had increasingly little in common with Sonia, they found they had even less in common with her friends. Mick enjoyed going to the Hare and Hounds, the large, mixed pub near the house in Garden Lane, but hated it if Sonia was with them and she fell into conversation with other teachers, as she inevitably did. 'All friends I've known that they've known have been bloody teachers an' stuff an' she's yappin' away to 'em, an' he'd be yappin' away to 'em an' all. Well that isn't my bloody idea of a good night. I'd just look at Susan as if to say, Sup off, and get up to bar for another one; just keep suppin'.

'Our lad'd say, "This is . . ." and I'd say, "Oh aye, I heard you say his name first time. I'm not interested at all. I'm just not fuckin' bothered." Long-haired bastards all talkin' down to us as if we know nowt.'

As a result of their obvious incompatibility, Sonia made no secret of the fact after a while that she had decided to see family and friends independently. Tackled by Mick on why it was only ever his family at Garden Lane 'do's', Sonia was unabashed in telling him in front of everybody that they entertained their 'professional' friends separately.

For Peter, though, the conflict was not so simply resolved. His attitude towards Sonia's pots was a typical example of the ways in which he found his loyalties divided. Enthusiastic, almost boastful, about them to her friends, he was apologetic, almost scoffing, when Sonia wasn't there. Under the pretext of taking him to look at something else, he would say to Carl, 'Come here, I'll show you. She's done another one,' and they'd both have to stifle their giggles. 'Me wife does these things,' he'd say almost immediately, looking embarrassed, if either of his brothers brought a stranger round to Garden Lane.

The amount of time Sonia spent on her own with her paints and clay in the attic room at the top of the house, furnished with just an old mattress and 'not even listening to radio or records or owt', amazed Carl as much as his presence irritated her. Looking up from working on a car with Peter, he would sometimes see her standing at the landing window, 'just watching, quiet as a little mouse'.

It often seemed to Jane that Sonia would have liked Peter to have been an only child so he didn't have to see any of his family, and she could have had him all to herself.

There were occasions, such as the time Carl roared up the newly-cemented drive at Garden Lane on a motorbike, creating a twenty-foot-long gully, when Sonia's resentment burst into the open. But most of the time it just hung like freshly sprayed deodoriser on the air.

In his late teens Carl regularly went over to Heaton to pull on a pair of overalls and strip down engines under the expert eye of his older brother, and it was a rare weekend when he didn't sense an 'atmosphere'. 'When you're working on an engine, you don't want disturbing, but she were always on at him. "Pete, Pete . . ." "What you want?" "Come and help me wash up." I mean, he's covered in oil up arms an' elbows and she's going, "Help me wash up." So then she'd be off in a huff.

'Same as if I ever went with 'im to scrapyard to pick up bits. He'd be watching his watch all the time – "I've got to get back by so-and-so." I'd say, "Why? Let's go for a pint." But it was, "Oh no, I've got to get back. She gets worried." So I'd tell him, "What the fuck should she get worried for? You've only gone for some parts for a car for fuck sake, and you're over thirty year old!"'

Those who only knew Sonia as the shy, softly-spoken schoolteacher – and they included Peter's father – found it difficult to imagine her in this other, dominant role for a long time. Listening to his complaints about her nagging, John once found himself saying as much to Peter, only to be assured that, at home, she was 'all mouth'. If that was the case, John later found himself thinking, then perhaps it was to do with her Eastern European background, 'where the men make all the show but the women rule inside the house'.

Being from a 'foreign family' is what Carl traced Sonia's frugality back to as well. He assumed that was the reason they sat on hard chairs in the kitchen most of the time, ignoring the bigger, more comfortable rooms in the rest of the house. 'You'd go up, say, in the morning, and you'd sit in there all through until 6.00. Then Peter might suggest having a look at what was on telly, but they would never ever put fire on an' it were freezing. *Really* cold. An' they'd have the telly on really quiet as well. You couldn't even hear it. You had to strain your ears.'

When there was only the two of them at home, Sonia frequently took exception to Peter having the television on at all and would snatch the plug from the wall. She would also 'tease' him by refusing to let him read a newspaper, swiping at his head and kicking him, and screaming at him so hard sometimes that he was sure the neighbours must be able to hear. But he would remain quite impassive, holding her arms at her side until she calmed down, but never hitting her. He would leave the house rather than raise his voice.

There was always 'hell to pay' if Peter ever entered the house with his boots on or put any of his clothes in the washing machine: he had remained sensitive about the smell his socks made anyway, and was happy to wash all his own clothes by hand in the kitchen sink. Sonia's obsession with cleanliness stretched to cleaning the carpets inch-by-inch with a brush and pan and working on the house at all hours of the day and night.

'I'd have buried her in back garden by now, if it were me,' was a thought that Carl shared only with Mick. Mick, on the other hand, never hesitated to tell Sonia herself exactly what he thought. 'Our Pete used to say to me, he'd say, "Bloody hell, just be a bit, you know, watch what you're saying." He wouldn't say owt at all to her, you see, but I just said, "Well, that up to you, but

I'm just going to tell her what I think, and you should do bloody same."

'If owt wanted doin', he'd do it for 'er, but then she'd have something else for 'im straight away. I'd say, "C'mon, we're going out for a bloody pint; we're goin' for a drink," which would get her goin' straight away. "He's not going anywhere. He's doing this, and when he's finished he's doing that and that . . ."

'Like, he might be out three nights wi' wagon around country somewhere an' he'd come back bloody jiggered about four in the afternoon, after driving all of the night and most of the day as well. Obviously he wanted to go to bed, have a few hours sleep, like, but, no, he had to come in an' start on bloody decorating. She used to start first thing in the morning and go right through day practically non-stop and all through night till mebbe five in the morning. Then she'd expect him to get straight on it, soon as he came in. She were cleaning fanatic. There were always sum-mat.'

It had relieved Mrs Bowman and the other neighbours on Garden Lane that the new people were so houseproud. They had had No. 6 re-pebble-dashed and had repainted the doors and windows themselves a smart black and white; Mrs Sutcliffe was always out weeding the garden, polishing the windows and even clearing the guttering around the roof. She had undertaken most of the painting singlehandedly in her first summer holidays from school, in 1978, and had caused a small sensation locally by shinning up a long ladder several days running in a bikini and bare feet: it occurred to Barbara Bowman that she had never seen the council workmen take so long to trim the verges, but Sonia hadn't appeared to mind.

Being of similar ages, Mrs Bowman and Sonia had struck up a casual acquaintance, based largely on teatime encounters in the street after school. Mrs Bowman had been able to deduce that Sonia was probably a teacher, largely on account of her 'arty' clothes and, having established that, had thought how useful it would be if she could give her youngest some extra tuition two or three nights a week. She had mentioned to Sonia that she was looking for somebody prepared to devote some time to their Robert – paid, of course – but Sonia, who Mrs Bowman had thought would have been glad of the cash, refused to bite. Robert was never invited into No. 6, and neither, despite repeated suggestions that she must come over and look at her pottery, was his mother.

Sonia herself was only in the Bowman's house once. She went across one evening to ask to borrow the ladder which she eventually used to paint the upper windows from, and four hours later was still sitting chatting in the back lounge. Peter had come across around midnight to fetch Sonia and, when they were finished with the ladder, it was Peter who had brought it back. He had given Robert 50p, which made Robert decide he was 'a nice man', but it did nothing to alter Barbara Bowman's opinion that, as far as the locality went, Peter still didn't really 'fit in'.

From how she had talked, however, Sonia seemed to genuinely love him, and there must have been some strength in the relationship to survive the amount of time they spent together in the house alone. Visitors at Garden Lane were few after the initial settling-in period, and became fewer as the years went on. His family still went on special occasions if they were invited, but Mick and Carl in the end usually only ever saw Peter on his own.

Even after his mother died, Peter liked to keep in touch with developments in Bingley. He dropped in regularly on his brothers and sisters and, whenever Mick had nothing better to do, which was often, he'd climb up into the cab and go off with Peter, occasionally staying away from home for two or three days.

They would sometimes pick girl hitchhikers up on the road. 'Look at these,' Peter would say. 'We'll get these in.' And he assured Mick that he often had sex in the cab. Mick thought it was strange though that, every time he was with him, the bunk-beds behind the driver's seat were only ever used for sleeping in.

Peter would invariably blame it on 'this fuckin' silly spot we're at' – usually a lay-by outside a quiet village.

Mick's favourites were the short runs to Nelson in Lancashire because they could be turned around and in Burnley by 2.00, and there was a pub in Burnley that stayed open all afternoon. They used to stay there, drinking steadily and playing dominoes, until about 4.30, which got them back to Clark's yard in Shipley just in time for Peter to clock off. Wherever they were, though, Mick noticed that his brother always tried to eat plenty of 'proper' food, before going home to whatever Sonia might have ready for him.

'She used to mek him little bowls of spicy stuff an' that that weren't fillin' or owt. I've known him have his dinner there then shoot out an' have fish and chips twice an' guzzle 'em, like, in motor. Sometimes he used to come to me mother's in wagon *starving*. If he hadn't picked owt up at chip shop, he'd come in, grab owt that were in fridge and be straight off.

'I told him, I said, if it was me, I'd say to 'er, "Never mind all that that you foreigners are used to eating. I want right dinners." That's what he should've said. But that weren't him. He never said owt to 'er, you see.'

The winter that Kathleen died was one of the worst in living memory in Yorkshire; in the week in which she would have celebrated her sixtieth birthday, Bradford had its heaviest snowfall for thirty years. The weather, followed by a national lorry-drivers' strike at the beginning of 1979, meant that Peter spent more lunchtimes than usual in the Belle Vue on Manningham Lane.

Working flat out the way he did meant that he often got his week's hours in in three days, and when this happened he would sometimes call on Mick and take him out for a lunchtime 'session'. He would then drop him off at home at the end of the afternoon with a few pounds shoved into his pocket so that he could go out again at night. Mick never ceased to marvel at the way money just seemed to 'build up on' Peter.

The Old Crown in the centre of Bradford, Yates' Wine Lodge opposite, and the Harp of Errin were some of their usual haunts, but the Belle Vue was the place where they invariably ended up. With their brother-in-law, Robin Holland, who was also a lorry-driver, and sometimes Trevor Birdsall, they were lunchtime regulars there while the bad weather and the drivers' strike lasted.

The Belle Vue in its day had been a rather stately public house, as uncompromising in its dourness as Drummond's mill in whose shadow it stood. In the mid-1970s, the new tenant, a Punjabi, had introduced a programme of 'Female Strippers' twice a day, seven days a week, and the Belle Vue had quickly become a favourite of lorry-drivers from all over the country as well as the Continent. With a smattering of local businessmen, students, Asians, West Indians and Chinese they made up the regular afternoon audience for 'Miss Abby Lane', 'Miss Ricci Lee' and the rest.

Yvonne Pearson, the Ripper's eighth victim, used to assist her husband who was the Belle Vue's disc-jockey in the days before the disc-jockey went 'topless'; and Tina Atkinson and Maureen Long also both used to be regulars.

In the winter and spring of 1979, however, all Bradford's prostitutes worked at the top end of Lumb Lane, near the park, where the police – although they publicly denied it – had granted them an 'amnesty' on the understanding that they only worked in a small, mutually agreed area during mutually agreed hours. In this way it was hoped that the 'Ripper', whose car number would have been noted by detectives covertly monitoring all traffic, would eventually be lured into the net. In other words, the prostitutes had tacitly agreed to act as live 'bait' in return for being allowed to earn their living without fear of prosecution.

As a result, there were few women in the Belle Vue most days that winter other than the disc-jockey with the often consulted fobwatch hanging between her pale, bare breasts and the performers in their gymslips, black leather, gold lamé and feather boas whom, every three quarters of an hour or so, it was her job to introduce. It was at this point that casual visitors would give themselves away by shuffling further into the room and craning their necks, while the regulars half-turned away from the raised stage with its guardrail and its single black plastic-covered chair and ignored 'Miss Abby Lane' 'masturbating' with a Johnson's baby oil bottle while squirting oil up on to her stomach and breasts.

They might look round if, as sometimes happened, she lifted the toupee off the head of a man at the front of the stage or removed somebody's glasses and placed them between her legs. But, otherwise, they assumed an air of studied indifference. 'When you've had as much cunt as I've had, you lose interest,' was typical of the 'men's talk' that circulated at the Belle Vue; impotence – 'old man's disease – I've to wind mesen up for three days wi' mucky books now' – was another perennial subject.

Further into 1979, Peter would confide in Mick that he'd 'caught a dose' and was trying to get as many overnight trips as possible so that he didn't have to 'go near' Sonia. But in company he rarely ventured far from the tried and trusted subject of motorcars and motor engines and, before the end of the winter, went up even further in the estimation of those who knew him by paying a West Country contact of Robin's £700 for a brown, K-registration Rover.

Robin hadn't found the readjustment to civilian life easy after his years in the army: he liked to drink and one morning John Sutcliffe spotted him slumped over the wheel of his wagon in the car park at the Fisherman, fast asleep when he should have been at the other end of the country. His marriage to Maureen would break up in the autumn of 1979 and he would drift out of Peter's life in the way that so many others had before him. The move from Tanton Crescent had more or less marked the end of Peter's association with the Barker brothers, and now he only saw them when, like other friends from his past, he happened to bump into them in a pub.

The Belle Vue was close to Bradford City's ground, and Ronnie and his brother often looked in for a game of pool and a few drinks on match days. Peter himself had never shown any interest in football or, for that matter, sport of any kind in the years that they had known him; and so it startled, and then intrigued, Ronnie to see him standing alone on the City terraces on one or two occasions after they had begun to go their separate ways. The black hair and sharply trimmed black beard were unmistakable in the sparsely populated stands on the far side of the pitch, even in the fading light of autumn afternoons.

Two more women would have been murdered by autumn, 1979. And 'Ripper eleven, police nil!' and 'There's only one Yorkshire Ripper!' were among the chants taken up at many football grounds in the North of England in the opening weeks of the 1979–80 season. 'Leeds United – more feared than the Yorkshire Ripper' badges could be bought outside Leeds' Elland Road ground.

26

Outside his family, Trevor Birdsall remained Peter's one link with his Bingley past. Trevor and Melissa had finally split up in 1978, a little over a year after appearing together at Wakefield Crown court on a number of charges, including breaking and entering, theft and attempt to defraud. The general view was that they were just unlucky to have been caught. Few of their acquaintances, including Peter, would have claimed to be entirely innocent of similar 'baby' crimes.

Carl had seen Peter go into an 'auto shop' and, under the pretext of buying something worth only a few shillings, slip a carburettor under his coat. He knew he sometimes stole the wheels off cars, leaving them jacked up on bricks. 'He were always nickin' stuff. He'd nick owt that weren't fastened down if it were any good to him. He used to nick all sorts.'

In the early hours of one New Year's Eve, ambling towards the high-rise flats in Bingley where Mick was then living with a girl called Lynn, Peter went through the boots of several cars, giggling and showing Carl what he'd found: 'He got a pair of women's tall zip-up boots, all sorts of stuff. He got a loada stuff, put it all in woods and collected it on way back up.'

On that occasion Carl had been about eighteen. Three or four years earlier, not long after Peter got married, Carl had taken him to an unoccupied house that he had come across up in Eldwick and, in the course of a number of trips, Peter had stripped it clean. He had sold a front-loading washing machine to his mother – 'He was a Jew. Right devious an' tight'; and the next time Carl saw the yellow Wilton was at Garden Lane, where it was fitted all over the top floor and up the stairs.

On the frequent occasions when Sonia was staying with her sister and her family in the northern suburbs of London, Trevor would move in and spend a few days with Peter at Heaton. Peter told Carl they had women in, and Carl believed him. 'I came round one morning on bike and there were Peter an' Birdsall in house and that little boy of Birdsall's who then must have been about three. I asked Pete where Sonia were, an' he said she were at Marianne's for the week. Then he says, looking round right nervously, whispering, "We just got rid of two birds. Just in time." An' they had, because he were telling me what had gone off.'

There was also the occasion when Peter told his 'kid' brother about how Sonia had nearly found him out. 'This bird he'd had in had taken the number with 'er when she left, and when she phoned up she'd got Sonia. He told me he'd convinced Sonia were a joke blokes at work were playing on 'im, getting a secretary to phone. He told bird that woman on phone were lunatic woman lodger who lived in room at top of the house, an' he were right pleased because he said they both believed him.

'He once said to me, "When she goes away, we'll have a week up there, get some birds round." But it weren't my scene, really. Age difference, I suppose. I used to like to go to different places than him. I didn't like wearing suits . . . I don't need to dress up in a suit to get a jump. I just go out an' get one.'

Sonia was still doing short-notice 'relief' work at the Sherrington nursing home in addition to her supply teaching (and nervously not declaring the extra income to the Inland Revenue). This usually kept her out of the house on Saturdays, although she did work some Tuesday and Wednesday nights, which left Peter at a loose end. On a Wednesday night in the week before Easter, 1979, he collected Trevor and they set off on one of their desultory rounds of the usual pubs.

It was six months since the death of his mother and almost a year since he had murdered Vera Millward in Manchester, but the Lumb Lane area was still full of 'undercover' police officers whose existence, in fact, everyone was aware of: they could be seen at the upstairs windows at the Perseverance and 'courting' in strategically parked cars; their 'secret' surveillance activities had even been the subject of a phone-in programme on the Bradford independent station, Radio Pennine. Similar schemes were in operation in Chapeltown and all the other red-light areas of the North.

It was a wet, miserable night at the tail-end of the long winter that, according to the calendar, should have been over, and shortly after closing time, Peter dropped Trevor off outside the place where he was then living. Instead of driving towards his own home, though, Trevor noticed that he had set off in exactly the opposite direction, but he closed the door against the cold and thought no more of it.

Halifax is the town where Peter Sutcliffe had attacked Mrs Olive Smelt, after identifying her to Birdsall in a pub as a 'prostitute', four years earlier. Halifax, in fact, had no prostitute population and no red-light area, and it was a quiet residential district called Bell Hall that he found himself in at 11.30 that Wednesday night. He had gravitated towards the playing fields of Savile Park, on which a few people were walking their dogs, and had made several circuits of it in his car before spotting a young woman walking alone.

He parked quickly and, after hurrying noiselessly to catch up with her, affected a casual approach. He asked her if she had far to go, and she said it was quite a walk. He asked her if she had considered learning to drive and she said she rode a horse which was the kind of transport she preferred.

She stepped on to the grass of Savile Park at that point to take a short-cut across the playing fields to Free School Lane and Ivy Street where she lived, and he expressed surprise, telling her you didn't know who you could trust these days. In his pocket were a ball-pein hammer and a seven-inch Phillips screwdriver which he had sharpened to a point on his garage floor.

When they were out of the range of the street-lamps, he asked her if she could tell him what time it was on a nearby clock-tower and, after she had, he congratulated her on her eyesight. He lagged behind then, pretending to squint at the clock himself but actually freeing the 'tackle' from his jacket.

He had knocked her to the ground before he noticed some-body walking along the pavement where they had been walking themselves only a minute or two earlier. He was also horrified to hear voices close behind and, turning around, saw two figures hurrying across the field; a man with a dog passed within five feet of him while he was crouched over the body, waiting to carry out 'the inevitable' in the dark.

At 7.00 the next morning a thirteen-year-old boy returning from collecting the papers that he delivered before school noticed a knot of men standing over something on one of the pitches. Seconds later, David Whitaker burst through the door of his home, speechless with shock. He had recognised the tan court shoe lying thirty yards from what was obviously a dead body as that belonging to his elder sister, Jo.

That evening, Peter Sutcliffe, along with the rest of Yorkshire, learned that he had murdered a nineteen-year-old clerk with the Halifax Building Society called Josephine Whitaker. At the time he waylaid her she had been on her way home from her grand-parents' house, where she had gone to show them the wrist-watch that had arrived in the post that morning, a gift to herself chosen from a mail-order catalogue.

Four days later, at the Palm Sunday service at St Jude's, near Savile Park, the vicar, the reverend Michael Walker, asked a packed congregation to adopt a truly Christian attitude and pray for everyone concerned, including the Ripper. 'He needs help, he is somebody's child, husband or father. Pray not only for Josephine and her family, but for the Ripper and his family. They may be unwittingly protecting him.'

Josephine Whitaker was not a prostitute; she was a 'decent, blameless' girl and the first 'totally respectable' victim of the Yorkshire Ripper since Jayne MacDonald, the young supermar-ket worker, in Leeds in the summer of 1977. Jayne had been the fifth woman to be murdered, and they were now dealing with the tenth. These were the points George Oldfield made repeat-edly in the days following the discovery of Josephine's body, and with encouraging results: for the first time in the hunt for the 'Ripper', the public responded instantaneously to his appeals for help.

Details were soon circulated of a number of cars seen in the area around the time of the attack, along with the Photofit picture of a man reported kerb-crawling in Halifax that night. He was described as being 'of scruffy appearance, with collar-length dirty blond hair, Jason King-style moustache and square-shaped face and jaw'. After being shown the Photofit, Marilyn Moore claimed to recognise the 'Dave' with 'come-to-bed eyes' who had tricked her by pretending to wave to a neighbour before attacking her with a hammer in Chapeltown, just before Christmas, 1977.

For the first time, too, there were important forensic clues. Traces of milling oil and tiny metal particles were detected in the many wounds inflicted on Josephine's body, as a result of which a confident-seeming George Oldfield called a press conference to announce that he now had 'a considerable impression' of the man he was seeking: he was 'white, aged between thirty and fifty-five, at least average to above-average height, an artisan or manual worker, either skilled or semi-skilled, with engineering or mechanical connections'. He was possibly 'a skilled machine tool-fitter, or an electrical or maintenance engineer'. But there were other reasons to account for George Oldfield's sense of renewed vigour, almost ebullience, which, for the time being, he was keeping to himself.

Eleven days before the murder of Josephine Whitaker, a letter had arrived at the Assistant Chief Constable's office in Wakefield bearing a Sunderland postmark. It was the same postmark, and the envelope was written in the same hand, as two letters which had found their way on to his desk almost exactly a year before. Posted within a week of each other in the Sunderland area and signed 'Yours respectfully, Jack the Ripper', they had been routinely checked at the time and dismissed as the work of a crank. There was enough detailed information in the latest one, however, to incline the officers of the 'Ripper Squad', and George

Oldfield in particular, to the view that they might not be the work of a hoaxer after all.

In the second letter, sent to the northern offices of the *Sunday Mirror*, the writer had urged 'chief constable' Oldfield to 'remember Preston 75', a clear reference to the murder of Joan Harrison, a prostitute addicted to the morphine in cough mixtures, whose body had been found in a lock-up garage in Preston, in Lancashire, in November 1975. Although there were marked similarities – Joan Harrison had been hit over the head with a heavy object; her clothing had been disturbed – her murder hadn't previously been regarded as the work of the 'Ripper'.

A semen test on Mrs Harrison's body, though, had indicated that the man who killed her, in common with only 6 per cent of the population, belonged to blood group 'B'; and a saliva test on the envelope containing the most recently arrived of the Sunderland letters showed that the writer of the letters was also a rare 'B'-secretor.

A rereading of the second letter, written two months before the murder, in Manchester, of Vera Millward, who at forty-two was the oldest woman in the series, also turned up references to going for an 'older one' in 'Liverpool or even Manchester again'. And then in the third letter the writer had revealed something which, as far as the police were concerned, only the 'Yorkshire Ripper' could have known: that victim No. 9, Vera Millward, had recently been a patient at the hospital in whose grounds her eviscerated body was found.

At a special press conference called two weeks after Josephine Whitaker's murder, George Oldfield made the first public reference to what was to become known as 'the Geordie connection'. He appealed to engineering firms on Tyneside to contact the police if any of their workers regularly visited West Yorkshire, and vice versa.

Squads of detectives were despatched to start the work of processing whatever information could be culled from the many thousands of potential sources in both regions. Like much that had preceded it in the previous four years, it was a long, slow, slogging process of elimination, inescapably low-key. And then, two months after the 'trawl' of the North East had started, the whole tenor of the operation suddenly – and irrevocably – changed. There was a development which convinced the men leading the search for the modern 'Ripper' that, 'in his arrogance', he had at last gone too far, and which instantly became not only national, but world, news.

At 2.00 p.m. on Tuesday, 20 June 1979, George Oldfield walked into the crowded press conference that he had called in the lecture theatre at the Metropolitan Police Academy in Bishopgarth in Wakefield. His cheeks flared as the television lights hit them and then, without a word, he pushed the 'Play' button of the portable tape recorder that was on the table in front of him. The hiss from the first few inches of blank tape, and then an unmistakable Geordie voice, filled the room.

> I'm Jack. I see you are having no luck catching me. I have the greatest respect for you, George, but Lord [the tone was intimate, gently goading], you are no nearer catching me now than four years ago when I started. I reckon your boys are lettin' you down, George. They can't be much good, can they? The only time they came near catching me was a few months back in Chapeltown, when I was disturbed. Even then it was a uniformed copper, not a detective. I warned you in March that I'd strike again. Sorry it wasn't Bradford. I did promise you that, but I couldn't get there.
>
> I'm not quite sure when I'll strike again, but it will definitely be sometime this year, maybe September, October or even sooner if I get the chance. I'm not sure where, maybe Manchester; I like it there, there's plenty of them knocking about. They never learn, do they, George? I bet you've warned them. But they never listen.
>
> At the rate I'm goin', I should be in the book of records. I think it's eleven up to now, isn't it? Well, I'll keep on going for quite a while yet. I can't see myself being nicked just yet. Even

if you do get near, I'll probably top myself first.

Well, it's been nice chatting to you, George.

Yours, Jack the Ripper.

No good looking for fingerprints, you should know by now it's as clean as a whistle. See you soon. 'Bye. Hope you like the catchy tune at the end. Ha-ha.

Three minutes and sixteen seconds of rehearsed but stilted monologue were followed by twenty-two seconds of a middle-of-the-road ballad called, with heavy irony, 'Thank You for Being a Friend'.

The first exposure most people outside the North of England had to the 'Yorkshire Ripper' was his voice, which led all news bulletins on television and radio that evening and the following morning, and dominated newspaper headlines for a week. It was also to be heard for the price of a telephone call on a special number which, despite the lines being doubled, was to be almost permanently engaged over the coming weeks and months.

That the voice on the tape was the authentic voice of the mass murderer, the public had little doubt. The envelope in which the tape cassette arrived at Wakefield bore the same handwriting as the Sunderland letters, it was explained, and the person who licked the envelope was also of the rare blood group 'B'.

Voice and dialect experts from the University of Leeds took six weeks to name the small mining community on Wearside that they were virtually certain was the Ripper's home town. And a Special Notice was soon issued by the Chief Constable of West Yorkshire to all forces advising them that a suspect could be eliminated from their inquiries if, among other things, he did not have a 'Geordie' accent.

Peter Sutcliffe was an almost immediate beneficiary of this directive: his high, flat, but undeniably Yorkshire vowels helped him survive his fifth police interview by the skin of his teeth.

On 29 July 1979, a month after the tape was released to the public, Detective-Constables Greenwood and Laptew called at 6

Garden Lane to talk to the owner, whose Sunbeam Rapier – swapped only the month before for a Rover – had been seen in the Lumb Lane area of Bradford no less than thirty-six times.

Like his predecessors, Andrew Laptew had no way of knowing that Peter Sutcliffe had already been questioned both about a red Corsair and in connection with the £5 note recovered near Jean Jordan's body, because his file in the Incident Room was almost two years out of date. Unlike them, however, Laptew sensed that there was something 'not quite right' about the lorry-driver married to the quiet schoolteacher, as he indicated in his report: Sutcliffe was vehement in his denials but at the same time appeared unusually quiet and seemed entirely lacking in a sense of humour – when Laptew joked to Mrs Sutcliffe that now was the time to get rid of her husband if she wanted to, neither of them seemed to find the remark at all funny.

Mrs Sutcliffe agreed to go out of the room at one point during the questioning, leaving her husband on his own, but he still denied using prostitutes and told the officers he had no need of such women because he hadn't been married very long.

Nevertheless, Laptew, continuing to follow his hunch, found out from the Regional Criminal Records Office that Peter Sutcliffe had a conviction for 'going equipped to steal' (although there was no mention that he had been equipped with a hammer), in 1969. This information, together with his general suspicions, was passed on to the senior detectives heading up the enquiry, who would finally get to see it nine months later. When they did, on the basis that Sutcliffe had lived all his life in Yorkshire and had produced a handwriting specimen that didn't tally with the Sunderland letter, Detective-Constable Laptew's report was routinely marked 'to file', where it was to languish with tens of thousands of others.

A little over a month after being visited at home by Laptew, and five months after murdering Josephine Whitaker, Sutcliffe went out and killed for the eleventh time.

The area which lies to the west of the twin domes of the Alhambra Theatre in the centre of Bradford contains the University, the Technical College and the Art College and many terraced streets comprised of mainly student accommodation. Where they aren't occupied by students, the houses of Little Horton are occupied by the Asian families whose shops and restaurants, together with the late-night restaurants owned by Italians, Greeks and Chinese, lend the area the relaxed, rather sophisticated ambience which sets it apart from the rest of the city.

Although close to his home and on the edge of the red-light district, Little Horton was not somewhere that Peter Sutcliffe often frequented. And yet the first Saturday in September 1979 saw him cruising the streets in the dark brown Rover of which he was so proud.

A little after 1.00 a.m. he saw a girl detach herself from a small group outside the Mannville Arms on Great Horton Road and go walking off on her own. Putting his foot on the accelerator he quickly overtook her and turned left into Ash Grove. By the time he opened the door to get out of the car she was walking towards him. He let her walk a few steps further before attacking her from behind with the hammer, and then dragged her into a back-yard where he stabbed her with the same cross-ply screwdriver with which he had stabbed Josephine Whitaker. The body was found hidden under a piece of weighted carpet thirty-six hours later.

With the murder of Barbara Leach, a third-year social science student at the University of Bradford, the ordinary women of the towns of West Yorkshire felt themselves to be at risk for the first time. It was with a sense of shock, gradually turning to outrage and anger, that they realised that nobody was immune.

Warnings to women to keep off the streets, to beware of the dark, came at them from all sides. 'We cannot stress how careful every woman must be. Unless we catch him, and the public must help us, he will go on and on. I warn all women to use lighted streets and to walk home with someone they know. In no circumstances accept lifts from strangers,' George Oldfield told the assembled press and television cameras.

'The Ripper could next kill in Bingley . . .', cautioned an editorial in the Bingley *Guardian*. 'The threat of this maniacal terror is as close as that. Despite the horror of the killings, and despite the frequency of the police warnings, it is still possible to see women walking through the streets alone late at night. The message is clear. The cost of ignoring it could be a hideous assault ending in death.'

If ever she had to walk along Mornington Road to the launderette or to her father's on her own in the dark, Maureen, John Sutcliffe's middle daughter, carried a carving knife up the sleeve of her coat. She warned her brothers never to come up behind her as a joke because, if she had to, she would use it. 'I'm for self-preservation, me,' Maureen said, and she was deadly serious, but still they all laughed.

Carl first heard the 'Geordie' tape on a transistor radio in a wood on the edge of Baildon Moor, where he spent a large part of 1979 sleeping rough. He was nineteen at the time, unemployed and with nowhere to live, his father having kicked him out of the flat in Rutland House.

As the 'baby' of the family – there was almost fourteen years between him and Peter, the oldest of his five brothers and sisters – Carl had always been especially close to his mother, who, everybody admitted, 'spoiled him rotten'.

None of her children had found it easy to come to terms with Kathleen's death, but Carl seemed to have taken it particularly hard. Whereas Peter had been able to drive over to Cottingley to pick up Marion, his father's girlfriend, on Boxing night, 1978, only six weeks after the funeral, and bring her down to the flat, Carl hadn't been able to accept another woman in his mother's place with anything like the same equanimity.

That New Year's Eve he had come back from a party drunk and put the glass panels of the front door in when he found himself locked out and nobody home. John and Marion returned in the early hours to find Carl, still in fancy-dress, lying in the hall, shivering. On another occasion Carl had hung out of the living-room window and been sick all over the windows of the people below; one or two of the dinners his father had served up to him had also gone out of the window and ended up on the patch of grass out at the back.

He was constantly complaining about what his father gave him to eat, and there were rows about the time he spent talking on the phone and about his father's attitude towards the girls Carl occasionally brought home. 'This really nice blonde bird were stoppin' in Bingley from Devon. She were really summat else. Everybody in pub fancied her. Anyway, I took her home to Rutland an' me dad, to my knowledge, were supposed to be away somewhere, so I were givin' this bird one on floor, watching telly, when fuckin' door opens an' it's him stood there.

'"Ooop, sorry," he says, has a good look an' out he goes. I carried on anyway; I thought, fuck it, I'm not going to stop. But afterwards, while I went off on motorbike to get some cigs or summat at shop, he had a go at her as well. "Your dad tried to grope me," she says when I get back, so I says, "Aye, he will do. You've got to watch him." You couldn't leave him alone with a female.'

Things finally came to a head in the winter of 1979 when John took to his bed with flu and Carl point-blank refused to carry so much as a cup of tea upstairs to him. It was his way of exacting revenge for the shabby way he believed his father had treated his mother all her life: 'She had a bad heart, she couldn't even walk, but she still had to go out cleaning while he went to pub wi' sixty quid in his pocket. He were always a skinny git with his money. She were always complaining that she never had enough. Every week she'd run out three days before next came in, but she would never ask him for any more. She were knackered but he never used to give her any help, so I thought, Why should I fuckin' look after him.'

At the heart of the problem, though, was Marion, who became semi-resident at Rutland House from the winter of '79. Although John remained a regular caller on Annie Rhodes after Kathleen's death, it was recognised within the family that Marion was the main woman in their father's life. A sunny, attractive, comfortably garrulous figure in her early sixties, Marion was easy company and quickly became a confidante of both Maureen and Jane. Even Peter seemed to prefer to see his father when Marion was there rather than when she was not.

It was Carl, though, who had to live with her, and he found it too much to take. 'Within two weeks of me mum dying he had that Marion woman in, and that really got me. It really vexed me.

'I come home a bit drunk one night just after he recovered from flu an' got off me motorbike an' he shouted something out

of window to me about mekkin less noise. So I told him to piss off an' it all happened from there. I'd always been wary of him all me life. It were all inside me for years, so I brayed shit out of him and left him on floor.'

Apart from the inky Sutcliffe hair and eyes which they shared, Carl and Peter, physically, didn't have a lot in common: at five feet eight, Peter had always been considered to be slightly on the short side, whereas Carl had passed the six foot mark while he was still at school; in his early thirties, Peter appeared thickset next to Carl, who was underdeveloped and 'like a lat'. In most important respects, however, the two of them were more like each other than they were like any other member of their family.

As a child, Carl had fallen as far short of his father's image of a 'proper lad' as Peter and, like Peter, had suffered at the hands of bullies both at the Sacred Heart and at Cottingley Manor Secondary Modern. Jane had come to his rescue at the junior school, much as Anne had acted as Peter's protector a generation earlier but, once at Cottingley Manor, he had been on his own. His solution, again like Peter's, had been to stop turning up. Unlike Peter, though, his 'blobbing' turned out to be chronic.

Most of the trouble took place at school-dinners where Carl told Maureen that he had to share a table with boys 'who ate like pigs and were right uncouth'. When he went to investigate, his father discovered that a gang from Shipley were spitting in his water and sprinkling pepper on his puddings, but it seemed to John the kind of thing that could be easily stopped if only Carl was prepared to stand up for himself. He was, after all, taller than many of the teachers. He put it down to Kathleen's 'molly-coddling' at home.

'The trouble wi' Carl was that he was too soft as a kid. He was ever so shy and soft. He were a pushover for anybody, up to being about fifteen or sixteen. Anybody had done anything like that to Mick when he was there, they'd have felt the weight of the table over their head. But Carl wasn't that sort of a lad. Like Peter, he was a rather gentle-mannered kid who didn't have the inclination to go and smack a kid in the teeth because he'd done

231

something to him. He knuckled under to everybody, did Carl. That was his problem.'

Mick did what he could, as he had with Peter, to instil a sense of combativeness into his brother, but to little effect. 'I told him, once you show 'em you're going to start tellin' tales you'll get even more stick. You're better off just sayin' nowt, just acceptin' it all. But he were soft as shit, like. He were a right mummy's boy.'

Every morning in the months before he was married, Peter would come in from working nights at Anderton International and drive Carl in his car up to Cottingley Manor. And every morning Carl would go in through the main gate only to abscond immediately through a back one. Maureen knew that her mother knew what was going on but had been pressured by Carl into saying nothing: 'She knew he hadn't been going to school, but she covered up to me dad, which she shouldn't have done. She covered up for him until things got really bad, and then he had to go away.'

Carl's first spell in approved school came a few months after his father's return to Cornwall Road after the episode with Wendy Broughton. He was approaching fifteen, and the only one then still living at home when he was made the subject of a 'care order' by the courts.

'First of all I went to a place called Tong Park, which is in Baildon, and that's really strict. I mean really strict. They treat you like shit; you're just called a number and you sit there with your arms folded until they say you can speak and if you don't they batter you. Oh it were lousy. You polished floors on your hands and knees and everything. They assessed me there for six weeks then decided there were nowt *wrong* wi' me, that I were quite intelligent, that I could do all silly lessons an' stuff, and should go back to school. Anyway, they sent me back to school and I went for a month or so and I got pissed off again, so they sent me back there, and they let me off *again*. Then third time they didn't. I knew they'd send me somewhere but I didn't think that far away.'

Mick dropped by his mother's one night at the beginning of 1975, only to be pounced on by two men who were lying in wait for Carl. 'I walked in door an' this stockyish bloke wi' beard grabbed me out of coats on wall. I thought it were our lad pissin' about at first. I were just about to plant the bastard when another one come flyin' out of other room. I says to me mother, "Who are they?" an' she says, "Oh they're waiting for our Carl." She were right upset about it, but they'd told her there were nowt she could do. And she really believed there *were* nowt she could do. But I says, "They'll fuckin' wait outside," an' they did.'

This was the only practical step anybody took to prevent Carl's removal to Richmond Hill, a barrack-like approved school standing in isolation on the North Yorkshire moors. Here, dormitoried with 'nig-nogs' and 'psychopaths', he was sent on cross-country runs, made to 'march like a silly soldier' and put to a trade. He was only allowed home for a weekend visit every four months, but his family could visit him.

'Bloody hell, this is a right place. It looks like Colditz,' was Peter's reaction the first time he drove his mother and father up, but he was an object of some interest himself: it took Carl weeks to live his brother's car down. 'He had this Capri then, lime green wi' black roof, only about a year old, and all lads in there thought I were right posh after, because most of them were out of *real* slums, or they'd been in homes and stuff all their lives and they knew nothing else. And to see a car like that arrive, which were posh sort of car, they thought I were right posh after that. They all used to tek piss.'

In the eighteen months he had to brood on it, Carl liked to blame his predicament on his father: 'Me mum, she didn't want me in there, it were him. She tried to stop him but there was nowt she could do. It was his idea.'

And while his father recognised the unjustness of what had happened – 'The victim got sent instead of the perpetrators' – he also came round to the view that it had probably worked out best for everybody in the long run. In this he was joined by Jane: 'Being sent away was the best thing that ever happened to Carl. He needed it. It was awful to see him there, and he'd cry, but he's the better for it.'

On his release from Richmond Hill, at the age of seventeen, Carl had acquired a toughened exterior that nevertheless cracked often enough to betray the essentially shy person who was still inside: he blushed easily, constantly gnawed the inside of his mouth and found it difficult to look at people when he was talking to them. In all these things, he reminded those who had known him of Peter at the same age.

His 'big' brother had been so successful in burying his former self that Carl didn't realise until he was quite grown up that Peter had had similar childhood experiences to his own. For many years, Carl just thought of Peter as 'the big tough thing' who roared round on a motorbike, told them ghost stories and walked up and down stairs standing on his hands. Only gradually, by piecing together snippets from elderly relatives at family gatherings, did Carl build up a picture of the weakly, put-upon youth that it was now impossible to detect in his brother's powerful chest and arms.

Peter had kept up his exercises with the Bullworker until even Mick was impressed with his strength; being left-handed, his left arm was remarkably powerful for a man of his size. He could lift himself the five feet on to the back of his wagon with a single push. Anybody, Maureen would say, would be proud to have a build like he had. 'He developed great big shoulders and an *enormous* chest. And you know how body-builders or weightlifters do, he used to walk like that.'

With his brother as an example, Carl set about building himself up. He started running and weight-training and taking part in traditional Bingley pursuits, like ratting on a local pig farm in the dead of night. 'I shot one fuckin' beauty last night,' he'd tell Peter. 'A really big, fat mucky-looking smelly rat. It were in these hens' food, bent over, an' its arse were stuck up, fuckin' huge thing, an' all rest scarpered when I put torch on, apart from this one that carried on eating. Then poof! Right up ring-piece an' out top of head.' Carl also became a dab hand at killing with his fist rabbits that he'd netted.

From approved school he had been sent to the technical college to take an electrical engineering course but had soon given that up in order to get a 'proper' job that would enable him to run a motorbike. The fact that he was unemployed when his father gave him forty-eight hours to get out of Rutland House at the beginning of 1979 only reinforced the 'rebellious' image Carl, as a nineteen-year-old not unacquainted with James Dean films and *Easy Rider*, was coming to have of himself. After seeing out the worst of a memorably severe winter in the homes of friends, he was happy to move into the woods with nothing but a sleeping-bag, a shotgun and his motorbike.

'People used to see me. I were sat there one day cooking some beans on this fire, unshaved an' all scruffy like a tramp, when these girls came up and said, "What are you, a Hell's Angel?" – "No, not really. I live here." They didn't believe me but they said, "Oh well, we'll come and see you tonight then, and bring you some food." So they all came, wi' big bags of food. They were from Baildon, all rich people. They buy in bulk, don't they, these snobs. And they just come down wi' big carrier-bags each, full of grub, tins an' . . . I were in me element.'

After a few months in the woods, Carl moved into the higher, denser forest surrounding a derelict mansion once occupied by the Victorian industrialist and philanthropist, Sir Titus Salt. Police cars used to patrol occasionally along the cobbled drive at night, but Carl would be able to hear them a mile away from where he was sitting in the ruins smoking 'dope'. Occasionally, though, it wouldn't be the police, but Peter, who would abandon his car and come walking through the trees out of the dark. Carl would emerge into the light cast by the fire once he had identified who it was.

'You shouldn't live here. There's loadsa nutters about these days,' Peter would warn his brother, who would nod at his gun and reassure him that he was capable of looking after himself. One night, though, when Peter called on him at about 11.30, Carl did take him up on his invitation to go back to Garden Lane for a bath, and returned to the woods the following day with some new red tee-shirts and other odds and ends of clothing that Peter had insisted that he take.

In these months, and in the months ahead, a bond was established between the two of them that hadn't been possible before because of the difference in age. But as Carl entered his twenties and the discrepancy in their ages started to matter less, they were able to do more things, and talk about more things, together.

Socially, Carl was less of a liability than Mick, whose idea of 'chatting up' a girl was to eye the front of her dress and tell her, 'You wouldn't get many of them in a bucket.' In fact, Carl, if anything, was more aware of social nuance and more ambitious than Peter; he was certainly just as aware of the importance of money as his brother.

It was of no little importance to Carl that his best friend was Robert Smith, show-jumping son of the horseman Harvey Smith, who was, without a doubt, the wealthiest man in Bingley. Carl helped out at the Smith stables at High Eldwick and went riding on the Smith farm and was a guest at parties which, in addition to numerous well-heeled daughters, invariably included a number of minor show-business 'names'. It gave Carl particular pleasure to be in the VIP enclosure on Bingley Show days when his father was confined to the bar on the other, public side of the fence. He used to like to say that he thought his family were 'peasants', 'doing peasanty jobs, going to peasanty pubs, leading peasanty lives'.

Although it irritated her that their only conversation was cars and they always seemed to be up to their elbows in grease, the fact that Carl was less gauche than his middle brother had helped lubricate his relationship with Sonia. Things improved noticeably while he was going around with a girl called Sue, the product of a 'good' Eldwick family, who was studying graphic design and so shared Sonia's interest in art. Sonia would always disappear upstairs with Sue to show her her latest work whenever they called.

About once a month the four of them would go out to a film together, but there was usually a certain amount of friction because Carl resented the way they almost always had to see what Sonia wanted to see. 'Me an' Peter either wanted a right good comedy or a horror film, *Alien* or summat. But she were into really heavy sorts of films. Crap. Things like *Kramer Versus Kramer*, which to me was just . . . boring, just about a couple getting divorced and the everyday routine that everybody goes through. She apparently saw that *four* times.'

Carl, like the rest of his family, was unaware that, by the autumn of 1979, Peter had been seen by the police on five separate occasions in connection with the 'Ripper' inquiry. Once, when Mick had been up at Garden Lane, Peter had ignored the telephone twice, saying it would only be the police, but adding, 'If they come up here, I'll get 'em in other room. They're coming to see us about something to do wi' motoring job.' He never mentioned to Mick that Clark's was one of the firms where the police thought the £5 note could have gone.

The 'Yorkshire Ripper' was something Peter never alluded to until it was the main talking-point in Yorkshire, and Carl remembers the first time: 'We were walking in this dark street in Bradford, me an' Pete, Sonia an' Sue. We'd parked Pete's car and we were walking down towards pictures and Pete says to Sonia, he got hold of her and said, "Oh he'll be lurking in here somewhere, Sonia. That Ripper. He'll be lurking in one of these alleys."'

The Odeon was a few hundred yards from where Barbara Leach's body had been found in a dustbin alcove, only a few weeks before.

28

By the late summer of 1979, the hunt for the Yorkshire Ripper had turned into the biggest police investigation in British criminal history: upwards of 150,000 people had been interviewed and eliminated from the enquiry: 27,000 house-to-house searches had been completed, 22,000 statements had been taken, more than £3 million had already been spent and George Oldfield, after working sixteen hours a day, six days a week for two years without let-up, was near to breaking point.

Since the arrival of the tape at the beginning of June – 'I reckon your boys are lettin' you down, George' – 'collaring' the man responsible had become a personal obsession, a fact which Oldfield himself was among the first to admit. 'Every time the phone rings I wonder if it's him,' he had told the *Yorkshire Post* in July. 'If I get up in the middle of the night I find myself thinking about it . . . I feel I know him already.'

The Assistant Chief Constable didn't set much store by the theories of psychologists. 'If we do get him, we'll probably find he's had too long on the left breast and not enough on the right. But it keeps the public happy,' he was overheard to remark characteristically at the end of one press conference. But after adopting a hard-line approach – 'This has become something of a feud. He obviously wants to outwit me but I won't pack it in until he's caught' – Mr Oldfield had slowly but significantly altered the tone of his public statements, in the hope of establishing the same sort of rapport with the murderer that kidnap and hostage victims were being advised to establish with their captors.

'I don't regard [the tape] as taunting or boastful. The voice is almost sad, a man fed up with what he has done, fed up with himself. A man who feels he knows me enough almost to take me into his confidence, confide in me,' was the sort of thing he started to say now. 'I'm sure he would like to cry on somebody's shoulder, but obviously can't. I am probably an obvious person for him to feel he has something in common with . . . I would like to talk to this man. And I feel he wants to talk to me.'

The fact that most of these statements were made on television and that George Oldfield had become, in the words of the same *Yorkshire Post* article, 'the most famous detective in the land', only served to increase the pressure. Behind the 'bucolic' public image, he had begun smoking heavily, eating and drinking too much and missing sleep and, one morning in the middle of August, was suddenly rushed to hospital. The official explanation was that he was suffering from 'pains in the chest' brought on by exhaustion, but it was an open secret within the police force and among the reporters assigned to the case that he had in fact suffered an almost fatal heart attack. Although he insisted on trying to make an early return, he was told to stay away from his post until at least the end of the year.

George Oldfield's emphasis on the search for the Ripper being 'a personal thing between him and me' had removed any remaining doubt members of the public might have felt about the authenticity of the tape and the letters, and the enquiry had proceeded on the basis that the man they were trying to track down was a 'Geordie'. When nobody was 'in the frame' by the end of the week of blanket interviews in the mining community which they had singled out on Wearside, though, the voice experts at Leeds University began to have their doubts. When Barbara Leach was murdered a few days later, they became virtually convinced that the tape had to be a hoax.

Three weeks after the Leach killing, at the beginning of September, the phoneticians put their views to the men who had inherited the responsibility of flushing out the Ripper: they were convinced that the person responsible for sending the tape had been interviewed within days of the police arriving in Castletown, they said, but had been eliminated because he had been able to come up with a cast-iron alibi and therefore couldn't have done the murders; more basically, none of the women who had survived attack had detected even the hint of a Geordie accent in the man who had attacked them.

These anxieties were shared by many of the officers in charge of the North-east operation, and in particular Detective Chief Inspector David Zachreson, who had taken the precaution of reviewing everything that had been reported about the York-shire Ripper in newspapers in the North and had come to the conclusion that everything in the Sunderland letters had appeared at one time or another in the press. The fact that Vera Millward had recently been a patient at Manchester Royal Infir-mary, the scene of her murder, which the West Yorkshire police maintained was something known only to the Ripper and to themselves, had actually been published at around the time of her death, in the *Daily Mail*.

Zachreson also pointed out the striking similarities between the Sunderland letters and letters sent by the original 'Jack the Ripper' to Scotland Yard in 1888, and drew what, to him, seemed the obvious conclusion: that the writer was a crank obsessed with the Ripper legend.

The Chief Constable of West Yorkshire, Ronald Gregory, how-ever, was not impressed by these arguments and, at the time they were put to him, was in fact about to embark on a course of action that was to unwittingly fuel the myth of the modern 'Rip-per'. Far from back-peddalling on the issue of the tape and stressing that the chances now were that the Ripper only *might* be a Geordie, Gregory committed himself one hundred per cent, and in the most public fashion, to the North-east connection.

At the beginning of October, against the advice of some of his own senior officers, including the still ailing George Oldfield, he launched an unprecedented media 'blitz' designed to ensure that nobody in the North of England could claim ignorance of the voice or the handwriting that he was personally convinced could lead them straight to the 'vicious, deranged maniac' who had already killed eleven, maybe twelve, women and could strike again at any time.

The head of a Leeds-based advertising agency volunteered his services, and a battalion of other professionals – printers, design-ers, site proprietors, photographers and distributors – were sim-ilarly persuaded to waive their normal fees. The slogan 'The Ripper would like you to ignore this . . .' went up on billboards on more than six hundred prime sites; a special four-page news-paper was delivered to every home in Yorkshire, Lancashire and the North-east; national newspapers donated advertising space; BBC local radio and local commercial stations ran tapes of the 'Ripper', along with police messages, sometimes as often as eight times a day . . . The tape was also played in pubs and working-men's clubs around the country, and over the loudspeakers at football grounds, where it was invariably drowned out by the derisory chanting of the crowd.

Mr Gregory had said that he was looking for 'dramatic impact' and the 'Flush out the Ripper' campaign achieved that. The result, as many had predicted, however, was pandemonium. The 'Ripper Room', still struggling to get to grips with informa-tion relating to murders committed as much as eighteen months before, was deluged with enquiries and offers of information. Many of the 'tip-offs' came from people with honourable motives, but it was also the perfect opportunity to settle old scores and, by mid-November, the list of possible suspects had shot up to 17,000.

The atmosphere in the cities of West Yorkshire as the nights started to draw in, meanwhile, was, for a time, one of near-panic. American observers – the Yorkshire Ripper was no longer a purely local phenomenon – likened Leeds and Bradford in the autumn of 1979 to Boston in the early 1960s, during the 'reign' of the 'Boston strangler'. Then, hospitals, universities and shop- and factory-owners had organised door-to-door transport for women who had to leave after dark; attendance at night classes, bingo sessions and any other activity that required women to be out on their own at night had plummeted; many previously crowded bars and restaurants had gone to the wall.

And, while all of this was duplicated in the North of England – the pupils of Leeds Girls' High School were given lessons in judo and karate; some women journalists covering the case asked for their by-lines to be omitted – there was one significant difference: the refusal of an increasingly vocal minority of women, who saw the Ripper as merely an extreme manifestation of men's everyday violence towards members of their sex, to be intimidated.

A notice from the Vice Chancellor of Bradford University, posted in university buildings in the week following Barbara Leach's murder, warning 'all women students that, until the person responsible for recent murders is brought to justice, they should under no circumstances be out alone after dark', quickly attracted the kind of slogans that were to be the rallying-cries of the 'Women Against Violence Against Women' and 'Reclaim the Night' movements in the coming months.

The students' union pledged itself to support any woman arrested for carrying an offensive weapon and, later, eleven women were arrested after picketing the Bradford cinema where a film called *Violation of the Bitch* was showing.

Women on their own, meanwhile, were left to cope with their fear as best they could. 'I walk the baby-sitter home, then I run back along the middle of the road carrying my little knife and wearing running shoes,' 'a single mother' told the *Guardian* in December 1979; and the wife of a Leeds University lecturer said she supposed there wasn't a woman in Yorkshire who didn't think about 'him' every single day.

Most women had to rely on male relatives to escort them if they wanted to go anywhere after dark, and requests for volunteers didn't always elicit a sympathetic response. The women of the Sutcliffe family, however, didn't have this problem.

Calling on her one night and finding that she was about to go out on her own, Peter not only insisted on giving Jane a lift to the pub in Shipley, but 'made a big drama' of going in to give the 'once-over' to the man whom she was supposed to be meeting. She got the definite impression on the way there that, had he decided he didn't the look of him, he would have taken her straight home.

Mick, too, never ceased to be impressed by his brother's regard for Sonia's safety: 'If I were up his house, he'd say, "I'll just nip out. I've to pick wife up and bring her back here from hospital. You don't know who's who wi' him walking about." An' I allus thought, Well you're doin' right, round here.' It was the kind of thoughtful act that had earned Peter his reputation as a 'gentleman' and the sort of thing Mick would have liked to have thought of himself doing.

Although marred by a bad timekeeping record, Peter's conscientiousness at Clark's, where he worked, was almost a legend. At the end of 1979, he had been employed by the father and son firm for three years, which made him the longest-serving driver on their books. He was the sole survivor of a recent 'purge' resulting from complaints made by Kirkstall Forge in Leeds, one of the Clarks' best customers, that drivers had been 'fiddling' their loads.

Peter's status as the firm's 'star' driver would soon be confirmed by having his picture taken at the wheel of his wagon and hung, enlarged and in full colour, in the small, otherwise unfurnished vestibule where visitors pressed a bell and waited to be attended to by the managing director's secretary.

Despite this close identification with 'the bosses', however, he was well liked by the other drivers, to whom he had been only too willing to show the ropes. He was recognised to be 'brilliant' at roping-and-sheeting large and often difficult loads, and was the person everybody turned to when they got a 'delivery ticket' for an unfamiliar town: he had 'A–Z' street-maps for every possible destination neatly stacked in his cab, and would happily draw anybody who needed one a map.

His patience, in fact, often staggered the other men. He didn't seem to mind how long it took to unload and, whereas they would be cursing and kicking the wall during any hold-up, he would sit quietly or 'rub and scrub' his wagon and not even want to know the cause. The thing about him, though, that they found even harder to understand was his 'neutrality' in the face

243

of what, to drivers like Allan Wright, seemed provocation: 'He would be all tarpaulined and roped and about to leave the yard when Clark would come out an' tell him to change the load. And, even on a right rotten day, he'd meekly obey.'

From this, Allan Wright and others drew the conclusion that Peter was probably 'a bit of a "Right" man'. They always suspected that, while he might declare himself to be on their side whenever they had a grievance, 'He used to shovel shit then jump on shovel.' In other words, confronted by the Clarks, he would back down.

Like everybody on the payroll, Peter had been seen by Manchester police, who were trying to trace the recipient of the £5 note found in Jean Jordan's handbag, and was, therefore, assumed to be in the clear. Nothing more had been heard about this line of enquiry for almost two years when, at the beginning of 1980, Detective Chief Superintendent Ridgeway and his team from Manchester suddenly reappeared.

Their arrival in West Yorkshire this time, however, was not accorded the kind of publicity that had marked their earlier visit. The re-enactment one Sunday morning of the day when the note had originally been issued, using the same tellers counting out the same number of 'dummy' £5 notes reprinted in exact sequence by the Bank of England, was conducted in comparative secrecy. The result was a whittling down of the number of firms who could have received the note from thirty to three, which included T. and W. H. Clark Ltd., of Canal Road, Shipley; and a whittling down of likely recipients from the high thousands to the lower hundreds. In addition, they also had the picture of a boot-print found close to Josephine Whitaker's body on Savile Park.

It was these boots that Peter Sutcliffe happened to be wearing on the morning of 13 January 1980 as he jumped down from his cab for questioning by policemen too preoccupied to notice. It was to be the first of three escapes from detection in the space of as many weeks.

On 20 January he was singled out by the police for attention, for the eighth time, when he was among Clark's employees who were taken home to have their clothes inspected and their wives questioned about their movements on specific dates and about any possible sexual deviations.

By the beginning of February, the Manchester police were showing interest in only two of William Clark's men. On 2 February, Peter Sutcliffe and another driver were escorted to Bradford police headquarters where they were photographed and obliged to submit to a handwriting examination. Sutcliffe had 'gone to pieces' when he was picked up, shaking and perspiring; but he was back at work later in the day, having his leg pulled by the men in the yard.

Although less wholeheartedly committed to it than his opposite number in the 'Ripper Squad', Ridgeway still basically felt he was looking for a man with a Geordie accent, which, of course, Peter Sutcliffe didn't have; and neither did his handwriting match the handwriting on the Sunderland letters. Just as crucially, the Laptew report 'fingering' Sutcliffe and submitted six months earlier still hadn't found its way into the system. The system had also swallowed most of the other relevant information relating to the lorry-driver living at No. 6 Garden Lane in Heaton.

It had become clear almost within days that Chief Constable Gregory's 'blitz' on the media had been a major miscalculation which, in the much-quoted words of his press spokesman, had produced 'one hundred per cent rubbish'. In November, following a visit to West Yorkshire by the then Home Secretary, William Whitelaw, Gregory had asked Scotland Yard to despatch a senior detective to Leeds to 'review' the investigation. And in February 1980, as the Manchester team prepared to return home for a second time empty-handed, the publicity machine went into sharp reverse. Information, which had flowed profligately for years, all but dried up; all press facilities were withdrawn.

The thinking behind the new move was that the 'Ripper',

starved of the attention which he seemed to crave, would be driven to communicate with police 'again'. It was the only way anybody could see out of the impasse. That, and the unspoken alternative of him killing another woman.

29

With the onset of winter, Carl had finally had to look for an alternative to the forest where he had spent the previous five months. And, thanks to his contact with the Smith family, at the beginning of 1980 he had found one.

Ray Kennan was an 'estate boy', a direct contemporary of Peter's, who had taken the sort of path to prosperity that Carl himself wouldn't have minded following. After involvements with pop groups and nightclubs in the 1960s and '70s, he had moved on to become Harvey Smith's personal and business manager and had property interests which included the large, rather gloomy corner house where Carl moved in to occupy the attic room.

No. 1 Priestthorpe Road was adjacent to Mornington Road Methodist Church, whose Victorian clocktower punctuated the day and night at quarter-hourly intervals, and diagonally opposite Rutland House. From the top-floor window, under which he slept and through which he occasionally threw teabags and jettisoned other rubbish, Carl could see the flats where his father lived. At the bottom of the bed was a small sink and a 'Baby Belling' cooker, while a 'leather-look' three-piece suite with screwtop lids on the armrests as ash trays accounted for most of the rest of the space. Horse-brasses and black-painted 'beams' crisscrossing the fireplace wall were the only decoration.

From the day he moved into it, though, Carl's 'flat' proved unexpectedly popular. Mick, for one, was quick to avail himself of the facilities. If he came round during the day with 'his bit on the side' and Carl wasn't in, he'd force the Yale lock on the attic door. And even if Carl was in, at nights after the pubs closed, Mick didn't let that stop him; he'd get down on the floor, between the gas fire and the settee, with whoever happened to be with him, while Carl lay in bed, staring at the ceiling.

Odd nights when Mick wasn't available, Peter would give his brother's 'regular knockings' a lift home from the pub to Eldwick. He seemed to be under the impression that she was a 'decent' girl, and when Carl told him what she was 'really' like – 'Right mucky. *Really* mucky. A right old slag' – he seemed genuinely shocked and disappointed. It was a reaction which was unexpected in the light of his own behaviour when he spotted a girl whom he thought 'looked fit': then, he'd get excited, giggling and wringing his hands up near his face in a way that reminded Carl of 'a right dirty old man'.

Peter seemed as taken with the idea of Carl having a place of his own as Mick, and was almost as frequent a visitor. He never brought women but, encouraged perhaps by the intimacy of his surroundings, women, unusually, became a favourite topic of conversation. Some months earlier, while making a delivery to the General Motors plant near Motherwell, in Scotland, he had met a 'cracker' of a girl in a bar and had managed to ingratiate himself not only with her but with her whole family. Between visits he bombarded Theresa with letters, telling her he 'missed [her] more than ever', and she wrote him 'steamy' letters, addressed to 'Peter Logan', at his father's flat.

He had shown Mick pictures of 'Tessa' and given him glimpses of her letters, from which he had deduced 'she were mad on him'. By the spring of 1980, though, he gave Mick the impression that he was trying to extricate himself from a situation which was getting out of hand: 'She wanted to move down to Yorkshire an' come an' see him, an' he were starting to sweat then in case she fuckin' turned up.'

But if it was a dilemma, it was one Peter was anxious to share with Carl, whom he also kept up-to-date with the progress of an 'affair' he said he was having with 'a blonde girl' in Bradford whose husband worked nights, and who, again, was 'mad' on him: 'She doesn't want any other fellers, only me,' he'd tell Carl, who thought it a strange thing to say.

'One time he came round and I knew he were after summat,

because he used to shift about if he were goin' to ask you sum-mat. "D'you fancy going out wi' me an' that bird I've got?" And he were looking round all time as if somebody were listening. "She's got this mate, a right cracker. You ought to come out with us." But I didn't fancy it. Birds he liked were always robbers' dogs.'

The reason he had asked Carl, Peter told him, was because you 'couldn't trust' Mick to keep his mouth shut. In the early sum-mer, though, when Peter travelled to London to 'keep an eye on' the house where Sonia's sister and her family lived while they were out of the country, it was Mick who went with him. The arrival of Mr Szurma the following day was an unexpected blow, but Mick didn't allow it to cramp his style: 'I went into Soho every day and night wi' our lad. Got pissed out of us heads and went wi' one or two birds. We used to get 'em in motor, like, an' tek 'em to this park going back towards Alperton. We just used to drop 'em off after, a few miles out.'

It was Peter's second visit to his sister-in-law's within the space of a couple of months. John and Marion had been sur-prised to receive an invitation from Peter to spend a few days of the Whitsun bank holiday with him and Sonia at Garden Lane, but they had only been there twenty-four hours when Mrs Szurma called to ask Peter if he would take a washing machine and a few other things down to Marianne in Wembley. He had immediately gone into Bradford to hire a van and, riding in the back on chairs from the house, Marion and his father had trav-elled down to London with Peter and Sonia.

Marion had been taken aback to find Marianne, who was mar-ried to an Asian, wearing a sari, but she had nevertheless been made to feel welcome. She slept with John on blankets on the floor of the living-room, while Peter and Sonia slept in the bed-settee; and the next day, Peter took her on a brief visit to her brother in another part of Middlesex before the return drive to Yorkshire.

By the time they got back to Garden Lane, they had all been feeling hungry. But there had been nothing to make a meal out of in the house – not a packet of soup nor a tin of anything – which Marion thought 'very queer'. The following night John and Marion had taken the four of them out to a sit-down fish-and-chip supper, which they felt they needed.

After returning Marion and his father to Rutland House the next day, Peter had called on Mick and Susan and suggested a 'run out' to Morecambe. At Morecambe, while Susan and Michelle spent some time at Anne's, Mick and Peter went off for a drink and, on the way back, paid what was to be the first of several visits to Tussaud's before the end of the 1980 season.

Peter seemed to spend most of the time when he was round at Carl's place, which he tended to be increasingly, complaining about Sonia's incessant nagging. 'She's been on at me again,' were often his first words after he'd sat down. And it seemed to get worse as 1980 wore on, until Carl got the impression that 'he were fed up wi' whole job, fed up wi' whole affair completely'. He had packed his bags on two separate occasions, intending to leave.

On the evidence of his own experience, Carl had started to feel that maybe Sonia was 'cracking up'. Always pernickety, by the beginning of 1980 she had started taking her obsession with cleanliness to 'weird' extremes: 'If she come to a chair, in a pub, the pictures, somebody's house, any chair, she wouldn't just sit down. She'd blow on it, an' start brushing and dusting it with her cuff. She'd spend a good two minutes going like that before she'd plonk herself down.'

But it was a single incident at the turn of the year that had resulted in Carl ceasing to go to Garden Lane altogether. 'I rang up for Pete one Friday and Sonia says: Is Sue with you? So I put her on an' they had a chat; then she came back to me an' said, Do you fancy coming up Sunday? She asked us up on Sunday for dinner, then we'd go out in a foursome to pictures . . . I said, Oh yeah, great.

'So off we went up to their house, knocked on door an' Pete come: "All right, Carl!" Then Sonia come, looked at us, and stormed off. So we went and sat down and she just sat in other room. She sat in dining-room and she wouldn't come in lounge at all. Then Pete kept going in and I could hear them arguing. I heard her say, Well I wish they'd let us know they were coming . . . She brought Pete his tea an' sort of slapped it on the table in front of him and stormed off out. She never said a word to us all night. After we left, Sue said, "I'm never going there again," and we didn't; we stopped going altogether.'

Peter found Priestthorpe Road a convenient refuge from the tensions at home. Although the landlord was always issuing warnings against it, the front door was left more or less permanently off the latch so that visitors could come and go as they chose. Carl was often surprised by Peter sticking his head around the door of his room to say hello and then disappearing downstairs to the recessed, linoleum-floored bathroom that was shared by everybody in the house: sometimes he would be in there so long Carl would think he must have gone.

Carl knew that Peter would occasionally call when he wasn't in, but one night he was in his room when he recognised the sound of his brother's Rover outside and heard Peter climbing the stairs long after most of the house had gone to bed. The footsteps stopped at the bathroom, though, and, after being in there for some time, Peter slipped out of the house again and drove off in his car.

Soon afterwards, towards the end of the summer, he turned up in the middle of the afternoon and asked Carl if he could change his clothes. He took off the clean clothes he was wearing and put on some dirty ones, which in itself wasn't remarkable: when they were working on engines at Garden Lane, Carl had often done the same himself. What struck him as odd was that Peter put the clean trousers behind the boiler in the bathroom at Priestthorpe and, when reminded that they were still there some months later, replied quietly, but firmly, that it didn't matter.

The police had always said the 'Ripper' would need somewhere to clean up in after the murders. And after letting this gnaw at him for some time, Carl felt he had to tell somebody. The only person he could think of to tell was Mick. 'I'm sure our Pete's bloody Ripper,' he blurted out to Mick one day when he called round, and was relieved by Mick's automatic, scoffing response. 'I just laughed at him an' told him he were stupid. I just said, "You're bloody daft you."' He reminded Carl that Peter didn't talk with a Geordie accent, and Carl was only too happy to agree that he was probably being stupid.

After Tong Park and Richmond Hill, Carl had found it difficult settling back into normal life. He had flitted aimlessly from job to job, and when he had finally found one which seemed to suit him – working in wall-cavity insulation – he had been forced to give it up because of losing his driving licence. Peter had come round intending to be 'big brotherly' and tear him off a strip, but instead had ended up lending him the £300 that he still owed on his motorbike. And then, shortly afterwards, much to his family's amazement, Peter had been breathalysed himself.

He had been out drinking on his own on the night of 25 June, and his last stop had been his old teenage haunt, the Royal Standard, in Manningham. He was spotted speeding on Manningham Lane by two policemen in a patrol car who followed him back to the house and approached him as he was getting out of his car at the top of the drive. Aware of the disastrous consequences for his work, he resisted breathing into the plastic bag that they offered him. But voices were raised and the test proved positive. Constables Doran and Melia submitted a report suggesting that Peter Sutcliffe should perhaps be seen by officers connected with the Ripper Squad, but word eventually reached them from the incident room that he had already been seen and eliminated.

Peter decided not to let anybody at Clark's know about the impending court case, bringing with it what he assumed would be the inevitable ban, because he knew that would result in him getting all the bottom-of-the-barrel jobs. He also didn't tell his father for some months that he had been breathalysed and, when he did, Marion noticed that Sonia quickly 'covered up' for him, saying that he'd drunk his usual modest amount, but that he'd been drinking on an empty stomach that night.

He had got on to the subject by saying that he might lose his job after Christmas, and had said it with his usual nonchalance; but Sonia knew how heavily the possibility had been weighing on him: he had had a couple of 'panic' attacks at home, and she had had to bring him round with mouth-to-mouth resuscitation.

On 13 August, Maureen noted in her diary that Peter had called to see if she wanted to go to the MFI furniture warehouse in Bradford with him, but she was in the middle of having the fireplace in her living-room pulled out and replaced with a decorative stone one, plus the house had just been flooded and so she had to tell him it was impossible.

The following Thursday, exactly a week later, he was driving through Farsley, a nondescript suburb of Leeds, on his way to Chapeltown, when the headlights of his Rover picked out the figure of a woman walking towards him. He parked the car and caught up with her over a distance of about four hundred yards. He hit her with a hammer and, looping and tightening a piece of hemp around her throat, dragged her into a high-walled garden, where he kneeled on her chest while he strangled her. He stripped the body once she was dead and left it partly covered in grass and leaves.

His twelfth victim was a forty-seven-year-old woman called Marguerite Walls, who had been on her way home from the Department of Education and Science's offices in Pudsey where she had been putting in some extra hours, in preparation for going on holiday the following day, Friday.

Sutcliffe had to scan Friday's evening paper thoroughly, though, to find this out. He had changed his method of attack in a conscious effort to mislead the police, and the 'demotion' of the Walls case by the press was an early indication that he had succeeded: West Yorkshire police had swiftly let it be known that they were not considering this latest murder as an addition to the Ripper series.

30

A week after the murder of Marguerite Walls, Mrs Szurma's mother, Sonia's grandmother, arrived in Yorkshire for a holiday from Czechoslovakia and, a further week later, the three women travelled to Morecambe where they had rented self-catering accommodation.

On the Sunday, after they settled in, it had been arranged that Peter was to pay them a visit and, once again, he stopped off in Bingley to collect Mick, Susan and Michelle. In addition, he squeezed in Maureen's two children, Rachel and Damien, who, since the break-up of their mother's second marriage, had grown to look forward to their trips to Morecambe with their uncle Peter.

He took them to the funfair and bought them toffee apples and paid for their rides, while Mick added an unintentional touch of light relief. He kept forgetting that Sonia's grandmother didn't speak a word of English and persisted in asking her if she was having a good time. 'How d'you like it in Morecambe?' he'd ask, raising his voice as if she was simply deaf; and Peter would remind him for the umpteenth time that she couldn't understand anything he said.

Seventeen days later, on the 24 September, he found himself alone again, in Headingley, which, thanks to the University and the Test cricket ground, was regarded as one of the smarter districts of Leeds. At around 10.30 he followed a woman taking a shortcut through a dimly-lighted 'snicket' and hit her twice over the head with a hammer after looping a length of rope around her neck. He was hiding the shoes and handbag which she had become separated from in the course of the struggle when a noise disturbed him and he fled.

Upadhya Bandara, a thirty-four-year-old doctor from Singapore visiting Yorkshire under the auspices of the World Health Organisation, later recovered in hospital and was not regarded, the police said, as 'a Ripper job'.

A few Sundays after their last visit to Morecambe, Mick was standing at the bar of the Harvester attempting to drown the hangover of the night before. He had had four pints within half an hour of the doors being opened when Peter strolled in and asked him if he wanted to go to Morecambe again.

Parked outside was a 'smart' red Mini with wide wheels and antiroll bars that Mick had never seen before and which Peter, trying to appear nonchalant but not succeeding, said he'd been doing up over the last few months. As a demonstration of how souped up the engine was, they 'screamed' to Morecambe in not much more than an hour. Their first stop was Anne's house, but Anne and her family were out which, by Mick's reckoning, meant they should just be in time for last orders. Peter, however, had other plans. He headed 'promptly' for Tussaud's wax museum.

'Steve Davis – Picasso – Jimmy Savile', a faded and rain-soaked poster announced over the door, but, once through the turnstile, Peter only gave a cursory glance to the models of Harold Wilson and Edward Heath in the downstairs gallery before ushering Mick with some urgency towards the staircase and onwards through the upper 'hall' towards 'the Macabre Torso room'. There, as his brother pored over the ancient exhibits with a more than usually 'salacious' grin on his face, it occurred to Mick for the first time that the purpose of these visits might be to show him the error of his ways: 'He seemed to me to be enjoying what he was trying to show me. He gave me the shivers. I've never seen a grin like it, pointing out each detail of what happens to a man when it's too late to control his self. Half-rotted penises . . . And all I wanted was to get back to the pub and have a good time.'

Tussaud's closed for the season on the last Saturday in October and, a few days later, on Bonfire Night, Peter clocked off work just after 5.00 but called Sonia to say he would be home late. By 8.00 he was in Huddersfield, shadowing a sixteen-year-old girl across a piece of open land close to her home. Theresa Sykes had reached the pavement of New Hey Road before she realised somebody was following her; as the shadow came level, she was hit with a hammer and, as she fell, she saw a man with dark hair and a beard. Her screams were heard by her boyfriend and father of her three-month-old baby, who tore after a figure rapidly melting into the dark. Sutcliffe hid under a hedge in a nearby front garden for some time until he felt it was safe to emerge.

In the summer, when it started to look certain that Peter was going to be banned from driving, No. 6 Garden Lane had been advertised for sale in the local paper, at an asking price of £37,500. The idea, as Sonia told Mrs Bowman opposite and Peter told various members of his family, was to buy a country property where Sonia could make pottery to sell to visitors in the summer and he could find a temporary labouring job until he got his licence back.

Returning from her holiday with her grandmother in Morecambe, Sonia had told her neighbour that she was undergoing tests at the hospital to see if she could have a baby. If the answer was 'no', and she had already had one miscarriage, then they were going to explore the possibility of adopting one or more Vietnamese 'boat children'.

The fact that no estate agent's board had gone up outside No. 6 had struck Barbara Bowman, who happened to be selling her own house at the same time, as odd. But then she rationalised that Peter probably didn't want people calling round at the house when he was away. How their respective sales were progressing was the main topic of conversation between Sonia and Mrs Bowman throughout the summer; and then Sonia suddenly announced in November that she had taken No. 6 off the market.

This coincided with a change in her appearance that left Barbara Bowman feeling stunned: Sonia came out of the house one day with the 'long, beautiful hair' that she had always worn down her back crudely hacked off: 'I said at the time, "That wasn't done by any hairdresser." She'd obviously done it herself. All that natural curl was gone, and there was just odd bits sticking up in different directions. She looked like one of these punks. I think she saw from the expression on my face that I was shocked.'

To Carl, Peter too seemed to be less and less himself as 1980 drew to a close. Seeing him talking to girls in the pub, he'd take Carl to one side and, seeming genuinely curious, ask him, 'What do you *see* in her?' He was always telling him that Sue was 'a *nice* girl'.

He also seemed concerned about 'the reputations' of Jane and Maureen, who, at the time, were living together, with Rachel and Damien, in Maureen's house on Ferncliffe Estate. He had dropped in one day and 'a bloke' was there having a meal, Peter told Carl, which to him didn't seem right.

At twenty-four, 'Janey' looked so much like her mother as a young woman that a former suitor of Kathleen's found it 'frightening – terrifying really'. 'A cracker. Beautiful big brown eyes. Beautiful smile. Real page-three material' was John's proud assessment of his youngest daughter, and few in Bingley would have want to contradict him: Jane could be seen with fairy-lights playing round her green plastic visor on Bingley Show night, surrounded by a crowd of admirers in the Fleece.

Legally separated and working full-time at Anderton's, where Peter had worked on the night shift for two years, Jane had made a conscious decision to carve out an independent life for herself, and this included, in her own mind, owning a car. She had fallen in love with the sporty red Mini that Peter had driven Mick to Morecambe in the minute she saw it and had quickly agreed to buy it from her brother.

It was transferred from Sonia's name to Jane's on the 1 November, and on 9 November, four days after attacking Theresa Sykes, Peter delivered the Mini to her door. It was a Sunday, and Mrs

Szurma followed Peter in her own car to Bingley to give him a lift back to Garden Lane.

The following Saturday, though, on her first attempt at a long run, the Mini broke down. Jane and Maureen had set out to visit Anne in Morecambe and had broken their journey to do some shopping in Blackburn on the way. They had only been back in it a few minutes when the engine spluttered and refused to start again. They got on the phone to Peter and, although he had just returned from a delivery in Lincolnshire, he agreed without hesitation to come and see to the car and ferry his sisters home. Forty-eight hours later he went out and murdered for the thirteenth time.

As far as the public was concerned in November 1980, the 'Yorkshire Ripper' had been dormant for fifteen months; and, inevitably, speculation that he had 'retired' or, as seemed more likely, 'topped' himself, was once again rife. The mood of indignation following Barbara Leach's death in September 1979 had abated, the police were maintaining their 'tactical' silence and the public's defences, with Christmas approaching, were down.

Peter Sutcliffe had had to make a delivery to Kirkstall Forge in Leeds on Monday, 17 November; and Leeds is where he returned in the evening, although he called his wife to say that he was still in Gloucester and not to expect him until late.

At 9.30 he was sitting in his car outside the Arndale Centre in Headingley, a quarter of a mile from where he had attacked Dr Bandara seven weeks before, eating a carton of Kentucky Fried Chicken and chips. He saw a young woman get off a bus at the bus stop opposite and watched her cross and turn into Alma Road, a left turning off the busy main road, straight ahead. He switched on the ignition and quickly overtook her and sat waiting in the Rover until she walked past. When she did, he got out and followed at a short distance and waited until she drew level with an opening before springing forward and delivering a crippling blow to her head.

Seconds later another woman walked into the well-lit street

and he had to hoist the unconscious victim into a standing position before dragging her thirty yards over a piece of waste ground, where he stabbed her repeatedly with a screwdriver in the lungs and once in the eye.

At 10.00, a male student found a cream raffia handbag on the pavement just beyond the entrance to the spare ground and, two hours later, having noticed what appeared to be spots of blood on one side of it, put in an emergency call to the police. The name 'Jacqueline Hill' had been found on a banker's card inside the bag and, when the Panda car arrived, the student suggested that they try to find out where Jacqueline Hill lived and establish that she was unharmed. Instead, the two constables satisfied themselves with a cursory search of the area; the beams from their torches failed to fall on an undamaged pair of spectacles or a woollen mitten, or Jacqueline Hill's body which was lying just thirty yards from where she had first been separated from her bag. Back at the station, it was logged as 'lost property' and shelved.

The following day, at teatime, eight hours after their daughter's body had been discovered only yards from where she lived in Headingley, eighteen hours after the first telephone call summoning the police, uniformed officers called at the home of Mr and Mrs Jack Hill in Ormesby, near Middlesbrough, and asked them to accompany them to Leeds.

They were back in Lealholme Crescent by Wednesday, 19 November, when it was announced that Jacqueline had been murdered by the 'Yorkshire Ripper'; and, following the announcement, they uncomprehendingly found themselves under siege: cameras started nosing at their back windows, notes offering 'a considerable sum' for their 'story' followed each other through the door, the telephone had to be left off the hook.

The Hill family expressed their revulsion through a family friend who also happened to be a solicitor, and a policeman was posted at the front gate. They didn't venture out of the house for two weeks in case West Yorkshire police called wanting information about Jacqueline's life and background, but they heard nothing at all. Finally, just over a week after her daughter's murder, and on the understanding that their film would be made generally available, Doreen Hill invited BBC television cameras in to record her grief.

A second-year student reading English at Leeds University, 'Jackie' had moved out of the flat where she used to live on the outskirts of the city into a hall of residence nearer the city centre in order to reassure her parents, who had expressed concern about her safety. She had made her mind up to become a probation officer and, on the night of 17 November, had been on her way home from a seminar which she attended on the probation service, in Leeds.

It was Doreen Hill's hope that, by demonstrating what 'a decent person' Jacqueline had been, and the anguish that her death had brought to her family, whoever was 'shielding' the man who killed her might be shamed at last into contacting the police.

The edition of BBC2's late-night news magazine *Newsnight* which went out on Thursday, 27 November also carried 'messages' spoken directly 'to camera' by some of the women who had survived attacks by the 'Ripper' and the families of other women who had died.

Olive Smelt, attacked in Halifax in the summer of 1975 said: 'Doesn't it bother you to think people hate you for doing this? It is nothing to be proud of, the things you do.'

The mother of Jayne MacDonald, murdered in Chapeltown in the summer of 1977, said: 'I think you are the Devil himself. You are a coward. You are not a man, you are a beast. I hate you and I believe the population hates you.'

Maureen Long, attacked in Bradford two weeks after Jayne MacDonald's murder, said: 'Someone wants to get hold of you and do some of the same things to you. If they come face to face with you, you had better kill yourself before someone else does.'

The stepfather of Josephine Whitaker, murdered in Halifax in April 1979, said: 'You are an inadequate person, physically and mentally. I think the person harbouring the Ripper is as bad as he is. I can't understand the mentality of anybody who can cohabit with such a loathsome creature.'

The mother of Barbara Leach, murdered in Bradford five months later, said: 'Look over your shoulder – many people are looking for you. They hate you.' And her husband added: 'You are an obscenity on the face of the earth. When they catch you, they should lock you away and throw away the key.'

A few hours before the programme was broadcast, Trevor Birdsall, believing that the brown, 'square-shaped' car spotted in Alma Road at the time of Jacqueline Hill's murder might be his friend's Rover, had sat down to scribble an anonymous letter to the police. 'I have good reason to now [sic] the man you are looking for in the Ripper case,' he began. 'This man as dealings with prostitutes and always had a thing about them . . . His name and address is Peter Sutcliffe, 6 Garden Lane, Heaton, Bradford. Workes [sic] for Clarkes Transport, Shipley.'

When nothing happened in the next twenty-four hours, Birdsall's girlfriend persuaded him, on the strength of a few drinks, to go with her to Bradford police headquarters. There he repeated what he had said in the letter, adding that he had been with Sutcliffe when he got out of his car to go after a woman in Halifax on 16 August 1975, the night Olive Smelt was attacked. He was thanked for his co-operation but heard nothing more from the police; his statement, if it was ever transcribed by the young constable on the desk who took it, was never seen again.

The familiar warnings to women, reiterated in the wake of Jacqueline Hill's murder, to stay off the streets after dusk led to a series of demonstrations by the 'Reclaim the Night' and allied movements in the towns of the North whose aim was to shock, and they succeeded.

Two hundred women marched on the Plaza cinema in Leeds, where *The Beast* and *Climax* were showing, chanting, 'Get men off the streets'; a screening of *Dressed to Kill* at the Odeon was terminated when several dozen women started throwing rotten eggs and 'paint-bombs' at the screen; a sex shop in Chapeltown, close to where Josephine Whitaker had been murdered, had its windows smashed and the slogans 'Women are angry' and 'No men after dark' daubed on the walls, and was later burned to the ground.

In a letter to *The Times* at the beginning of December, Professor Hilary Rose of the University of Bradford articulated the thinking behind these apparently spontaneous eruptions: 'It is important to stress that the "Ripper" only makes public and unavoidable that which, as a whole, society tries to avoid thinking about, namely the high level of violence against women whether within the home or on the streets,' she wrote.

'Meanwhile the commercial pretence that sex and violence go together only in fantasy is reflected in the cinemas and the bookstalls. Almost the entire media persist in speaking of "prostitutes" and "innocent" women. Murder is murder regardless of the occupation of the victim. The "Ripper" hunt is not only an urgent matter in its own right, but it has become part of a long battle against the sexual violence which deforms our society.'

Professor Rose added that, far from women giving in to intimidation, she saw 'a tremendous number of support networks springing up, of shared cars, telephone links, shared journeys on foot', all of which made for 'something of that sense of community which was shown in the "blitz".'

But the centres of Bradford and Leeds, even as Christmas approached, were deserted every night by 7.00. Every man out alone was suspect, and any Geordie asking for a drink in a pub was likely to feel a tap on his shoulder before he had drained the glass. In the climate of suspicion that the murders engendered, countless marriages faltered and relationships fell apart.

West Yorkshire police had been willing to try anything that might help run the 'Ripper' to ground, including clairvoyants from all over the world: Mrs Doris Stokes had advised them through the medium of the *Sunday People* that the man they were looking for was likely to be called Ronnie or Johnnie, while a Dutchman said the murderer would turn out to be a twenty-seven-year-old washing-machine mechanic living in Aberdeen.

But as 1980 drew to a close, there was enormous public pressure on Ronald Gregory to produce concrete results. A week after Jacqueline Hill's murder he announced the formation of a 'think tank' of senior officers drawn from outside his own demoralised force, which the papers quickly dubbed the Super Squad. George Oldfield's deputy, Jim Hobson, was to be in charge of this 'unique' new team. Oldfield himself was quietly dropped from the case.

31

A couple of days before Christmas, Carl climbed the stairs to his bedsit at Priestthorpe Road to find that Peter had called while he was out: a bottle of Brut aftershave, which is what he always got from Peter and Sonia for Christmas, plus some Hai Karate soap-on-a-rope and a card were lying on the bed.

Carl hadn't seen Peter for nearly two weeks, and on that occasion they had parted on an unsettling note. Carl had always found it difficult to draw Peter on the subject of the 'Yorkshire Ripper': 'I'd say, "What d'you think then, Pete? D'you think he's a Geordie?" An' he'd just go, "Oh no," but he would never discuss it. He used to always nip to next subject, like "How's bike coming on?"'

There was a Geordie who lived at the top end of Priestthorpe Road, for instance, who Carl was convinced must have been 'tapped' by the police 'dozens' of times: 'He just talked like that tape an' I'd never seen him with any women or any friends or owt; he lived in a flat on his own an' he used to walk with one of them Adidas bags all time, an' I were sure it were him. I were going to follow him about.' Carl had mentioned this man to Peter and, one afternoon in October, had pointed him out from the top-floor window. As usual, though, Peter hadn't shown much interest.

But in mid-December, four weeks after Jacqueline Hill's murder, Carl came across something in the paper that he was idly flipping through which made him say how much he would like to get his hands on the Ripper, and watched a change come over his brother: 'I were telling him what a bastard I thought Ripper were, about how I'd cut his bollocks off an' all that if I caught him. And whereas usually, whatever you said to him, he'd laugh right loud an' crack some sort of joke, this day he went right strange, did our Peter. He got right nervous. Right edgy. *Really* edgy and uncomfortable.'

He had said he better be off then and, on his way out, halfway down the stairs, turned to Carl, who was immediately behind him, and mumbled something about not wanting to lose Sonia, about Sonia being all he had left, and seemed on the verge of crying. 'It were like he were goin' to burst into tears. He were really shekkin an' his voice were breakin' when he shut door.'

On 18 November, the day after Jacqueline Hill's murder but the day before it was confirmed as a 'Ripper' murder in the press, Robin Holland had made a similar remark and had watched Peter react in a similar, if less extreme, way, although it had seemed to him at the time to be none of his business. Robin had brought Rachel and Damien back to their mother in Bingley and had been quite pleased to bump into Peter, whom he hadn't seen for some time. He had appeared more or less his normal self but had then suddenly got up from the armchair where he had been sitting with Robin's dog in his lap and started walking up and down in front of the window, wringing his hands, which Robin had never seen him do before.

Once again Carl felt stirrings of unease. He would be absent from the various family gatherings over Christmas, giving as his excuse the fact that he couldn't bear to be with more than two of his family at the same time.

Shortly before Christmas, Peter had been shaken to find himself face to face with Maureen Long, a woman he had attacked three and a half years earlier, in the Arndale Centre in Bradford. She hadn't given him a second glance, however, and had walked straight on.

At around the same time, he had been given a January date for his appearance in court on the drunk driving charge, and had handed his notice in at Clark's. On Christmas Eve he sat in the cab of his wagon in Clark's yard, sharing the liver sandwiches that Sonia had made him and discussing his future with one of the other drivers, Allan Wright. He said that he had been to see a cottage in Ripon which they had decided to buy, and that 'three or four vans' came with it. He outlined the scheme for selling Sonia's pots to summer tourists and added that he was also thinking about going into partnership with Carl, doing cavity-wall insulation.

'If you get up there and you get on your feet, don't forget me,' Allan Wright said as he slammed the cab door. He was back in Bingley for morning opening time. Peter, on the other hand, stayed behind 'rubbing and scrubbing', putting in the hours.

Christmas Day was a Thursday, and Peter and Sonia, who had delivered their presents personally earlier in the week, spent it quietly at Garden Lane with Mrs Szurma. Sonia's mother was also with them on Boxing Day when they travelled to Bingley to have lunch with Maureen and the children, plus Jane and her boyfriend, Eddie. At teatime they were joined by Peter's father and Marion, and then, at about 7.30, Sonia and Mrs Szurma went off with Peter on his traditional 'duty' visits to the old people.

They called on Josie London, leaving her a small present and a card, and stayed to have a cup of tea with his Grandmother Sutcliffe after seeing her safely into bed. The atmosphere on the drive back to Heaton, however, was not all that it might have been because of an incident that had taken place before they left Maureen's: Mrs Szurma later told Carl that his father had 'groped' her in an 'upsetting' way as she was walking downstairs.

Two days later, Sunday, 28 December, it was Peter's turn to play host to his family at Garden Lane. But, at lunchtime, he left Sonia preparing the evening meal while he went out for a drink in Bradford with Trevor Birdsall and Birdsall's girlfriend, Gloria. It was only three weeks since the two of them had walked into Bradford police headquarters and named Peter Sutcliffe as the Yorkshire Ripper, but the fact that he was still free to stand at a bar reassured Trevor. Gloria, however, would later claim that she had had 'a feeling of apprehension' and 'a churning' in her stomach all the time they were in his company that day.

It took two taxis to bring the members of his family over to

Peter's at the end of the afternoon, and they travelled back to Bingley from Heaton several hours later the same way, so that Peter could drink with a clear conscience. Afterwards, they would be united in their opinion that the 'foreign' food Sonia had cooked them was 'not that nice', but nobody spoiled the atmosphere by saying so at the time.

It was a pleasant, if not uproarious, occasion and, when it was over, Peter walked them all out to the cars, kissing his sisters and wishing everybody a happy New Year.

The next morning, his first back at work, he was late. 'Where the bloody hell have you been?' Willie Clark barked at him when he eventually rolled in and was astonished to see tears welling in Sutcliffe's eyes. He mumbled that he would be back in the New Year and left the yard saying he had 'things to do'.

Maureen was surprised to open her door the following afternoon, Tuesday, 30 December, to find Peter standing outside in the gathering dark. When they were at his house a couple of days earlier he had been upset to hear that Anne's kids hadn't got their presents and wanted to know whether Maureen felt like 'going on' to Morecambe with them now. She piled into the Rover with Jane and Rachel and Damien, ran into Rutland House to pick up her father's gifts and stayed at Anne's just long enough to see the Christmas wrappings removed, before turning round and coming home.

Once again Marion was impressed. 'There's not many blokes would do that,' she said to John as they heard the car drive away.

Depressed about his job and fed up with Sonia's 'constant nagging' ever since he'd been breathalysed, Peter walked out of the house just after 4.00 p.m. on 2 January 1981, the first Friday of the New Year, saying he was going to collect the key to Jane's Mini which had broken down again. He didn't drive to Bingley, though, but to Mirfield, outside Leeds, to a scrapyard, where he picked up a number plate which had fallen off a Skoda and wrenched off the other one to make the pair. He called Sonia at 9.00 from a service station on the motorway to say that he was having trouble with the car and, an hour later, fixed the stolen plates with black electrical tape over the registration plates of his Rover before heading for Havelock Square, the red-light area of Sheffield, thirty miles from home.

A few minutes past 10.00 he drove up to a young West Indian woman in Broomhall Street and asked her if she was 'doing business', but after a close look she simply said 'Sorry', and walked away. Her friend, though, who was also black, couldn't afford to wave good-bye to £10 so casually. And when the car reappeared a few minutes later, she climbed in and directed the driver towards, and then through, the stone gateposts of a well-screened private-looking road just half a mile away. He backed into the drive attached to a large stone building, which no other 'punter' had ever done in her experience, and turned off both the ignition and the lights.

On the way, 'Dave', as he called himself, had talked about his wife, about her miscarriages and about how she nagged him and, even now that they had reached their destination, still seemed more interested in talking than in sex. 'Sharon' listened politely for some time but eventually asked him if he would like to pay her now, and passed him a 'rubber' once she had taken possession of his £10 note. She removed the pants she was wearing under her dress and, having taken off a black plastic carcoat and laid it carefully across the back seat, he unzipped his trousers, placed one hand on the gearlever and the other behind her head and, with no real enthusiasm, lowered himself across her.

Unlike the 'big, fat taxi driver smelling of sweat' whom she told him she had been with earlier, and who, she assured 'Dave' in response to his suggestion that they get into the back seat, hadn't seemed hindered by the dashboard, she sensed that 'Dave' was 'nervous' and tried reassuring him, insisting that there was 'nothing to worry about'. But when, after ten minutes, he was still 'cold as ice', she stopped and said, 'I don't think we'll be able to do it.' Rather than being upset or embarrassed as she would have expected, he simply said, 'It looks like it.'

268

They had picked up the threads of their earlier conversation and 'Dave' was telling her about 'not being able to go with' his wife when the interior of the car was suddenly illuminated from in front. Even without clearing the condensation from the windscreen, it was possible to see that it was a police car that had turned into the drive and parked nose-to-nose with the Rover.

Sergeant Bob Ring, twenty-six years with South Yorkshire police, and Probationary Constable Robert Hydes had reported to Hammerton Road police station for the nightshift just over half an hour earlier and, as often happened at weekends, had made Melbourne Avenue one of their first calls.

It was the younger officer who approached the well-maintained car parked in the shadow of Free Trades House, and seeing him coming, 'Dave', suddenly galvanised, said, 'Leave it to me. You're my girlfriend.' Winding down the window, he told the constable what he had just said he was going to, plus the fact that it was his car and his name was 'Peter Williams'. An openly sceptical Hydes sauntered back to rejoin his partner, who, via police headquarters, checked the Rover's number plates with the national police computer in Hendon. The information came through within a couple of minutes that the plates belonged to a Skoda.

'Dave', meanwhile, had asked the woman still sitting next to him whether she felt able 'to make a run for it', and she had told him there wasn't much point, seeing that she was hardly unknown to the local vice squad. The more experienced of the two officers now approached the Rover. He reached through the window and removed the keys from the steering column; PC Hydes, having established that the false plates were only held on with tape, unpeeled the tax disc, and both men escorted the woman, whose true identity was quickly established as Olivia Reivers, currently serving a suspended sentence for soliciting, back to the patrol car.

Sutcliffe immediately saw this as his opportunity. Grabbing the ball-pein hammer and single-bladed knife that were concealed under his seat, he made for the stone porch abutting on to the building some yards behind him and, out of sight of the police, who were prepared to take his word for it when he explained that he had been 'bursting for a pee', threw the 'tackle' behind a small oil storage tank, on to some leaves. There was a second wood-handled knife in his jacket on the back seat of the car, accessible through a hole in the pocket, but he would get rid of that in a cistern at the police station later.

At Hammerton Road police station, he owned up to being Peter Sutcliffe, of No. 6 Garden Lane, Bradford, without a great deal of pressing, and also admitted that the false number plates on the Rover were stolen. He explained that this was because he was due in court on a drunk driving charge in less than two weeks, and his insurance had lapsed the night before.

He was asleep in his cell by 2.30 a.m. and, at 5.12 a.m., Dewsbury police in West Yorkshire, who, it had been discovered, were responsible for the area where the number-plate theft had occurred, were informed of his arrest. They said they would send somebody to collect him from South Yorkshire after the new shift had come on at 6.00 a.m.

The normal procedure in a case involving the theft of property worth only 50p would have been an immediate remand on bail. But, discomfited by the sloppy groundwork in the hours immediately following Jacqueline Hill's murder, Ronald Gregory had been at pains to emphasise to the 5,000 members of his force the importance of forwarding all information regarding prostitutes and red-light areas, no matter how apparently inconsequential or trivial, to the Ripper Incident Room at Leeds. Consequently, at 8.00 a.m. on Saturday, 3 January, the station sergeant at Dewsbury police station informed the duty officer with the Ripper Squad of Sutcliffe's impending arrival. He actually arrived at 8.55 a.m., closely followed by his brown Rover, and was logged in at the station desk at 8.59 before being escorted to the interview area in the basement.

He remained genial and apparently unsurprised by the attention being lavished on such a minor offence, and volunteered the information that he had been interviewed by Manchester police as part of the £5-note enquiry, as well as being questioned as a result of the surveillance operations in red-light areas, inside the first hour. It was also noted that his foot-size matched the size of the bootprint found near Josephine Whitaker's body, as well as at the scene of two of the other 'Ripper' murders. And at 10.00 a.m., the detectives at Dewsbury contacted the Ripper Room to confirm that they might very well be interested in 'clocking' the Bradford lorry-driver arrested with a prostitute in Sheffield the night before.

Ten miles away, meanwhile, in Bradford, Sonia, thinking it was Peter, was studiously ignoring the hammering at her door. She did pick the phone up, however, when it rang five minutes later, and a voice on the other end told her that the police were outside her house and that she should open up. When she did, a uniformed officer informed her, wrongly as it turned out, that her husband was being held in custody in Sheffield, which was the first clue she had been given as to where he was. She would hear nothing further for twelve hours, when the police called a second time to say that they would take her to see Peter the following day, Sunday.

At lunchtime on Saturday, Det. Sgt. Desmond O'Boyle arrived at Dewsbury police station to begin questioning the suspect who, on paper, seemed no more likely to be the Ripper than the many dozens of others he had seen already in the course of the enquiry.

Introducing himself as a member of the Ripper Squad, O'Boyle started off slowly, and spent most of the afternoon trying to build up a picture of the 'pleasant, co-operative' man sitting across the table from him – education, interests, friends, social life, home life, previous employment, present place of work. One of the things O'Boyle asked Sutcliffe was whether he had been having 'normal sex' with his wife and he said yes: 'The last time was about four days ago.' Questioned further about having sex with his wife even though they were constantly rowing, Sutcliffe said: 'We forget about rows when we go to bed.'

By 5.30 p.m. O'Boyle was prepared to write Sutcliffe off as

another false alarm and was about to recommend his release when the Chief Superintendent in charge at Dewsbury took matters into his own hands. He ordered O'Boyle to convey to the duty officer at the Incident Room in Leeds his 'displeasure' at the lack of rank of the man sent to interview what, to him, was still a major suspect in the Ripper case.

As a result, O'Boyle, who should have finished his shift at 6.00 p.m., was instructed to stay with Sutcliffe and, when he resumed the interview, started 'going in' harder. The circumstances surrounding his visit to Sheffield the previous evening were explored at length. Sutcliffe was anxious that his wife should not be told about a prostitute being in the car with him when he was arrested, but O'Boyle informed him that his car had previously been seen in red-light areas and that, as far as he was concerned, Sutcliffe was a 'regular punter'. Questioned about a previous denial that he had ever been to Manchester, although his Rover had been logged on Moss Side, he said that he had left it in the car park at Bradford Central Library one night after it had broken down in the city centre, and that 'someone must have used it to go to Manchester and put it back on that spot'.

At about 9.00 p.m. Sutcliffe was asked to give a blood sample, which at first he resisted. 'What if it's the same as the one you're wanting?' he asked O'Boyle, who simply said to him: 'Are you the Ripper?' He co-operated with the police doctor and, once again, the atmosphere lightened. 'I'd get them, but they might be cold by the time I got back,' Sutcliffe joked when it was decided to send out for fish and chips. He was bedded down in his cell by 10.00.

At the 10.00 p.m. 'parade' at Hammerton Road police station, back in Sheffield, Bob Ring picked up the news that the man he had 'collared' twenty-four hours earlier in the company of Olivia Reivers was still in custody at Dewsbury police station, being questioned by Ripper Squad officers.

An hour later, Ring was back in Melbourne Avenue, scene of the arrest, exploring the area beyond the stone porch at Free Trades House where he remembered Sutcliffe had gone to have a 'pee'. By 11.05 p.m. Hammerton Road were on to the Ripper Room to inform them about the knife and the hammer that had been found lying in a pile of leaves and were told to leave them *in situ* until a picture had been taken.

As soon as he put down the phone, Inspector John Boyle jumped in a car and was rushed from Leeds to Sheffield, where he ordered a more extensive search to be made and reinterviewed Olivia Reivers. At midnight, he telephoned Dewsbury to tell them the news, and then called the head of the Ripper Squad, Det. Chief Supt. Dick Holland, at home to fill him in on the dramatic developments of the previous twenty-four hours. Sutcliffe was put under constant surveillance throughout the night, with one man inside, and another outside his cell.

Sonia rose early on Sunday morning. She was following a German-language series on television and did little to conceal her irritation when she was interrupted by knocking at the door at about 9.30. She opened it to admit Dick Holland, Det. Sgt. O'Boyle, Chief Inspector George Smith, and Detective woman-constable Jenny Crawford-Brown. Then, wearing a green corduroy topcoat over her day-clothes, Sonia picked up an exercise book and went back to watching her programme.

She lowered the sound but declined to give the police her undivided attention until Det. Chief Supt. Holland walked up to the set and turned it off. She would eventually report him to his superiors for 'discourteous behaviour'.

They quickly embarked on a search of what one of them would later describe as 'one of the most meticulous – as well as one of the coldest' houses he had ever seen: 'There wasn't a thread out of place. Everything, from the face-cloths in the bathroom to worn-out clothes down to shoe rags, was folded to a sharp crease. There were crochet-covers over the covers over the living-room suite.'

A collection of tools had already been retrieved from Sutcliffe's Rover, including three screwdrivers found in the glove compartment; and a hacksaw and a yellow-handled screwdriver were among the items that Dick Holland and his colleagues removed from his home. Mrs Sutcliffe accompanied them to police headquarters in Bradford, where they arrived shortly after 10.00 a.m., and started the questioning that would go on until 8.00 that night. After several hours of questions designed to build up a 'profile' of her personal life, Sonia, who it was known had alibied her husband on at least three separate occasions, was asked about Peter's movements on specific dates during the previous two months. She was also shown the knife found in Sheffield and identified it as one she had bought for her 'bottom drawer' before she was married.

This information was relayed to Dewsbury, where Sutcliffe had been up since 8.00 and was into his second full day of questioning. Confronting him this time were Inspector John Boyle and Peter Smith, a young detective from the Ripper Squad with an unparalleled knowledge of the background to all the attacks.

Sutcliffe was still polite and composed, and the questions were still of a general nature until, after lunch, Boyle and Smith started to quiz him on his whereabouts on dates relevant to the Ripper enquiry. Bonfire Night, for instance, two months earlier, when Theresa Sykes had been attacked in Huddersfield. He had been at home with his wife at 8.00, he said, when the attack was taking place. Asked how he could be so sure, he said that if he had been out he would have remembered seeing fires. Sonia had already told police in Bradford that she remembered him walking through the kitchen door at 10.00 on 5 November.

Sutcliffe was then asked where he was on 17 November, the night Jacqueline Hill was murdered, and he again replied that he was at home at Garden Lane with Sonia. 'Every time you have been seen, you always seem to have the same alibi – that you were at home with your wife,' Boyle said. 'I find that rather strange. How can you be sure that's where you were?'

'I'm always at home every night when I'm not on an overnight stay,' Sutcliffe said, but his composure was showing the first signs of slipping. Boyle switched his attention to Friday night then, and the arrest in Sheffield. Sutcliffe had claimed he had driven the thirty miles south because three hitchhikers whom he had picked up had offered him £10 to take them there. Boyle told him he thought this was 'rubbish'. He said: 'I believe you went to Sheffield on Friday night with the sole purpose of picking up a prostitute.'

Sutcliffe said: 'That is not true.'

Boyle continued: 'I believe you put the false number plates on to conceal the identity of the vehicle in the red-light district.'

SUTCLIFFE: 'That is not true. To be honest with you, I've been so depressed that I put them on because I was thinking of committing a crime with the car.'

BOYLE: 'Why did you leave your car and go to the side of that house?'

SUTCLIFFE: 'To urinate.'

BOYLE: 'I think you went for another purpose. Do you understand what I am saying? I think you are in serious trouble.'

SUTCLIFFE: 'I think you have been leading up to it.'

BOYLE: 'Leading up to what?'

SUTCLIFFE: 'The Yorkshire Ripper.'

BOYLE: 'What about the Yorkshire Ripper?'

SUTCLIFFE: 'Well, it's me.'

He remained totally calm and unemotional, as he was to remain throughout the almost sixteen hours that it would take for him to dictate a detailed statement. 'They are all in my brain, reminding me of the beast I am,' he said. 'Just thinking of them all reminds me of what a monster I am.' He made only one request: that he be the one to tell Sonia.

At 5.00, as Inspector Boyle paced around the main CID office at Dewsbury asking questions while Det. Sgt. Smith took down Sutcliffe's 'confession', Sonia was still at police headquarters in Bradford. 'Has Pete had anything to eat?' she wanted to know when a policeman brought her a hamburger, and the policeman told her: 'We're not inhuman, you know.'

She was driven to Dewsbury at 10.30 and an hour later saw Peter for the first time in two days when he was escorted into the functional, tungsten-lit room in the police station where she was waiting. He was still wearing the blue sweater with a light band at the neck, the white shirt and the grey trousers that he had been wearing when he walked out of the house at 4.00 p.m. on Friday.

'It's me . . .' he said, and she said: 'Is it? Is it really?' The several pairs of eyes monitoring her reaction inhibited her from crying or from saying anything more.

She didn't break down for an hour and a half after being handed a glass of Scotch by George Smith, her interrogator. She was having 'a two-minute sob' on policewoman Crawford-Brown's shoulder when, out of the corner of her eye, she saw 'some of the top brass' slip into the room and then out again.

A quarter of an hour later, at 1.15 a.m. on what was by then Monday, 5 January, George Oldfield returned and sat down next to her, saying, 'You know who I am, don't you?' Although no longer concerned with the day-to-day running of the case, he was still Assistant Chief Constable, and he seemed to her to be working hard at presenting 'a concerned image'.

'My priority,' she said, staring straight ahead rather than at him, 'is to let my parents know.' She felt that such news should be broken face to face and not on a telephone and at first couldn't understand his obvious reluctance to let her do it.

'Oh no, I wouldn't advise you to do that,' he said. 'The press will get you.'

'What on earth are you talking about?' She looked him straight in the face for the first time. 'What do you mean?' And so he spelled it out: 'We've had a press conference. They're all waiting outside.'

As word had spread that a suspect was clearly 'in the frame' for the first time, the men who had led the hunt for the 'Ripper' for five and a half years had started making their way to Dewsbury police station throughout Sunday afternoon. Ronald Gregory had sent a cadet out for a bottle of Scotch on arrival, and the atmosphere in the second-floor conference room where the rest of the team had assembled around their Chief Constable was already celebratory when, at about 3.00 p.m., Det. Sgt. O'Boyle burst in, beaming. 'It's definitely him. He's started to cough and tell us where the murder weapons are hidden.'

The scene was suddenly like the victors' dressing room in the minutes following the FA Cup Final at Wembley, with the all-male company playfully punching each other and hugging each other and pumping each other's hands.

It was a mood that inevitably spilled over into the press conference that was eventually convened in the television lounge downstairs and watched incredulously that evening in millions of homes. Flanked by two rows of florid, chuckling lieutenants, an unashamedly euphoric Ronald Gregory confessed to being 'absolutely delighted, totally delighted' with developments and said that the hunt for the Yorkshire Ripper was now 'being scaled right down'. They were remarks that, in many quarters, were seen to be flying in the face of the country's long-established contempt laws and were the cause of immediate concern.

'It was unnecessary for [the police] to have held a press conference at all. It was irresponsible for them to have done so in the way they did . . .', Wednesday morning's *Times* concluded. 'They praised the two young policemen who had carried out the arrest, and those officers then gave press interviews in which they professed their own satisfaction. The police did not quite go as far as saying that they had caught the Ripper. They did not need to.'

The most damaging consequence of Mr Ronald Gregory's 'overenthusiasm', *The Times* pointed out, was the example it set for representatives of the press 'and the media in general', who, in the forty-eight hours following the announcement of Sutcliffe's arrest, proceeded, in the words of another observer, 'to drive a number of coaches and horses through the contempt laws: the popular press seems to have decided that this was such a fantastic story that they would publish what they wanted and let the lawyers pick up the pieces later'.

Believing this to clearly be the case, the Solicitor-General issued an urgent warning to all newspaper, radio and television editors, reminding them of 'the vital principles embodied in

English law that a man accused of a crime, however serious, is presumed to be innocent and is entitled to a fair trial and of the responsibility which the law accordingly places upon editors'. The horse by then, however, had already bolted.

It was a matter of some pride to journalists on West Yorkshire's rival daily papers – the *Telegraph and Argus*, based in Bradford, and the Leeds-based *Yorkshire Post* and *Yorkshire Evening Post* – that they 'scoop' not only each other, but also the 'big hitters' and 'buy-up' men from Fleet Street responsible for the teams of reporters who, by midnight on Sunday, were invading their 'patch' in their hundreds.

The identity of the man assisting police with their enquiries had not been revealed at the Dewsbury press conference. But even before the conference was over, reporters from the *Yorkshire Post* were finding their way, via the telephone directory, the electoral register and reliable inside information, to a quiet street in the 'select' Bradford suburb of Heaton. By midnight, and still many hours ahead of the competition, they had located the neighbour with whom Mrs Sutcliffe, a schoolteacher living at No. 6 Garden Lane, had left a telephone number in case of emergency. And, at 1.15 a.m. on Monday, as George Oldfield made Sonia understand that she wasn't going to be allowed to break the news to her mother and father in person, two young men walked up the path to the front door of 42 Tanton Crescent and lifted the freshly painted black knocker.

When an elderly woman in a nightdress appeared at the upstairs window they told her they were from the press. 'We have some news for you. It's about Peter Sutcliffe, your son-in-law.' But it was clear from her confused expression that Mrs Szurma still didn't understand. 'Has there been an accident?' she said. And then, in faltering English: 'You could be anyone. You could be crooks.' She closed the bedroom window and called the police.

A uniformed constable arrived in a patrol car in a very few minutes and they satisfied him that they were from the *Post*.

'They're all right,' he told the woman, who by now had put on a dressing-gown, and her husband, who had pulled on a sweater and trousers. 'You can let them in.'

Squeezed into the small kitchen at the side of the house, the journalists explained to the Szurmas that Peter had been arrested in Sheffield on Friday evening with a girl in his car, and tried to suggest the implications of the arrest. Mrs Szurma, however, remained confused. 'It must be Sonia, surely?' she said, adding that she had been expecting both of them over for tea several hours earlier, after *Gigi* had finished on television. She had spoken to Sonia on Saturday and there had been no mention of the fact that Peter hadn't come home on Friday night.

Realising that they must by now be only hours, perhaps only minutes, ahead of 'the pack', the reporters' main priority was a picture. After some persuading, Mrs Szurma finally produced a photograph of herself and her son-in-law, taken the previous Christmas: it showed a small woman in a sleeveless embroidered jacket, her features bleached out by the flash, and an unsmiling, rigid young man with both hands plunged deep into the trouser pockets of a three-piece suit, standing either side of a large Christmas tree which looked like a third person in the picture. By 5.00 a.m. it was in the safe at the newspaper's Leeds offices, although the journalists, determined to maximise their advantage, continued to sit it out with the Szurmas through the night.

At 6.45 a.m. on Monday, the radio news finally confirmed that what the newspapermen had been intimating was true: Peter Sutcliffe, a thirty-five-year-old lorry-driver of Heaton, Bradford, was to appear in court later that day charged with the murder of Leeds University student Jacqueline Hill. At 7.45 a.m. Mrs Szurma was sufficiently recovered to ring Bradford police to ask where her daughter was, and a few minutes later they rang back and put Sonia on the line.

At 2.30 a.m., following her conversation with George Oldfield, Sonia had been given a bed in police accommodation next to Dewsbury police station. Jenny Crawford-Brown, the policewoman who had been with her all day, went to sleep in an adjacent room, but Sonia was assigned another woman constable whose instructions were to sit up with her until the morning: the door had to be left open when she took a shower and a light was left burning all night.

At 6.00 a.m. there was a change of shift and Sonia, who hadn't been able to sleep, got up and dressed. The day shift officer absently handed her a newspaper but, as soon as she realised what she was reading with such concentration, hurriedly snatched it back. Sonia was incensed. 'Come on, you've just passed me your paper. You've just handed it to me,' she said. 'Everybody else in the street is able to read the papers. I don't see why I shouldn't be allowed to.' She said she thought it was ridiculous. The policewoman said it was orders. Similarly, when she wanted to take some exercise, she was told she couldn't leave the room.

At 7.45 a.m. she talked on the telephone to her mother and immediately afterwards rang her sister in London in an attempt to save her from having to hear the news from the radio in the same way. 'Is it true?' was all Marianne, like Sonia herself, could say at the beginning, and Sonia had to tell her it was. When she asked her how she could be so sure she said: 'Because Pete said it. Why should he say it if it wasn't right? And he is honest.' As they spoke, they kept reverting to their native Czech, and the police, who were monitoring the conversation, kept threatening to cut them off.

At 9.00, the *Yorkshire Post* reporters were still firmly entrenched in Tanton Crescent and they had the satisfaction, as the day wore on, of picking up the handwritten pleas and offers from virtually every newspaper in the country, as well as many from abroad, as they tumbled through the Szurmas' front door. By Wednesday, the *Post* itself would be being accused by its local rival, the *Telegraph and Argus*, of 'being thrown out of the home of Bohdan and Maria Szurma, after spending more than twenty-four hours in the house, after a row over a photograph' (an accusation the *Post*'s editor was to hotly deny).

An editorial in the same issue of the paper pointed out that 'chequebook journalism – the buying of people with a special story to tell by an individual newspaper to the exclusion of all others' had 'raised its ugly head in Bradford over the past few days' and was a practice to be roundly deplored. 'Responsible journalists,' it went on, in a tone that, to the 'irresponsible' journalists whom it was aimed at, smacked of sour grapes, 'base their case for unimpeded access to information on the people's right to know. When other so-called journalists come along to corner the market on the basis of how much money they have to spend, they have discarded the basic principles for the morals of the marketplace. We can do without them in Bradford.'

That same Wednesday evening, at the Norfolk Gardens Hotel, fifty yards from where the Bradford *Telegraph and Argus* was printed, the thirty-two representatives of the *Daily Mail*, the fourteen representatives of the *Sunday People* and eight from the *Daily Mirror*, just a few of the 200-strong press corps who had descended on the city, were recuperating from another day 'on the knocker' by laying false trails for one another and 'bravuraing it out' in the bars. The *Daily Express* team were loudly ordering bucket after bucket of champagne to 'celebrate' their 'signing up' of Sonia. The fee, it was rumoured, was to be £200,000, plus sixty per cent of syndication.

There weren't two women in Yorkshire more interested in the 'Ripper', Maureen would say, than her and Jane. Jane had been reading *I'm Jack*, a paperback book about the case, over the Christmas holiday and had passed it on to her older sister, who had been halfway through it on Sunday evening when the news came on the television that a man had been arrested. Jane was ecstatic. She told Maureen she would take her out 'for a big, slap-up meal' the following night, to celebrate.

Shortly after returning to Bingley from Germany in 1978, Maureen had been startled by a Photofit picture of a man police wanted to interview in connection with the Ripper murders while watching television. 'That's Peter' had been her immediate thought, but she had almost as immediately dismissed it as nonsense. It was Jane who, as Sunday evening started to wear on, and more became known about the man being questioned at Dewsbury police station, started to have misgivings.

The fact that he had been arrested in a Rover V8 saloon instinctively made her think of Peter, and after a while she told Maureen she was going to call Garden Lane. She didn't, when Maureen pointed out that she would worry even more if he turned out not to be in, and Jane let it drop. Privately though, for some reason she wasn't able to put her finger on, her thoughts kept returning to Peter all night.

On Monday morning Jane got up early and crossed the road to work at Anderton's as usual. Stocktaking, weighing out scoops of metal and hearing a male voice somewhere behind her reading aloud from a newspaper – 'Heaton . . . lorry-driver . . . married to a schoolteacher . . .' – was the last thing she remembered before passing out. She was carried over to Maureen's where she was sedated by her doctor and put to bed.

Jane's father had caught the first bus out of Bingley and had been at work at Drummond's mill on Lumb Lane by 6.00 a.m. He was on his tea break two and a half hours later when a workmate mentioned that the man they'd got for 'the Ripper job' was a Sutcliffe and jokingly asked him if he was any relation. He instantly recognised the tall, detached, pebble-dashed house pictured on the front of the *Yorkshire Post* as the paper was passed to him, and his works manager quickly drove him home.

That night, John, with Marion and all of his daughters and grandchildren, including those from Morecambe, slept at Stirk House, a country hotel buried in the Dales near Skipton, as guests of the *Daily Mail*. The following morning, Tuesday, 6 January, John signed an agreement worth £5,000 with what had always been his regular morning paper, by the terms of which he undertook 'not to speak to any other news organisation or to provide them with photographs or to pose for pictures', and agreed to 'use my best endeavours to persuade all members of my family' to follow suit.

*

Following Doreen Hill's appearance on *Newsnight* five weeks earlier, a Leeds businessman had paid for 8,000 posters to be printed bearing the legend 'The Ripper Is A Coward'. A number of these posters, now also scrawled with the words 'Hang him!', sprang up among the crowd which started to choke a narrow street at the side of Dewsbury Town Hall many hours before Peter Sutcliffe was due to appear in the magistrates' court, effortlessly accommodated in the enormous Victorian Gothic building.

By the time the representatives of the world's press were admitted to claim their seats in the first-floor public gallery just before 4.00 p.m. on Monday, the crowd had turned into a swaying mob more than 2,000 strong. The TV lights singled out a number of skinhead gangs brandishing oily ropes fashioned into crude homemade nooses; and the arrival of the convoy with the van carrying Sutcliffe at its head was the signal for a riot of jeers and abuse in the suddenly floodlit dark: 'Hang the bastard!', 'Killer!', 'Die, die!' were cries that penetrated the thick stone walls and tall arched windows of the court to spiral round the pastel dome high above the dock.

At 4.54 p.m. the journalists packed into the public gallery rose to a half-standing, half-sitting position as Sutcliffe's wife and her father were ushered into court, and a minute later they rose as one and pressed forward excitedly as Sutcliffe himself took his place in the dock below. His curly black hair, thick when viewed from the side or the front, could be seen to be thinning slightly at the crown; his face, which seemed to reflect the courtroom walls, looked pale yellow.

He stood to be charged by the Clerk of the Court with murdering Jacqueline Hill between 16 November and 19 November 1980 'against the peace of our Sovereign Lady the Queen' and with stealing 'two motor vehicle registration-plates to the value of 50p' and eight minutes later was gone. Some reporters fancied that he 'sagged against the wall' as, still handcuffed to Desmond O'Boyle, he was taken downstairs to the cells.

Several hours earlier, a local reporter had tracked Kathleen's sister and her husband down at their house in Rotherham. Hearing the name and address of the man being held for questioning on the morning news, she had walked over to where Peter and Sonia's Christmas card was still standing on the mantelpiece and thrown it into the dustbin. She intended to live her life, please God, as if she had never known the Ripper or any of his family.

PART THREE

Other Rooms

32

A comment often heard in Bingley in the forty-eight hours after the news broke was that the town had never seen so many men in suits during the day. The reporters, for their own part, advised each other that the best way of avoiding trouble was not to arrive in Bingley wearing a sheepskin coat.

Whatever they wore, though, they were instantly identified and themselves came to recognise – in many cases too late, and at some cost – 'the strong sagacity and the dogged power of will which seem almost the birthright of the natives of the West Riding'. As they chased leads and ran down contacts on blowy council estates and in outcropped moorland villages, or hovered uneasily at the bars of local pubs and Working Men's Clubs in the (usually forlorn) hope of unearthing a retailable anecdote or an unfingered picture, the reporters also learned what Mrs Gaskell had learned about 'this wild, rough population' a century and a half earlier: that 'they have a quick perception of character, and a keen sense of humour' and that, consequently, 'the dweller among them must be prepared for certain uncomplimentary, though most likely true, observations, pithily expressed.'

By the time of his arrest, Peter Sutcliffe had become an occasional, sometimes only a dimly remembered, presence on the periphery of the lives of those who had once been his closest friends. The last time Eric Robinson had seen him had been from his ladder in Bingley Main Street where he was cleaning the windows of the old library building, soon to become 'Porky's Nite Scene'.

Reading his name in the newspapers and hearing it repeatedly on the radio and television had pulled that, and Eric's youthful memories of Peter, into sharp focus.

'I just saw wagon, and Peter's eyes in cab an' you could see them right plain as he was passing,' Eric remembered later. 'His eyes lit up . . .' On the morning when he heard 'who they'd got for Ripper', Eric had to come down off his ladder and go into the Working Men's Club 'for a couple of stiffs' which he had to steady with both hands.

Keith Sugden, married for many years to Peter's former neighbour from Cornwall Road, was no less stunned. 'Peter bloody Sutcliffe,' he kept repeating to Doreen after hearing it on the 7.00 a.m. news. 'I can't believe it. I can't believe it of him, knowing him as I knew him.' To his amazement, though, Doreen, whom he had shaken awake, hardly turned a hair. 'I aren't bloody surprised,' was all she said.

'When I went into work, I says to other girl who I knew knew him as well, I says, "Have you heard they've got Ripper?" And she says, "Yes, but they haven't given his name yet." I says, "They have." And she says, "Who?" I says, "You know 'im." And she's a lot older than me. "John Sutcliffe's lad. Oldest." And she goes, "Oh Doreen, it isn't him." I says, "It is Nancy, an' me an' Keith used to go around with him and I can bet my bloody life now he done it." She said, "Don't you ever say that." But I says, "I don't care. I *know* 'im."'

When they heard, Laurie Ashton and his wife, Cath, who, like Doreen Sugden, had always had a sixth sense about Peter even in their 'Gravediggers' Corner' days, couldn't believe that it was the same Peter Sutcliffe they knew, now living in a £35,000 house in Heaton. Within hours, though, the newspaper and television people started finding their way to the modest terraced cottage commanding a spectacular view across the Aire valley to Haworth. Employed part-time as a 'lollipop lady' in the village, Cath arrived home to find cameras of all descriptions set up in the garden. Several men and women were peering in through the downstairs window at the rock'n'roll mementoes, the Elvis Presley commemorative plaque and 'In Memoriam' mirrors, the Gene Vincent and Eddie Cochran photographs and album covers pinned to the Ashtons' living-room walls to indicate that,

288

even as they entered middle age, they were still 'keeping the faith'.

Laurie's musical tastes were immediately seized on by most representatives of the media as a way of breaking the ice: a surprising number of them had been reduced to tears by the news of Elvis's death. By Tuesday they were turning up in such droves that Laurie nailed a notice to the gate warning 'No TV or Press'. But it didn't stop them sending bouquets of flowers and boxes of chocolates with business cards attached, as well as toys for the kids and offers of more money than the out-of-work welder and his family had ever seen – or were ever likely to see – in their lives.

'I imagined him to be an ugly hunch-back wi' boils all over his face, somebody who couldn't get women and resented 'em for that. Somebody with totally nothing going for him.' Carl's mental picture of the Ripper, largely based, as it was, on information issued by the police, was one shared by many other people in Yorkshire. It was shattered, though, the minute he picked up a newspaper in the reading room at Bingley Library and saw his own brother's name leap out at him. 'He had everything going for him,' Carl found himself thinking obsessively, and then repeating aloud. 'Nice house, steady job, enough money, good looking . . . He were totally different to what I imagined this murderer to be.'

By lunchtime on the Monday, it had been borne in on Carl that, overnight, he had turned into something of a 'property'; and a visit to two *Daily Star* reporters at their hotel in Bradford hammered the point home. 'I went to Norfolk Gardens Hotel one night, only a couple of days after they'd caught him,' Carl later said, 'and I walked in there and there were hundreds of reporters. I shot off upstairs, 'cause I knew where their room were, and they chased me, brayin' on door, shoving notes underneath, all scraps of paper . . . They were fanatical to sign me up.'

Unlike Mick, who was happy to accept enough 'readies' to keep him in drink, Carl insisted on doing everything through a solicitor. The *Star* bought him a 'swanky' new wardrobe before leaving Bingley and then, with Mick in tow, he embarked on what was to be an itinerant existence for the next four and a half months. 'Nurse-maided' by the two reporters, they checked into hotels all over England under assumed names, only to check out again the minute it looked as though another newspaper was on their tail, attempting 'a spoiler'. The hotels were three- and four-star and no expense was spared, and Carl would later claim that the experience had almost turned him 'into an alcoholic'.

'We'd get up every night an' leave nine wine bottles on table, then go to a club. When we got back, I'd go to bed with a bottle of Scotch an' Mick would have a bottle of Southern Comfort. Every morning he'd wake up an' just throw up everywhere an' start over again.'

Within hours of him being 'spirited' away from Bingley by the *Star*, Carl's room at Priestthorpe Road was broken into and ransacked. His landlord recognised the men responsible through his show-jumping connections and immediately reported them to their editor in London.

Sonia had vowed to her father-in-law at the outset that 'Peter pulled me through my trouble and I'm going to pull him through this.' In fact, by the time a date for the trial had been set – 29 April 1981, an almost unprecedentedly brief three months and twenty-seven days after the arrest – Sonia was the only one still seeing her husband.

The family's verdict was that she had always wanted him to herself, and now, by 'poisoning his mind' against them, she had got him. No member of his family ever saw Peter while he was on remand in Armley without Sonia also being present. 'I never got the chance to really talk to him in depth, because she kept this running commentary going all the time,' John later complained. 'She'd arrive with probably a dozen headings on a piece of paper, and every one of these headings led to half a page before she'd finished. "Oh, and I must tell you . . .", and away she'd go again, leaning across the table, speaking to him in a very pianissimo-type whisper. None of us ever got a chance to say owt to lad because she just kept it going, reading from this little list of nonsense until fifteen minutes visiting were over. I could never take Jane and Maureen, or Mick and Carl and meself could never go because three was the limit and she was always there.'

What 'finally killed the pig' for Peter's father, though, was the morning he turned up outside Armley with Maureen and Maureen's two children and waited for an hour and a quarter in the rain, only to be told that Peter had left instructions that he only wanted to see his wife that day. As they turned to leave, Sonia brushed past them without speaking and rang the bell to be let in. 'That were when I realised she controlled him,' John said. 'Controlled his mind. She'd twisted him.' It was the last time he was to see either Sonia or his son.

Mick, too, would be dropped from the visitors' list on Sonia's insistence, but not before he had had the chance to set his mind at rest about a few things. The first visit to Armley could have been tense and embarrassing for all concerned, but Peter made it easy by smiling and laughing and cracking jokes about trying to escape. As soon as he could, though, Mick said his piece: 'I says, "I've just one thing to ask you first, Pete, before we get goin'. 'Cause they can say what they want in papers an' that, but I aren't going to believe it till I hear it from you. When you tell me, then I'll start tekkin it in. So, have you done it or what?" An' he says, "I haven't done 'em all. I'll tell you that now. But I've done six or seven of them, aye." So I says, "Well, that's it then," an' we sat down.'

About a year earlier, with the hunt for the Yorkshire Ripper at its height, Mick had come across a ladies' handbag while he was 'rooting' on the corporation tip at Dowley Gap. He had disposed of the contents – two Ronson cigarette lighters, a man's and a woman's, and about £20 worth of 10p pieces – and, a few weeks later, had surrendered the bag itself, after incautiously mentioning it during a drinking session, to Bingley police. Following Peter's arrest, stories had appeared in the local papers about Sutcliffe's brother Michael trying to assist the enquiry by taking a handbag in for examination, and it had since occurred to Mick that perhaps Peter had 'planted' it as a roundabout way of putting some money in his pocket. Peter laughed appreciatively, but noncommitally, when Mick put this theory to him, but he was quite positive when Mick enquired, as casually as possible, whether it was him who had 'topped' the Bingley bookmaker whose murder the police at one time seemed to suspect Mick himself of having committed: that, he insisted, had nothing to do with him whatsoever.

After these brief exchanges, Sonia had produced her notebook and taken charge of the conversation but, although it irked Mick to see her 'still on at him', he was prepared to make allowances and, in fact, promised Peter before leaving that he would 'keep an eye on poor lass'.

The following Sunday Mick drove over to Tanton Crescent in the Cortina Estate that he had on the road at the time and, leaving Susan and Michelle behind in the house with Mrs Szurma, took Sonia and her father for a two-hour walk through the snow on Queensbury Moors. 'Everything went well. I took 'em back home and had summat to eat an' a drink of coffee. But next thing I knew when I went in to see Pete was she'd told him I'd had all cameramen hiding in bushes, photographing us both, so I could sell pictures an' get some money . . . I said to our lad, "This is bloody stupid, this. I try and do her a good turn and this is the thanks. Well I'm afraid that's it. Finish. She's twistin' everything all time to get family. She's twistin' things round her way so we don't get any visits and she gets 'em all."'

Bradford, in the first weeks of 1981, was alive with rumour and counter-rumour, speculation, misinformation and lies, and they all, sooner or later, found their way to Sonia's ears. She didn't know how much Peter's family had been paid – estimates had it as high as £400,000 – but her view was that, by taking any payment at all, they had forfeited their right to continued prison visits.

Kerry Macgill, a young man with mutton-chop whiskers who described himself as 'a straightforward provincial solicitor' and whom Peter had chosen more or less at random to represent him, from a police list, advised Sonia from the beginning that, as a potential witness in her husband's defence, it would be wrong for her to sell her story to any paper. But the press, in her experience, had anyway shown themselves to be 'absolutely despicable':

'They made me endure having my supposed refuge – the home of my parents – totally besieged,' she later complained to the Press Council. 'Hordes of reporters clambered one over the other banging at the door, windows and letterbox; shamelessly yelling that they would pay more than the next man or woman for my story. The scene was akin to a frenzied auction, with wild attempts to outbid each other in shouts of "I will top any sum the rest of you care to name . . ."

'Not only did we have to keep the curtains continuously drawn, but we were not even able to leave the house to do our shopping. Our oppressors fared rather better. To accommodate this media mob some enterprising person found room amongst the streetful of press cars to set up a caravan selling food and hot drinks to provide the said gang with further stamina with which to continue their abysmal performance . . . On venturing to open the curtains a chink, vigilant photographers were immediately at the ready . . . This extremely inhuman harassment resulted in my mother (the only breadwinner) having her nerves so badly shattered that she needed two months off work and still now has to take tranquillisers.'

In a second written submission to the Press Council, who had promptly announced their intention of conducting an enquiry into the case, Sonia described how she had had to 'escape' from her mother's home on the eve of the trial at the Old Bailey.

'The press, knowing of my intention to travel, and also knowing that I was stranded, cornered and trapped, did not let up in their hectic intense oppression of trying to urge and compel me into going with them – the very people I most wanted to avoid.

'Ultimately, I had to abandon plans going in the comfort of my mother's car – firstly because I was physically prevented by the hordes and crowds outside the house, and the constant press guard outside Ma's garage. And secondly, it would have meant a journey fraught by being tracked, monitored, photographed, filmed, and possibly even ending up in a crash.

'The day was wearing on – still the vigil continued. Under this over-powering pressure I was left with no alternative but, come nightfall, to climb out of the back window like a burglar – simply to escape the organised sentry. Then creep furtively through the muddy back garden with only the bare minimum of belongings, in a constant fear of being fallen on at any moment by the multitude of press . . .

'I had to resort to public transport – that is, the last train, which I just caught by the skin of my teeth. The whole of that night journey was spent in a disturbed sense of continual dread – not only the likelihood of a passenger being press, but also being recognised by a member of the public and being exposed to a barrage of abuse and hatred, and possibly injury . . .

'Arriving, unslept in the early, dark and frosty hours of the morning, I had to wander the streets, still enveloped in this tense and suspended state of terror. In this helpless and solitary position, my aged mother – a person more vulnerable than myself – had to serve as my bodyguard.'

At 6.00 a.m., Sonia finally called Kerry Macgill at his hotel but, instead of getting her solicitor, was put through to his brother, Ian, a sub-editor on the Sheffield *Star* and in London for the trial. Ian Macgill arranged to meet her, and that day, and in the days ahead, helped her run the gauntlet of the pressmen eddying around the Old Bailey. He was offered £10,000 for the rights in the article which he was to eventually write for his own paper, and another journalist on *The Star* was offered £5,000 in the street outside the court in return for the secret address where Sonia was staying in London: he was shown the money in banknotes in a briefcase.

Curiously, given the sensational nature of many of the revelations, money was a subject that regularly preoccupied the court in the opening days of Regina versus Sutcliffe.

On 20 February 1981, two and a half months before the trial was due to open, Mrs Doreen Hill, the mother of Jacqueline Hill, Sutcliffe's thirteenth and final victim, had launched a campaign to outlaw chequebook journalism with a press conference at the offices of her solicitor in Middlesbrough. Mrs Hill had been moved to act by a report in the magazine *Private Eye* at the end of January, alleging that the *Daily Mail* appeared 'to be leading in the squalid race to tie up the Sutcliffe family'. A specific sum of £250,000 had been mentioned in connection with Sutcliffe's wife.

Hard on the heels of the press conference, Mrs Hill and her husband had written to persons of influence in industry, the trade unions and Parliament, as well as in other areas of public life, and the campaign had quickly gained momentum: a number of petitions were delivered to the headquarters of the Press Council in London deploring the payment of 'blood money' to the family and friends of Peter Sutcliffe and, indeed, of anybody accused of any crime.

And on Wednesday, 6 May 1981, the second day of the trial, a Commons motion was tabled by Conservative backbenchers calling for legislation which would make chequebook journalism illegal.

It was another development the same day, though, which grabbed the headlines and had immediate repercussions inside Number One Court at the Old Bailey.

Among those canvassed for support by the Hills had been the Queen. And most newspapers on 6 May, and again the following morning, carried on their front pages the text of a letter, dated 26 February 1981, from the Queen's deputy private secretary, Mr William Heseltine, to Mr and Mrs Hill expressing the Queen's 'sense of distaste', if, as reported, substantial sums were being paid to members of the Sutcliffe family for their story.

At 4.36 p.m., when Trevor Birdsall, the second witness for the prosecution, took the stand, he was immediately asked by the Attorney-General, Sir Michael Havers, QC, to state whether he had entered into any agreement with a newspaper 'about your knowledge in the matters concerned with Peter Sutcliffe'; and

Birdsall, trembling perceptibly, the artificial sheen of his toupee unhappily reflecting the overhead lights, admitted that he had. He said that the *Sunday People* had helped pay his bills, had given him £500 and had been paying him £65 a week since the beginning of January. He also said that the *People* were picking up his hotel bill during his stay in London, and that the woman with whom he lived had an exclusive rights contract with the paper worth £2,000.

The next day, Ronnie and David Barker, and then Olivia Reivers, were all required to declare how much they had received for their stories before giving evidence. Ronnie Barker, well scrubbed behind a walrus moustache and, unlike Birdsall, who had had to be provided with a chair in order to complete his evidence, clearly basking in the attention, said he had received £700 from the *Sun* for photographs of Sutcliffe's wedding, and added that he was expecting a further £400 from the *Sunday People* for pictures they had taken of him at the scene of Jayne MacDonald's murder in Chapeltown. His brother, who had been brought to the Old Bailey from the prison where he was serving an eighteen-month sentence for grievous bodily harm, said he had received £20 from ITN and £10 from the BBC. Olivia Reivers said she had already received £1,000 of the £4,000 she was expecting under the terms of her contract with the *Daily Star*.

Sir Michael had made clear his motives for asking these questions by gravely explaining to the jury, none of whom could have been expected to have brushed with this sort of thing, that 'if money has been paid and more is available, it is one of the considerations which might tempt a witness to gild the lily, to make his story worth more money . . . The jury must always be satisfied there was not some ulterior motive such as money which might be persuading someone to tell a story which is much worse or much better because of the cheque at the end of it.'

The Attorney-General, Conservative MP for Merton, Wimbledon, was the son of a High Court judge and the father of the actor Nigel Havers, currently enjoying a West End success in the film *Chariots of Fire*. And in his courtroom demeanour, both elements of the lineage were apparent: although he was quietly authoritative – so quiet, in fact, that halfway through the second week a man in the public gallery would stand up and shout, 'Excuse me, my Lord, I can't hear,' only to be unceremoniously ushered outside for his trouble – Sir Michael gave the distinct impression that, shorn of his robes, he would exhibit the discreet Jermyn Street dandyism characteristic of the upper reaches of the acting profession.

What was faintly astonishing to those who had been in court exactly a week earlier, however, was that Sir Michael should be leading for the Crown against Sutcliffe at all. Shortly before midday on Wednesday, 29 April, Sutcliffe had been brought up into a silent, almost fearful court and, when asked thirteen times how did he plead, had replied thirteen times, occasionally stumbling over the words, 'Not guilty to murder but guilty to manslaughter on the grounds of diminished responsibility.' Then – that is, just seven days earlier – Sir Michael, as most of those in court had been led to expect him to, had indicated that he was prepared to accept the lesser pleas of manslaughter on the grounds of the defendant's paranoid schizophrenia.

He had then proceeded to put his case before the judge, Mr Justice Boreham, who had listened politely for two hours, scratching at a ledger with a fountain pen as the Attorney-General gave a resume of the medical evidence which all pointed, he said, one way: 'that this is a case of diminished responsibility'. The judge had then laid his pen aside and, with the infinite courtesy that would be extended to everybody in Number One Court over the coming weeks, had advised Sir Michael of his 'grave anxiety' about the pleas and his belief that 'it would be more appropriate if this case were dealt with by a jury'.

A ninety-minute adjournment allowed the implications of the decision to sink in. From the conversation drifting out of the many urgently conferring groups in the marble hall outside the Old Bailey's infamous 'show' court, it became clear that, because the facts were not in dispute – Sutcliffe had after all just admitted the manslaughter of thirteen women and the attempted murder of seven others – what a jury was going to be asked to reach a verdict on was his state of mind. Was he 'suffering from such abnormality of mind as substantially impaired his mental responsibility in doing the killings', in the words of the 1957 Homicide Act? Or was he a calculated and premeditated killer?

Before lunch, the Attorney-General had seemed in little doubt that the answer to the latter question was 'no'. When the court reconvened after lunch, however, Sir Michael informed Mr Justice Boreham that the Crown would be prepared to proceed before a jury within forty-eight hours on the thirteen original charges of murder. And, at 11.00 a.m., on Tuesday, 5 May 1981, just six days after arguing the case of the forensic psychiatrists who had examined Sutcliffe and independently but unanimously diagnosed schizophrenia, Sir Michael rose and informed the six men and six women who had just been sworn in as a jury that it was their job to decide whether these same psychiatrists 'might in fact have been deceived, whether (Sutcliffe) sought to pull the wool over their eyes, or whether the doctors are just plain wrong'.

It would be emphasised a number of times in the course of the next three weeks, both by Sir Michael and by the judge, that it was not the psychiatrists who were on trial. Few of those in court, however – least of all the doctors themselves, who had never expected to have their diagnoses submitted to cross-examination – were inclined to believe it.

Monday, 4 May 1981 was a Bank Holiday in England, and several dozen people chose to spend it on the pavement outside the Old Bailey queueing for a ringside seat at the opening of what was being bruited as 'the trial of the century'. A retired butcher and his wife from Harrogate, whose boast was that they had attended all Sutcliffe's appearances in court; a mother and her teenage son from Essex, who told newsmen they were 'going to come every day if we can get in', and a twenty-eight-year-old chef from Shepherd's Bush were among those who camped overnight with stoves and sleeping bags in order to have first claim on the thirty-four seats in the public gallery – a narrow, cramped space wedged in under the ceiling.

They made up what *The Times* the following morning called 'a motley rabble . . . that could have come straight from a Newgate public hanging with only a quick change of costume'. This was in marked contrast to the sweeter-smelling occupants of the VIP benches, directly below them. 'A succession of well-groomed middle-aged women with Harrods carrier bags and winter suntans sat there with their daughters or their best friends from 10.30 in the morning until the curtain fell at 4 [every] afternoon,' the *Guardian* reported.

'There were free seats for the manager of the hotel where the Yorkshire police were staying, for MPs, councillors, sundry lawyers with their children, the Arsenal goalkeeper, Pat Jennings, and for three men who were commended in another court for tackling a bank robber.'

On the opposite side of what was a vaulted and light but surprisingly small room was the box where the jury sat and, running between, deep in the well of the court, was a long oak table on which Sutcliffe's 'killing tackle' was exhibited: seven ballpein hammers, a claw-hammer, a hacksaw, a long, thin-pointed kitchen knife, several carving knives, eight assorted screwdrivers, a wooden-handled cobbler's knife and a short rope, all affixed with neat yellow labels, were watched over by a group of impeccably (in a few cases, elaborately) coiffed detectives from West Yorkshire.

(There would be gasps when, in the course of his long opening address, Sir Michael Havers selected a rusty screwdriver painstakingly sharpened to a point – 'one of the most fiendish weapons you have ever seen', he called it – and passed it into the reluctant hands of the jury.)

The dock and the bench faced each other across the width of the table at a distance of some thirty feet and elevated at unequal heights above it. The judge sat in a towering oak-and-leather chair, the sword of justice in its jewelled scabbard on an oak panel above him, effulgent in scarlet and silk moiré and white linen. The prisoner, wearing the same outfit every day of the trial – pale blue open-necked shirt, dove-grey suit, bright tan high-sided boots of the kind worn by all the farmlads around Bingley – sat on the same wooden seat sat on by Crippen seventy years before, and in the judge's direct line of vision.

The minute he stepped into the dock, the effects of imprisonment were already clear on him. His face, familiar already from the papers, had lost the angularity of the early pictures and was turning fuller and more flaccid; he still had the look of the gypsy about him, but being shut up had robbed his skin of its natural greasiness and pigment: it looked stale and unhealthy, like the sole of a recently unbandaged foot.

The extra weight was also noticeable about his body. Each time he stood up to leave the dock the waistband of his trousers would be twisted and buckled, a result of his newly acquired paunch. He was apparently less conscious of this, though, than of his hair which, presumably in an attempt to disguise its decreasing volume, he had started to brush forward in coarse ripples from the crown.

In his first hours in the dock, however, there was a curious reluctance, even among the eighty or so representatives of the world's press crowded into the court, to scrutinise Sutcliffe at any length. When the clerk of the court rose and called for silence on the first morning and, a few seconds later, Sutcliffe and his five attendant prison officers were heard mounting the stairs from the cells, only the members of the public gallery showed any inclination to gawp. (As word had got around that Sonia was in court, the people in the front row of the gods had started hanging over the balcony in an attempt to catch a glimpse of the small figure in the Alice-band and what the press would call 'granny shoes', sitting quietly with her mother.)

Plucked virtually without warning from their normal lives – and the sense of disorientation was clear on many faces – the members of the jury at first stole only shy glances at the man whom even the Attorney-General referred to as 'the Ripper', as if afraid of engaging his attention. They need not have worried. In the fourteen working days that the trial was to last, Sutcliffe's eyes rarely strayed from a spot several feet above the head of Mr Justice Boreham. Even when pictures of the mutilated bodies of his victims were circulated in court, the defendant maintained the unwavering, dissociative gaze adopted by celebrities in public places and passengers on the London Underground.

The jury were required to examine the blue-bound albums of photographs which Sir Michael Havers assured them they would 'become immune to quite quickly', in the course of his four and a half hour opening peroration.

'The reason for this trial is simple,' Sir Michael had stated within minutes of rising to his feet. 'There is a marked significant difference between the version [of events] which Sutcliffe gave to the police and the version he gave to the doctors. You have to consider whether, as a clever, callous murderer, he deliberately set out to create a cock-and-bull story to avoid conviction for murder.'

The doctors who had examined him, Sir Michael said, were all agreed that Sutcliffe was suffering from the imbalance of the mind known as paranoid schizophrenia. What Sutcliffe had told them, in effect, was that he had had 'messages from God' to kill prostitutes and that what he did was part of 'a divine mission', and the doctors believed him.

'But,' Sir Michael added, 'none of that detail was told to the police at all.' Sutcliffe told the police he had had urges – hallucinations – but of a different kind to the ones he described to the doctors and he didn't even tell the police that straight away. After his arrest, he had made a statement to the police which it had taken the best part of two days to take down. 'But that confession is curious, you may think. It is by no means wholly frank. There were twenty murders and attempted murders. He only spoke in his confession of fourteen.' Sutcliffe, when first arrested, did not in any sense say to the police: 'I have a divine right to do this. I am responding to God's orders.'

'What he did say, he told a whole series of lies as to how he had been caught and why he was in the car with a prostitute and why he had weapons in the car and why he had a rope in his pocket and gave a cock-and-bull story about how he came to be there.'

It may be, Sir Michael told the jury, that the discrepancies between what Sutcliffe told the psychiatrists and what he told the police were going to 'cause the greatest anxieties in this case and that they will be the most relevant facts to the issue of whether the medical evidence should be accepted by you or not'.

He emphasised that, while the Crown intended to demonstrate that Sutcliffe had 'duped' the doctors and was a 'sadistic killer', the burden of proving that he was suffering from diminished responsibility lay with the defence. Unless the defence could satisfy them that Sutcliffe genuinely believed that he had heard the voice of God while working at Bingley cemetery, they must find him guilty of murder on all thirteen counts.

The Attorney-General's opening speech continued late into the afternoon of the second day, when the first prosecution witness was called. Sutcliffe had told the doctors that in his late teens he had been involved in a motorcycle accident in which he suffered a severe blow to the head, implying that this might in some way account for his later actions; and Donald Sumner confirmed that he had been riding pillion behind Sutcliffe on the night the accident happened. 'We had a puncture while we were going along and came off the bike. Peter went into a lamp-post and I went sliding down the road . . . Peter hit his head and was bleeding. There was damage to his crash-helmet. He looked a right clown.' Sutcliffe had since claimed he was 'knocked unconscious for hours' and afterwards became prone to 'hallucination and bouts of morbid depression – my mind was in a haze and I didn't know what was right or wrong. I didn't know whether I was acting rationally or not.' But, Sir Michael had suggested to the jury, 'you may think he was embroidering this story.' (No member of his family has any recollection of the episode or can ever remember Peter injuring his head.)

Sir Michael then went on to question Trevor Birdsall and the Barkers about their late-night tours of the red-light districts in

Peter Sutcliffe's car. Birdsall described the 'rock in the sock' incident in 1969 in Bradford, and the night when Olive Smelt was attacked in Halifax in 1975, but said that his friend had never indicated a hatred of prostitutes to him.

Consulting a pocket diary for 1977, Ronnie Barker told the court about the visit to York with Peter in May of that year and the detour on the way home to take in Chapeltown. He also looked up the entry for Saturday, 25 June 1977, the night the young supermarket worker Jayne MacDonald was murdered in Chapeltown, and said he had gone on a pub-crawl with his brother and Peter around Bradford.

Cross-examined by Mr James Chadwin, QC, for the defence, Barker said that he had never seen anything in Peter Sutcliffe which might suggest he had an aggressive attitude towards women.

'In fact, he was a rather quiet, even shy, man?'

'I would say so, yes.'

The Barkers were followed into the box by Olivia Reivers and, after three days of almost total immobility, Sutcliffe turned and stared at Reivers intently for a few moments as if trying to recollect where he might have seen her before, while she recounted what had taken place on the night of the arrest.

Det. Inspector John Boyle, the police officer to whom Sutcliffe had finally admitted being the Yorkshire Ripper, told the jury that, in the course of giving his sixteen-hour statement, Sutcliffe had commented: 'I would have killed that girl in Sheffield if I hadn't been caught,' and agreed with Mr Chadwin that Sutcliffe had said a number of other things which did not 'show him in a very good light'.

Of the Helen Rytka killing, Sutcliffe had said: 'I had the urge to kill any woman. The urge inside me to kill girls was now practically uncontrollable.' And of the Vera Millward killing in Manchester: 'The urge inside me still dominates my actions. Following Millward the urge inside me remained dormant, but then the feeling came welling up. I had the urge to kill any woman. It sounds a bit evil now. There I was walking along with a big hammer and a big Phillips screwdriver in my pocket ready for the inevitable.' He added: 'I have been taken over completely by this urge to kill and I cannot fight it.'

He had forced Jacqueline Hill's bra over her head to expose her breasts after she was dead so he could stab her more easily, he had said. He had used a screwdriver to stab her through the eye: 'I just put it to her lid and with the handle in my palm I just jerked it in.'

Mr Chadwin asked Boyle whether Sutcliffe had dealt with all the offences he committed in a way which did not 'tone down or soften the enormity of them', but the judge interrupted, saying that that was a matter for the jury to decide, not Mr Boyle.

The final witnesses for the prosecution were a number of prison officers from the hospital wing at Armley, where Sutcliffe had been held on remand. The first of them, a Mr Leach, was handed the hospital logbook and asked to look at a particular reference dated 8 January 1981. Sir Michael asked him: 'Do you remember anything of significance that Sutcliffe said to his wife (while she was visiting him) that day?'

To which Leach replied: 'What I have written down here, yes, sir . . . They were left for a short while together. Mr Macgill wasn't there. Mrs Sutcliffe used to run the visits, in as much as she used to take the lead very much. She brought pieces of paper with itemised things on them . . . I think personal matters between Sutcliffe and his wife. Sutcliffe said at one stage. "I wouldn't feel any animosity towards you if you started a life of your own. I'm going to do a long time in prison, thirty years or more, unless I can convince people in here I'm mad and maybe then ten years in the loony bin."'

A second prison officer from Armley, a Mr Fitzpatrick, told the court that on the evening of 5 April 1981 he had noted in the log that Sutcliffe seemed 'unusually cocky'. He later discovered that this was because Sutcliffe claimed an agreement had been reached between the defence and the prosecution for a plea of diminished responsibility to be accepted, and a bed had been reserved for him, he said, at Park Lane Special Hospital in Liverpool. He also said a psychiatrist had told him he would have to do no more than ten years 'to satisfy the public'.

Mr Fitzpatrick refuted the defence's suggestion that, when Sutcliffe talked about 'an agreement', what he had actually meant was that the doctors all agreed on their diagnosis. (Sir Michael Havers, at a later stage of the trial, would deny absolutely that any agreement had been reached regarding Sutcliffe's plea.)

A third, and final, prison officer from West Yorkshire described how, on 14 April 1981, just after Leeds Crown Court had moved the trial to the Old Bailey, he had found Sutcliffe 'cheerful and bright'.

'He told me that he was going to the Old Bailey for trial and he was very pleased with that news. He was saying to me that the doctors considered him disturbed and he was quite amazed by this and was smiling broadly and leaning back in his chair. He said to me: "I'm as normal as anyone."'

The Attorney-General said that that completed the case for the prosecution, and the judge announced an adjournment until after the weekend.

At the weekend, 'a firebug' caused an estimated £1,000-worth of damage at the house the Sutcliffes had shared at Garden Lane and extra police were drafted in to keep 'sightseers and ghouls' away. Neighbours were quoted in the popular Sunday papers saying that 'Sick people have turned the Sutcliffe home into a terrible shrine.'

On Monday, and every day for the remainder of the trial, a group of women representing the English Collective of Prostitutes joined the general pandemonium in Newgate Street outside the Old Bailey: they carried placards which, among other things, accused the Attorney-General of 'condoning the murder of prostitutes' by drawing a distinction between prostitutes and 'respectable women' when cataloguing the Yorkshire Ripper's crimes.

Meanwhile, inside the court that morning, speculation was rife following Mr James Chadwin's request for an adjournment 'to take more detailed instructions', just seventeen minutes into Day Five. On the press benches this was taken as a signal that Sonia was about to give evidence. But when the hearing resumed fifty minutes later, it was Sutcliffe himself who was called in his own defence.

The sense of apprehension which had characterised the first couple of days had gradually given way to an atmosphere in which the media contingent at least felt free to swap wisecracks under their breath and move around at will. All movement ceased, however, on the morning of 11 May, the second it became clear what was about to take place. Accompanied by two men in petrol-coloured uniforms, the Ripper left the dock with its enclosing, antique, sanitising glass screen, and passed between the jury and the exhibits table to the canopied witness box in the far left-hand corner to be sworn in.

Although in reality this took only seconds to complete, it seemed to be in progress for a long time; and, although it was the most pedestrian of events – a man taking two dozen paces across a room – it seemed far and away the most dramatic thing that had occurred. Even those who felt that they had long ago reconciled themselves to the fact that the Ripper was manifestly a man like other men felt hairs rising involuntarily on their necks.

His voice, as he took the oath, came out as a piping treble which could easily be imagined abstracting itself into the familiar high-pitched giggle that would be one of the things by which his family would choose to remember him. And his face, even when discussing the most sordid details of his crimes, seemed to constantly flirt with the idea of a smile.

In profile, which is how most of those in the lay areas of the court had been seeing him, he had looked stooped and stale and bovine. Now, head-on and liberated from the dock, he could have been merely a near relative of that other self. His eyes, unfastened from the spot where they had rested for the whole of the first week, flashed inquisitively around the room, returning repeatedly to the space occupied by his own empty chair. The small deceit by which his hair seemed to retain its youthful

306

height and body was not apparent from in front, and below it was a face transformed by its own liveliness into something pleasant, unalarming, almost personable.

Led by Mr Chadwin, Sutcliffe spent the rest of that day and much of the next telling the court about his 'divine mission' and how the failure of the police to catch him, even after interviewing him many times, seemed to him confirmation that he had been chosen as the instrument of God's will. 'It was a miracle that they didn't apprehend me earlier. They had all the facts. They knew it was me. They had all the facts for a long time, but then I knew why they didn't catch me. Everything was in God's hands. The way I escaped, the way they went away satisfied. There was no chance of them getting me.' He said he thought the episode of the hoax letters and tape recording was 'an indirect line to God'. He thought it had been a diversion 'so that I could be left to carry on'.

'What was it,' Mr Chadwin began by gently prompting him, 'that happened at Bingley cemetery that you particularly remember?'

To which Sutcliffe enthusiastically replied: 'Something that I felt was very wonderful at the time. I heard what I believed then and believe now to have been God's voice.' He said that he had been digging a grave in the Catholic section at the top of the cemetery. 'I was digging and I just paused for a minute. I just heard something – it sounded like a voice similar to a human voice – like an echo. I looked round to see if there was anyone there, but there was no one in sight . . .

'Then I got out of the grave and walked – the ground rose up. It was quite a steep slope. I walked to the top but there was no one there at all. I heard again the same sound. It was like a voice saying something, but the words were all imposed on top of each other. I could not make them out; it was like echoes . . . coming directly in front of me from the top of the gravestone, which was Polish. I remember the name on the grave to this day. It was a man called Zapolski.'

Shown a photograph of Bingley cemetery, Sutcliffe indicated

the crucifix-shaped headstone from which he claimed the voices emanated, then continued: 'It had a terrific impact on me. It was starting to rain. I remember going to the top of a slope overlooking the valley and I felt as though I had just experienced something fantastic. I looked across the valley and all around and thought of heaven and earth and how insignificant we all were. But I felt so important at that moment . . . I felt I had been selected.'

He said this had happened in 1967, when he was about twenty, and that, although he heard the voice 'hundreds' of times over the coming years, he mentioned it to nobody.

Sutcliffe explained how, in 1969, his brother Mick had told him that Sonia, who at that time he had been courting steadily for more than two years, had been seen in the company of an Italian. This information, which Sonia didn't deny when he confronted her with it, had stunned him: 'I was so depressed, in fact, that this led to my first encounter with a prostitute.'

He recounted his experiences with the 'coarse and vulgar person' who, first, tricked him out of the change she owed him and then made a laughing-stock of him when he approached her in a pub two or three weeks later and asked for his money back. The voice, which had previously been benign and 'reassuring', now started instructing him on his mission: 'This is what I believed was the voice of God saying it was prostitutes who were responsible for all these problems . . . It kept saying I had got to go on with a mission and it had a purpose. It was to remove the prostitutes. To get rid of them.'

Soon afterwards, he attacked a prostitute with a piece of brick in a sock in the Manningham area of Bradford, and was cautioned by the police about it. About a month later (in October 1969) he was arrested and later found guilty of 'going equipped for theft' but admitted that the real reason for carrying a hammer that night was because he intended to kill a prostitute with it.

Asked by his counsel what he felt about the fact that the woman whom he hit with the sock had not pressed charges, Sutcliffe said he felt it meant he 'was not meant to be caught or punished'.

There had been no further attacks on women for six years,

until 1975, when, in the space of a few weeks in the summer, he had tried to murder both Olive Smelt and Anna Rogulskyj. Of the Smelt attack, Sutcliffe said that, earlier that night, he had felt very strongly that he must kill a prostitute. He had hoped that the feelings would subside, but they didn't. 'Consequently I did it with Trevor still in the car. I knew that was my mission. I heard voices – echoes. Sometimes it was the voice, sometimes an echo, sometimes it was very clear, sometimes not.'

Two and a half months later he killed the first of the thirteen women. 'Before doing it,' Sutcliffe said, 'I had to go through a terrible stage each time. I was in absolute turmoil. I was doing everything I could to fight it off, and asked why it should be me, until I eventually reached the stage where it was as if I was primed to do it.'

Mr Chadwin asked if he ever tried to resist what he had been told to do and Sutcliffe said yes, he had, once: 'I was on my way to the Leeds red-light area. I got halfway there and I was still in a turmoil. I do not think I was quite in that state where I could possibly do it. I was arguing all the time. I was not always getting answers, and there was a lot I did not understand. I finally stopped the car and turned it round. I was shouting in the car. I set off back, and was changing up and down the gearbox. Eventually I got back home, locked the car in the garage, and went to bed. I felt a great sense of achievement at that stage.'

Mr Chadwin reminded Sutcliffe that, at first, he had only admitted twelve killings and two attempted killings to the police. Was this because he thought he would be making things worse for himself by admitting all twenty attacks?

– 'No, not at all.'

'One thing you don't mention is the incident in Bingley cemetery. Why not?'

– 'I didn't want [the police] to find out about the mission. I was by no means convinced it was finished . . . God was in control of the situation and anything was possible. I didn't want them to have the faintest idea about the mission . . . I just thought it was wiser to steer clear of the place altogether.'

Mr Chadwin then asked Sutcliffe whether he had had it in mind at any time to pretend that he was mad, and Sutcliffe said he had not.

'Do you think you are mad?' – 'No.'

'Do you think there is anything wrong with you mentally?' – 'Nothing serious at all, no.'

'Do you think you will spend less time in custody if people think there is something wrong with you mentally?' – 'No. There would be something wrong with me mentally if I thought that.'

This last was the sort of exchange that, as Mr Chadwin, a school-masterly, bespectacled figure, sat and Sir Michael rose, was – astonishingly – to be characteristic of the Attorney-General's cross-examination. Being matched against one of the pillars of the British legal establishment might have been expected to faze Sutcliffe; on the contrary, it put him on his not inconsiderable mettle – which, attempting as he was to demonstrate that the accused was no stranger to creative extemporisation and 'devious cunning', may have been part of the Attorney-General's purpose. 'I do not claim to be stupid,' Sutcliffe was stung by him to declare at one point; and later in the week one of the doctors would confirm that, although 'not a genius', he was, with an IQ of between 108 and 110, 20 to 25 intelligence points above the average.

In order to demonstrate Sutcliffe's impressive ability for thinking on his feet, Sir Michael's first questions concentrated on the night of the arrest. Sutcliffe agreed that he had picked up Olivia Reivers in Sheffield on 2 January intending to kill her, and that he had suggested to Miss Reivers that she run away from his car when the police suddenly turned up. He also agreed that it was his instinct to protect himself that led him to say that he had gone behind an oil tank to urinate, when in fact he was hiding his weapons, and to conceal a knife in the cistern at the police station upon arrival.

SIR MICHAEL: 'Then, for a considerable time you lied, and lied, and lied again?' – 'Yes.'

'All to protect yourself?' – 'The mission . . .'

'All to protect Peter Sutcliffe?' – 'Yes.'

'Then, when found out, you decided to tell the truth, like any other criminal?'

– 'Like any criminal – not any other.'

Sir Michael next turned to the events in Bingley cemetery and made no attempt to disguise the tone of heavy irony which cloaked his every statement. He expressed curiosity as to why Sutcliffe had kept the 'mission' a secret until his eighth interview with one of the psychiatrists in Armley at the beginning of March. Why was it, for example, that, during the otherwise exhaustive police 'confessions', he had never mentioned a word?

'Because I was waiting for a direct message saying that it was over, to fully convince me that the mission was terminated,' Sutcliffe said.

– 'What you are saying is that you had to have a "mission finished" or "mission terminated" signal? Did you ever get that?' Sutcliffe said he hadn't.

'Do you mean *never*? You still haven't had it?' Mr Justice Boreham enquired over the rims of his spectacles, and Sutcliffe shook his head, no.

SIR MICHAEL: 'To this day, you believe you are an agent for God in a mission only partially fulfilled?'

SUTCLIFFE: 'That's right.'

The Attorney-General then reminded him about the first time he had heard 'the voices' and how he had described being 'transfixed' and had felt he had been chosen to hear the words of God.

Answering questions from Sir Michael, Sutcliffe acknowledged that Sonia was his girlfriend at the time of the graveyard 'revelation' and that he 'loved and trusted' her; that his mother was then still alive and that he was 'devoted to' her; that, as a lapsed Catholic, he had no priest to turn to but that he did have a best friend, Eric Robinson.

'This is the most stunning thing in your life and you did not tell Sonia?'

'No.'

'You didn't tell your devoted mother?' – 'No.'

'You didn't tell anyone until years and years had gone by and then you told them on the eighth interview in Armley jail? . . . What was so secret about this marvellous message?'

SUTCLIFFE: 'The first two years were the best. There were no signs of the purpose or why I had been chosen to be here. None whatsoever.'

SIR MICHAEL: 'Then there was nothing to be ashamed of in telling Sonia, your mother, your priest or anyone?'

He wanted to know what the words of the message were, and Sutcliffe said he hadn't heard them. But Sir Michael was intent on an answer: 'The first time the line was clear,' he asked critically, 'what was said?'

– 'That I should have faith and that I should believe and that there was no need to be so depressed.'

'Should that not have encouraged you to go back to the Catholic faith?' Sir Michael now wanted to know.

– 'No, because I had been chosen when I was out of the faith.'

'But you have gone back now?'

– 'Yes.'

'So for all these years this miracle – and to you it must have been a miracle – was kept entirely to yourself?'

– 'Yes.'

Sir Michael asked when it first occurred to Sutcliffe that the God he was in touch with was a very evil God, quite contrary to the sort of miracles he had surely been told about as a boy in the Roman Catholic Church. Sutcliffe's reply was that, to him, it seemed similar to the contradiction between the Old Testament and the New.

There was what the newspapers next day would call 'a terse exchange' when Sir Michael suggested that 'God had jumped on the bandwagon' only after Sutcliffe had *already* developed a hatred for prostitutes. He had told the court, had he not, how he hated prostitutes after he was taunted by the first one he had dealings with, following his row with Sonia?

'You came out frustrated and tormented . . . Humiliated, outraged and embarrassed? . . . You felt a hatred for her and her kind. That is a fact.'

– 'Yes.'

'So, God jumped on the bandwagon after that, and says, "You have a divine mission, young Peter, to stalk prostitutes and avenge me by killing them"?'

– 'It is a very colourful speech, sir,' – Sutcliffe tried, but ultimately failed, to dampen a smile – 'but it does not apply.'

After lunch on what was Sutcliffe's second full day of testimony, Mr Justice Boreham reiterated for the benefit of the jury, and at the jury's own request, the definition of the particular defence in the case. 'What has to be established,' the judge told them, 'is, first, that at the material times – that is, at the times he killed – the defendant was suffering from abnormality of the mind. Secondly, that that abnormality was caused or induced by inherent causes or disease, mental disorder or illness; and, thirdly, that that abnormality was of such proportions as substantially diminished his mental responsibility for what he did – for the killings.'

In other words, looked at another way, if it could be shown that Peter Sutcliffe killed any woman knowing that she was not a prostitute, or that he derived sexual pleasure from any of the thirteen killings with which he was charged, then 'the divine mission' and, with it, the defence of diminished responsibility due to an 'abnormality of the mind' – in this case, paranoid schizophrenia – effectively crumbled.

These were to be the twin prongs of the prosecution's all-out assault on the doctors. But it became plain that the Attorney-General planned to rehearse the arguments in his cross-examination of their patient in the course of the afternoon. Sir Michael put it bluntly to Sutcliffe that, having decided to 'pull the wool over the doctors' eyes' by persuading them that he was mentally ill and that his whole thing was a mission, the mission collapsed if he had to admit to the doctors that five or six of the murdered women were not prostitutes.

'Is that why you had to maintain through thick and thin, in the face of the clearest evidence, that these six women were prostitutes?'

'No,' Sutcliffe retorted, 'I knew when I did it that each one was.'

'Your story would have gone straight down the drain if you had to say to the doctors that six of them were not prostitutes?'

– 'It is not a story.'

'But the mission requires them to be prostitutes?'

– 'It didn't require them to be, they were.'

Sir Michael referred Sutcliffe to the killing of Josephine Whitaker and read from his statement to the police the phrase: 'I realised she was not a prostitute.' He asked Sutcliffe why he had told the police that.

He said it was because he 'couldn't divulge anything else'. He had believed that she was not a prostitute until he received a message. The message was that she was a prostitute and not to believe her (when she said she was on her way home from visiting her grandparents). She was very clever.

Sir Michael recalled what Sutcliffe had said to Miss Whitaker shortly before killing her: 'You can't trust anyone these days.' 'Can you think,' he asked, addressing his question to the jury as much as to the man in the box, 'of a more horrible and cynical thing to say to someone you were just about to murder?' He asked Sutcliffe why he had said it, and then supplied the answer himself. 'You were trying to convince her she was safe with you?'

– 'Yes, in a sense.'

Sutcliffe agreed that what he told the police about the attack on Miss Whitaker was a confession of 'a cold-blooded, calculated, sadistic murderer'. He also agreed that he had feigned poor sight and asked her to look at the time on a clock to get her to stop.

'Was this a sort of macabre play-acting while you got her jock-eyed into the right position?' Sutcliffe conceded it was.

'Did God tell you to tell that poor girl to look at the church clock?' Sutcliffe said He did.

He admitted removing his victims' clothes after they were unconscious, but only so that they 'would not hinder' him when he stabbed them, and 'to show them for what they were'. There was nothing at all sexual in his actions.

When it was put to him that he had stabbed his victims 'in areas of sexual attraction in order to get sexual gratification', he denied it. Asked why he had placed a piece of wood against Emily Jackson's vagina, he said that he was 'just pushing her out of sight with it. I pushed her with it because I could not bear to touch her again.'

But he had had sex with Helen Rytka. 'Surprise, surprise,' Sir Michael taunted him. 'Pretty little Helen Rytka. You went and had sex with her. Why?'

'I didn't have sex,' Sutcliffe replied. 'I entered her, but there was no action. It was to persuade her that everything would be all right.'

He was asked if he had any regrets about putting a screwdriver through Jacqueline Hill's 'accusing' right eye, and hesitated before giving his answer for an unusually long time. 'It's difficult for you, isn't it?' Sir Michael asked him, and Sutcliffe agreed that it was. 'Because you're not sure what is the right answer to give to the jury and the doctors.'

It was Sutcliffe's turn to be sardonic this time: 'You're much quicker than I am, sir,' he said.

Returned to the dock, he returned, upon contact with his firmly bolted seat, to his former, entirely impassive self, and sat out the rest of the trial like a seaside cabinet doll that has known better days.

'The poor psychiatrists,' Ferdinand Mount was to write two weeks later in the *Spectator*. 'The whole court is well aware that it is they who are on trial. The policemen sitting in the dock around the defendant exchange smiles every time a shrink is made a fool of; after lunch, two of the policemen nod off.'

In the final words of his cross-examination – 'The mission was the floater and the bait on the end of the hook was God's message, and [the doctors] fell for it hook, line and sinker' – Sir Michael Havers had prepared the stage for what, in retrospect,

315

would be regarded as the most ruthless – and, in the opinion of many, the most damaging – examination psychiatry had been given in any British court.

Three of the four forensic psychiatrists who had interviewed Sutcliffe in prison would be called in his defence. And Sonia was in court for the first time in six days to hear Dr Hugo Milne of Bradford immediately speak for all of them when he declared that he did not believe the accused was simulating mental illness but was suffering from 'schizophrenia of the paranoid type'.

Answering questions from Mr Chadwin, Dr Milne said he had interviewed Sutcliffe on eleven occasions at Armley jail and had 'always been very much on my guard' about attempts by the defendant to persuade him that he was mentally ill: 'There was no evidence whatever to say he was simulating. I had been looking for this all the time, and I cannot accept that, in the sequence his symptoms were made known to me, that he could have been simulating.'

(Later, answering questions put to him by the prosecution, Dr Milne would say that, from twenty-nine years' experience, he would have expected anyone trying to simulate schizophrenia to show outward symptoms, such as jumbled speech, irrational behaviour, excessive moving and running about, and frequent dressing and undressing. During her illness in 1972, Sutcliffe's wife, Sonia, had been at times violent, aggressive, restless and would often dress and undress at inappropriate times. Sutcliffe had shown none of these signs, despite the fact that he had probably seen them in his wife.)

Dr Milne told Mr Chadwin that he believed Sutcliffe had been a paranoid schizophrenic since the age of nineteen or twenty – from the time of what he referred to as 'the primary experience' in Bingley cemetery. Hearing voices was the 'classic' symptom of the many symptoms of schizophrenia that Dr Milne enumerated for the court.

The cross-examination of the expert witness was conducted by Mr Harry Ognall, the small but pugnacious Yorkshire-based QC on the Attorney-General's team. Cross-examining Sutcliffe two days earlier, Sir Michael had touched on Sonia's 'breakdown' in

316

the early 1970s. Mr Ognall now pressed Dr Milne for the symptoms of Sonia's illness.

After consulting the judge on the ethics of the matter, Dr Milne said that Sonia had suffered from schizophrenia and had complained of 'hearing voices talking to her'.

MR OGNALL: 'Sonia is described as having grandiose ideas. That is what this man has set out to display to you. This man has spoken of being in communication with the Almighty and Jesus, hasn't he? . . . Sonia had the delusion that she was the second Christ, didn't she?'

Dr Milne agreed that she had and that it was just possible that he could have been 'duped' by Sutcliffe into thinking he was a paranoid schizophrenic.

MR OGNALL: 'Prison officers have told us that six days before you first saw Sutcliffe, he had said: "I'm going to do a long time in prison, thirty years or more, unless I can convince people here that I'm mad. Then I'll do ten years in the loony bin." What are we to make of that, Dr Milne, in the context of your evidence?'

– 'I think it is a very straightforward decision to make. Is this man pretending to be mad and has duped me and my colleagues? Or am I, from my clinical experience and clinical examination, right in saying that he is a paranoid schizophrenic? As far as I can see in this particular case, either he is a competent actor or I'm an inefficient psychiatrist.'

– 'It is possible that he was very much on the alert as to what you and other doctors wanted to hear?'

– 'If he knew the symptoms and signs of schizophrenia and he was as cool and calculated as he might have been, then it is possible.'

'"Morbid depression",' Mr Ognall said. 'That's a very learned phrase for a lorry-driver? And "pathological hatred". That's a rum phrase for a lorry-driver to use?'

– 'He is an intelligent lorry-driver.'

– 'Yes he is.'

– 'And articulate.'

– 'Yes.'

– 'And astute.'

– 'He *is!*'

Mr Ognall then turned to the timing of the twenty attacks. Exactly half of them had taken place on Friday or Saturday nights when Sutcliffe's wife was working at a nursing home. 'This is a man,' he told Dr Milne, 'who is prompted by God, the hapless and hopeless victim of God's will. This is a man who believed he was God's instrument. Why did God only direct him on Friday and Saturday nights?'

Dr Milne said he didn't think God had; that paranoid schizophrenics are 'extraordinarily cunning, extremely involved in premeditation and determined not to be found'. Mr Ognall put it to him that that wasn't the hallmark of the schizophrenic so much as of the normal criminal – 'the badge of a premeditated killer'. The doctor said he didn't agree.

Dr Milne did accept, however, that the fact that Sutcliffe had neglected to tell him about his arrest in a red-light district in 1969, when he had been equipped with a hammer, showed that he did tell lies.

Mr Ognall went further. Sutcliffe was a selective liar to suit his own purpose. He had told deliberate lies to police and doctors and had said that his first attack was on Wilma McCann when, in fact, he had attacked four times before then. The central weakness of Dr Milne's diagnosis was that it was based almost exclusively on what the defendant himself had told him, and the doctor now admitted that he could have told him lies.

Dr Milne could only stress once again that he didn't feel that he had been 'wilfully misled'.

'You take the view,' Mr Ognall now put it to him, 'that, so far as this man is concerned, there is no underlying sexual component in his attacks?' (In a detailed report, read to the court by Mr Ognall at the beginning of the trial, Dr Milne had said Sutcliffe consistently denied that the killings and attempted killings had given him sexual excitement at the time or that afterwards he had used the incidents to 'help in the sexual situation' at home. Dr Milne had also stated that there was no suggestion that Sutcliffe's habit of stabbing his victims through the same hole on repeated occasions 'had a specific sexual symbolism'.) Mr Ognall now asked him what he meant when he talked about there being no sexual component?

Turning to the judge, Dr Milne replied: 'In simple terms, although his victims were female and it might be thought to provide the suggestion that he must be a sexual killer, I am of the opinion that he is not primarily a sexual killer.'

Mr Ognall suggested that, if Sutcliffe was disposed to mutilate his victims or show any unhealthy interest in their sexual parts, that would be a minus against Dr Milne's diagnosis. If there was a sexual component, that tended to go against the 'divine mission' argument? Dr Milne agreed.

Mr Ognall held up a seven-inch sharpened screwdriver which had been used to attack Josephine Whitaker. 'There is absolutely no doubt that this wicked agent was introduced deep into the vagina with almost no injury to the external parts. That indicates the most fiendish cruelty deliberately done for sexual satisfaction. Do you agree?'

DR MILNE: 'It may be a most vicious and foul thing to do, but not necessarily for sexual satisfaction. Mutilation of the genitalia for sadistic satisfaction would have to be repetitive, and there is no evidence, as far as I know, that this man has attacked any of the other victims in this way. There is no other evidence that he has in any way despoiled them or carried out any unnatural acts with them during the killings.'

Dr Milne, in his report, had said he believed that the injury to the lower part of Josephine Whitaker's body was accidental, but the judge asked him whether, if Mr Ognall was right, the observations made in the report would still stand. Dr Milne said that it would seem not to be as accurate as it should be and he would withdraw the observation that it was accidental.

Mr Ognall asked what else the screwdriver attack could be but sexual.

DR MILNE: 'It may well have been sexual.'

MR OGNALL: 'What else could it have been? I will have an answer.'

DR MILNE: 'I don't think it could have been anything else other than sexual.'

Mr Ognall commented that it was not the only example, although by far the most horrendous, of a sexual component. He asked Dr Milne whether Sutcliffe had told him that this injury had been an accident. Dr Milne said he had not.

'Did Peter Sutcliffe tell you there was no sexual element in the attacks?'

– 'Yes.'

– 'Well, that doesn't seem to be right, does it?'

– 'No.'

– 'He deceived you. Why did he do that?'

– 'Perhaps he might have been very reluctant to talk about this because of what people might think of him.'

– 'He had admitted thirteen killings and seven attempted killings. But he thought he might be worse thought of because he stabbed one of them in the vagina? Is that a considered reply?'

– 'It is a considered reply. He has said he never ever wanted to be seen as a sexual killer.'

– 'I expect he has never wanted to be seen as a sexual killer because, if he puts himself forward as a sexual killer, the divine mission goes out of the window. That's why, isn't it?'

– 'It could be.'

– '*Could* be!'

Dr Milne, a small, neat man with heavy lips and the vestige of an Edinburgh accent, looked momentarily as if he thought he was going to be allowed to stand down. But that was to underestimate the stamina of Mr Ognall, whose finely orchestrated attack was just moving towards its crescendo.

'If you were to find a number of instances of sexual molestation,' he said, 'the more instances you find, the more it would erode the validity of the diagnosis?' And Dr Milne agreed with a heavy heart that, yes, it would lead to an erosion.

Mr Ognall reminded the jury of how Sutcliffe had stabbed Jacqueline Hill through the breast and told police that he did it because 'It's just something that comes over me.' 'Unless I'm very naive,' Mr Ognall said, 'that betrays a specific, clear sexual element in his killing.'

DR MILNE: 'If you interpret it in that way, it does suggest that there may be a possible sexual component.'

Mr Ognall again asked him if he thought there was no suggestion that Sutcliffe had specific sexual reasons for the killings. Dr Milne again repeated that he still did not think that Sutcliffe was a sexual sadist.

Mr Ognall asked the jury to recall how Sutcliffe had attacked Olive Smelt and then scratched her buttocks with a hacksaw blade. He asked Dr Milne what he made of that, and Dr Milne replied: 'I don't make very much of it, apart from the fact he thought she was a prostitute and I don't see any particular sexual significance, certainly not as a sexual sadist.'

Mr Ognall said that when Sutcliffe killed Emily Jackson he had pushed a two-foot to three-foot piece of wood against her vagina.

DR MILNE: 'If in fact you believe what he said, then it obviously could imply a sexual component.'

Mr Ognall described the killing of Helen Rytka, whom Sutcliffe had hit with a hammer. When she was near to death he had had sex with her, but complained that she 'just lay there limp and didn't put much into it'. 'Could you think of anything more obscenely abnormal than his behaviour with that unfortunate girl?'

– 'I entirely agree with you, but I still think that this was a use of sexual behaviour for entirely the wrong reason – to avoid detection, quieten her and get away.'

MR OGNALL: 'I don't suppose he could have just put his hand over her mouth?'

Dr Milne said he thought Sutcliffe had had intercourse with Helen Rytka because it was 'what the girl expected'. At which point a politely incredulous Mr Justice Boreham interrupted to enquire: 'At that stage did she *really* expect it, doctor?'

Dr Milne conceded that he didn't know whether she did or not.

Mr Ognall said the killing of Marguerite Walls also had a sexual component because Sutcliffe had left fingernail scratches at the entrance to her vagina. He asked Dr Milne if he agreed there was an underlying sexual component in that case, to which, with resignation creeping in, he replied: 'You may possibly be right.'

MR OGNALL: 'I put it to you that the injuries to these women betray quite clear sexual components in the attacks. Do you agree?'

DR MILNE: 'Yes.'

Mr Ognall told the jury: 'This isn't a missionary of God, it is a man who gets a sexual pleasure out of killing these women.'

DR MILNE: 'I don't accept that.'

MR OGNALL: 'It is not God telling the tortured soul, "You must kill." It is a man who craves for it like an addict for the next shot of heroin. What he is saying is: "I am hooked on it."'

Mr Ognall suggested that the 'mission to kill' was central to the diagnosis, and the doctor agreed. Dr Milne also conceded that, if the divine mission did not stand up in the eyes of the jury, then his diagnosis lay 'very simply, nowhere'.

MR OGNALL: 'If the jury were to decide that Sutcliffe knew full well that the last six women he attacked were not prostitutes, then the divine mission to kill prostitutes as a theory lies in smithereens?'

DR MILNE: 'I agree. If he knew they weren't prostitutes, and killed them knowing they were not, then the diagnosis fails.'

MR OGNALL: 'He then becomes a murderer.'

DR MILNE: 'Yes.'

Mr Ognall then reminded the jury of three comments Sutcliffe made to the police about the attacks. After the Millward killing he had said that 'there was a compulsion inside me. Sometimes it would lie dormant but eventually it would come welling up, and each time they were more random and indiscriminate. I now realise I had the urge to kill any woman.'

He had also said that before he killed Josephine Whitaker he had driven round aimlessly: 'The mood was in me and no woman was safe.' He later said: 'I realised she wasn't a prostitute but at that time I wasn't bothered, I just wanted to kill a woman.'

Mr Ognall pointed out that Sutcliffe had completely changed his method of operation, and, on the last six occasions, instead of going into red-light areas and luring prostitutes into his car, had driven to an isolated spot, parked and attacked innocent women. 'I suggest that the circumstances of these last six killings show this man, with compelling clarity, to be a liar and a fake.'

Dr Milne, nearing the end of his fourth day on the stand, said he did not agree.

A few hours before the trial was adjourned for the second weekend, the second medical witness, Dr Malcolm MacCulloch, medical director of Park Lane Special Hospital in Liverpool, was sworn in.

A quietly spoken, moonfaced man, Dr MacCulloch sent many correspondents hurrying to the telephone when he told the court that he had interviewed Sutcliffe in Armley on three occasions and had concluded after only half an hour that he was suffering from paranoid schizophrenia. (An example of 'overcompetence' the judge would call it in his summing-up.) Dr MacCulloch then added – a touch defiantly – that nothing he had heard in court had caused him to change his mind. On the contrary, in the past week he had seen certain signs which were consistent with schizophrenia.

One was Sutcliffe's persistent and repeated looking up, on about thirty-eight occasions, to the same spot – a light cluster about ten feet above the judge's head. He had also seen how Sutcliffe showed an abnormal lack of emotion, especially during heated exchanges about the weapons he used and the wounds inflicted by them.

Prompted by Mr Chadwin, Dr MacCulloch said there were eight 'first rank signs' which aided diagnosis. If a patient had just one of these, it would be fair to say he would be diagnosed as a paranoid schizophrenic. Sutcliffe had four. These included:

(i) Bodily hallucinations, which involved a sensation of being touched, or an electrical sensation, or feelings deep in the chest or abdomen. (Sutcliffe had talked of a hand gripping his heart.)

(ii) Influence of thought. Sutcliffe believed his thoughts were being influenced or tampered with, or that he could read the thoughts of others. (Exemplified best in the case of Josephine Whitaker.)

(iii) Delusional perception. He had read in a newspaper that a priest had said Manchester was a wicked place and had interpreted this as a message from God to go to Manchester and kill a prostitute. 'Prostitutes should be exterminated,' Sutcliffe had said. 'They corrupt men. It affects their lives. The mission is from God. I have read something in the Bible which confirms these women should be shown up.'

(iv) The final symptom was passivity, where a patient believes his actions are being controlled by others.

Dr MacCulloch said that he regarded Sutcliffe as 'an extremely dangerous man', and the best that a hospital could hope to do was turn him into simply a 'dangerous' one.

Cross-examining him for the prosecution, Mr Ognall drew from Dr MacCulloch the admission that the first time he had considered the Crown's case against Peter Sutcliffe had been the day before Sutcliffe was due to stand trial. Mr Ognall affected outrage that the doctor had offered a diagnosis without availing himself of the details of what the defendant was alleged to have done. Dr MacCulloch said that he had examined the defendant's mental state and 'taken a history', but the judge interrupted to enquire whether there are not 'truly occasions when that homely old phrase applies, that a man's acts speak louder than his words?'

Dr MacCulloch said that he was sure there were, and the judge said well, he thought that was what Mr Ognall was getting at.

When the court reconvened after the weekend, at the beginning of its tenth working day, Dr MacCulloch was again in the box, and Mr Ognall was again performing like a terrier.

'Your diagnosis stands or falls by what this man has told you,' he barked. 'That is the beginning and the end of it.'

The doctor replied: 'I don't think it's the beginning and the end, but it is substantial.'

The final witness for the defence, and the final witness before both sides began their summings-up, was Dr Terence Kay, a tall, kindly-looking man who had originally been engaged to examine Sutcliffe by the Crown.

Like his colleagues, Dr Kay maintained, while being questioned by Mr Chadwin, that his faith in his original diagnosis of Peter Sutcliffe was unshaken. He believed that Sutcliffe thought he had heard the voice of God in Bingley cemetery and that he was suffering from paranoid schizophrenia.

Dr Kay said that at times Sutcliffe's manner did not match the seriousness of what he was talking about. 'At times he smiled, almost giggled, when we were discussing very serious things. Sometimes he treated it almost as a joke and laughed.'

He said that he had asked Sutcliffe what brought on his depressions and was told: 'Quarrels with wife, worries, problems losing licence. Two or three occasions packed my cases. Wife has had a nervous breakdown. Hell to pay if I enter house with boots on.' (In his report, Dr Milne said he had interviewed Sonia three times at the beginning of the year and found her temperamental and difficult: 'She admitted that she teased and provoked her husband . . . He told me that she was over-excited, highly-strung, unstable and obsessed by cleanliness.')

Dr Kay said he asked Sutcliffe if his wife was worried about excessive cleanliness regarding sex. It would have told him a lot about his wife if she had insisted on him taking baths before sex, Dr Kay explained, but Sutcliffe had told him that she didn't, though she did use towels on the bed when she had just put clean sheets on.

Mr Chadwin asked if, given what the doctors knew of Mrs Sutcliffe's own illness, there was anything Dr Kay might have expected Sutcliffe to do if he was attempting, as the prosecution had suggested he was, a copycat version. 'Yes,' Dr Kay replied. 'She had shown terror, aggression, dismay, a fatuous smile, things that could be seen on her face.'

If Sutcliffe wasn't schizophrenic, Mr Chadwin wanted to know, what was he? 'If he is not schizophrenic, only a psychopath would kill this many people,' Dr Kay said, 'and the origins of that must be sexual.' He said he had asked Sutcliffe about 'his lifestyle and daydreams' and he did not believe that he came into the category of a sadist-killer. There were a number of reasons. Firstly, a sadist-killer can very rarely relate to adult women and therefore is very rarely married; secondly, he has a rich sexual fantasy life, dreams about sex and is usually very anxious, given the opportunity, to discuss his fantasies; thirdly, such people would stimulate their fantasy with pornography and would be interested in torture, whips and female underwear. Dr Kay said he was not aware of any evidence of that nature in Sutcliffe's case.

Asked by Mr Chadwin whether there was anything that struck him about the killings in that context, he replied: 'I would have expected the sexual aspect to be present in all except the first one or two cases, and I would have expected it to spread so that in the last killing there would have been greater mutilation than in the earlier ones.'

He added that the use of the hammer also did not suggest a sadist-killer, because of its speed: the usual emphasis was on slowness of death and the agony of the victim. The sadist-killer needed to see the suffering and he needed to control the terror of the victim. Referring to the hammer blows, Dr Kay said the speed and need to see the face of the victim would appear to contradict the sexual pleasure in doing it.

Mr Chadwin turned to the injuries suffered by Josephine Whitaker. 'I suppose it is obvious to all of us why a sadistic killer would inflict that injury – why would a schizophrenic inflict it?'

Dr Kay explained that as a schizophrenic went on, his sensitivity would be eroded.

After several days of silence, Sir Michael Havers decided to unburden his junior colleague of the cross-examination of this final representative of the medical profession. Immediately homing in yet again on the ways in which the Crown maintained Sutcliffe had 'duped' the doctors, the Attorney-General referred the court to a controlled experiment in America in which psychiatrists were fooled by a team of researchers pretending to be schizophrenics. Before he could get into his stride, however, Sir Michael was diverted by the unaccustomed gust of laughter which blew through the court following Mr Justice Boreham's observation that he must not blame Dr Kay for what happened in America.

Sir Michael then set about convincing Dr Kay of the likelihood that Sutcliffe was, despite all the doctor had already said, a sadist-killer. Dr Kay conceded that Sutcliffe's sexual involvement with Helen Rytka as she lay dying was 'a very unusual act', but he added that he would have expected that sort of thing in not just one, but in every case from a sadist-murderer.

Next, Sir Michael turned to the case of Josephine Whitaker, who had been stabbed with a screwdriver in the vagina. Wasn't it much more like the work of a sadist-killer than somebody on a mission?

Dr Kay replied: 'I have to balance whether this was done for sexual excitement or pleasure, or whether it is the act of a man whose feelings for human beings are blunted by schizophrenia.'

The doctor was then handed the screwdriver with which Sutcliffe had attacked Miss Whitaker and told by Sir Michael, lacking the *brio* of Mr Ognall, that 'there must be a sexual component there. That was introduced inside the vagina three times through the same entry hole.'

Dr Kay agreed, and said that when he asked Sutcliffe about it Sutcliffe had said he 'waggled it about two or three times'. It didn't, however, significantly affect his diagnosis.

SIR MICHAEL: 'Why would any man want to do that to a girl?'

Dr Kay acknowledged that a sexual motive was the most likely but insisted that he could not know what went through a schizophrenic's mind all the time. 'I do not know what particular thoughts they have in regard to sex or anything else under every condition.'

He agreed with the Attorney-General that if Sutcliffe was 'a

327

cold-blooded killer who had an enormous desire to kill prostitutes or just to kill women, he could be bad rather than mad.'

This was the point, to nobody's surprise, to which Sir Michael returned shortly before the adjournment for lunch on Tuesday 11 May, when he began his closing address to the jury. In a ninety-minute speech, he told them it was up to them to decide whether Peter Sutcliffe was mad, as the doctors believed, or 'a sadistic, calculated, cold-blooded murderer who loved his job', as the Crown maintained. Somebody who was 'just plain evil'.

'It is the doctors' belief in what he said about Bingley, the voice of God and the mission which leads them to their diagnosis. If you do not believe that he is telling the truth, then the doctors' diagnosis collapses. If you are not satisfied that he did hear voices of God or he did have a mission, that is an end to it,' Sir Michael said.

It might be the most notorious or infamous multiple murder of the decade, he told them, but it was in essence no different from any other case. They must not flinch or feel afraid to allow the presence of the world's press in court to affect them.

In a characteristically unflamboyant but well-argued closing speech, Mr Chadwin explained to the jury that he was in the unusual position as defence counsel of having to prove the defence case, while the prosecution didn't have to prove anything. 'Because Peter Sutcliffe has admitted these killings, and has said they were done with the intention of killing, it follows that they are murders unless I can persuade you that, because of the evidence, it is probable that Peter William Sutcliffe at the time of these killings had a sick mind, a diseased mind which had the effect that it substantially impaired his responsibility for what he did.'

Mr Chadwin challenged the theory put forward by the prosecution that Sutcliffe attacked women because he had a grudge after he was belittled by a prostitute in 1969. He asked what happened to Sutcliffe's seething hatred of prostitutes between 1969 and 1975. 'If this man had been activated merely by resentment, then by 1970, 1971 or 1972 the matter would have been over.'

Mr Chadwin said a man with a healthy mind as opposed to one which was diseased would have been most unlikely to start killing and attacking prostitutes in 1975 because of an incident that had taken place six years earlier. 'But a man who had become convinced through sickness of mind that it was God's will that he should attack prostitutes might well have taken time to become so convinced to start his attacks.

'This man was obsessed by prostitutes,' he continued, 'paranoid about prostitutes, and would see special significance about a part of a prostitute's body. But is there anything to suggest he enjoyed anything sexually?' Mr Chadwin suggested there was not. He drew the jury's attention to Sutcliffe's own explanation of why he placed one victim in a humiliating position, 'to show them for what they are. To show them as a disgrace.'

'He loathed their bodies and he attacked in many cases with excessive violence – one woman having something like fifty-two stab wounds,' Mr Chadwin went on. 'But bear in mind that, whether stabbing or strangling, the pattern was always blows to the back of the head. Is it even probable,' he asked, 'that this is a pattern of someone who enjoys to see the suffering of his victim, or enjoys killing? Or is consistent with the feeling that he was destroying what he, in his own way, regarded as the scum of the earth who were responsible for all the ills of the world?'

In conclusion, Mr Chadwin told the jury that the responsibility shouldered by the defence counsel in the case was a heavy one, but that he asked for no sympathy 'because your responsibility is heavier than mine'.

This, of course, was mere rhetoric. As Piers Paul Read pointed out soon afterwards in the *Observer*: 'Barristers may pretend that it is the jury which decides a case such as this, but the facts at the jurors' disposal are filtered through the rules of evidence, and because of this they were denied quite crucial information – notably about [Sutcliffe's] childhood and married life.

'The contentions of both prosecution and defence in this case,' Read went on, 'both seemed inadequate explanations for what had happened, and the issue became less and less a question of fact, and more a philosophical riddle: Was he a sane man pretending to be mad? Or a mad man who thought he was sane? Or a mad man who thought he was sane and was pretending to be mad?'

It was the judge's purpose, of course, to convince the jury that their verdict turned on less arcane distinctions than these. And often during a summing up which took him from Wednesday afternoon to the morning of Friday 22 May to deliver, Mr Justice Boreham seemed like the head of a family lately returned from a long holiday in a strange land, trying to remind the younger members of all that they had seen. 'This was the one killed in her flat, d'you remember?'; 'This was the one where he waved at the window to reassure her'; 'you know, the little twin'; 'that ligature, the cord, do you remember it?' he gently prompted the jury, turning the pages of the ledger that he had been assiduously, and rather hypnotically, blotting with the heel of his right hand, day by day.

Having devoted several hours to the factual evidence and *what* Sutcliffe did, the judge turned to the evidence as to *why* he did it, still counselling the jury that 'If you keep your feet firmly on the ground it will stop you from getting your heads into the clouds.' The point at issue, Mr Justice Boreham said, was reasonably simple: did Sutcliffe lie to the police in order to divert them from his 'mission'? Or did he lie to the doctors in order to persuade them he was mad?

It was Sutcliffe's own testimony here that was 'crucial'. It was Sutcliffe himself who had decided to give evidence; nobody had been in a position to make him. He was capable of it because, according to the doctors, his schizophrenia was of the rare type known as 'encapsulated', which means that the rest of his personality is intact. The jury were advised to 'weigh him up as you would any other witness – not just what he said but how he said it'.

'If the doctors have been told the true story – that he was deluded into thinking he had a divine mission to kill prostitutes – then nobody challenges the diagnosis they have built on it,' Mr

Justice Boreham said, and the defence was made out: they must find him not guilty of murder but guilty of manslaughter. 'But if the factual basis is not reliable, then their opinions fall to the ground.' He is guilty of murder on all thirteen counts.

The judge gave the jury a clear indication of which way his own mind was working on at least two occasions during his summing-up. Reminding them of the several times Sutcliffe had talked about 'an inner compulsion to kill any woman' in his statement to the police, and of how the defence and the medical experts agreed that too much notice should not be taken of such comments because Sutcliffe was wanting to hide his divine mission, Mr Justice Boreham remarked: 'I don't know, you must judge, but do you necessarily have to say things like: "I realise she wasn't a prostitute but at the time I wasn't bothered and I just wanted to kill a woman"? Why say that if it isn't right, and why go to that length if all you are trying to do is simply hide the mission?'

Reviewing Dr Milne's evidence, in which he had said that there was nothing the defendant had told him which in the end he didn't accept, including the experience in Bingley cemetery which was central to his diagnosis, Mr Justice Boreham told the jury: '[Sutcliffe] says he worked in the cemetery. I do not know how far that takes you, but you must judge. I don't wish to be flippant in a case such as this, but it is very much like claiming to have swum the Channel and when your friends doubt you, you take them to see the Channel. It doesn't prove very much, does it?'

Not a great deal hung on the verdict of the jury in the case of Regina versus Sutcliffe. Whether he was found guilty of manslaughter or murder, nobody doubted that Peter Sutcliffe was going to be locked away for the rest of his natural life. But proof that the last act of a famous murder trial still exercised a profound fascination for the public was to be found in the number of people who arrived with their sleeping bags for what was expected to be the trial's final day, even before the afternoon sitting on Thursday, 21 May was over. Even the rain which lashed them for most of the night didn't seem to lower their spirits.

Mr Justice Boreham concluded his summing-up within half an hour of the court reconvening on Friday morning, and at 10.21 a.m. sent the jury to their room to seek a unanimous verdict. Five hours later, at 3.28 p.m., they returned to the court to tell the judge that unanimity was proving impossible, and the judge said that in that case he would accept a majority verdict.

By now it was after closing time, and so the journalists and other spectators milled impatiently around the grand muralled hall outside Number One Court, discussing deadlines. If the atmosphere stopped just short of the circle-bar at *No Sex Please, We're British*, this was out of deference for the relatives of some of the dead women who were present. Below in the cells, the defendant was said to be happily whiling away the hours with his favourite author, James Herriot.

At about 4.15 there was a buzz of excitement when an usher appeared and unlocked the doors of what from the outside gave every appearance of being a superior department-store of the old school. And at 4.19 p.m. the foreman of the jury, a young red-haired man with a beard, rose at the invitation of the clerk of the court and took seven minutes to deliver thirteen verdicts of murder by a majority of ten to two.

As the foreman sat, Sutcliffe himself went to sit down but was prevented from doing so by the two prison officers pressed on either side of him. They urged him closer to the rail of the dock, where he stood without registering a blip of emotion as Mr Justice Boreham pronounced sentence on him.

'Peter William Sutcliffe, the jury have found you guilty of thirteen charges of murder, and, if I may say so, murder of a very cowardly quality. It is difficult to find words that are adequate in my judgement to describe the brutality and the gravity of these offences and I say at once I am not going to pause to seek those words. I am prepared to let the catalogue of your crimes speak for itself.'

The judge said that in deciding on his sentence he had considered the depth in human terms of the terror which Sutcliffe had brought to a wide area of Yorkshire. 'It is a population which to my knowledge does not lack fortitude. But I am left in no doubt that women from a wide area were in the deepest fear, and I have no doubts too that that fear spilled over to their menfolk on their account.'

He said he had also considered the danger which Sutcliffe would represent in the future if he were at large. 'The sentence for murder is laid down by the law and is immutable. It is a sentence that you be imprisoned for life.'

He told Sutcliffe that he would recommend to the Home Secretary that he should serve at least thirty years. 'That is a long period,' he said, 'an unusually long period, but I believe you are an unusually dangerous man. I express the hope when I have said life imprisonment it will mean precisely that.'

The final remark addressed by Mr Justice Boreham to the man who had sat virtually motionless under his gaze for fourteen days was that the seven charges of attempted murder to which he pleaded guilty at the start of the trial also incurred life sentences. 'You may go,' he said, and a bolt was drawn loudly in the door at the bottom of the dark flight of stairs leading from the dock.

When news of the verdicts reached the crowds in the street outside the Old Bailey, *The Times* reported next day, there were three cheers for the jury.

'I would like him to be hung. I could kill him myself,' Mrs Doreen Hill told awaiting newsmen. 'I want him in a normal prison so other prisoners can get him.'

'I wish he was going to the gallows,' Mrs Irene MacDonald, Jayne MacDonald's mother, said. 'I hope other prisoners have the decency to make every minute he is inside a living hell for him.'

'I hate and loathe him,' were Mrs Beryl Leach, Barbara Leach's mother's, parting words.

That night, both the BBC and the ITV network ran hour-long documentaries about the case. John Sutcliffe was in both but watched neither (although a friend videoed the Yorkshire Television programme for him). He started watching YTV's film at home but 'got bored' after about ten minutes and went down to the pub. He had made no bones about the fact that he thought the 'voices from God' story was 'bunkum'. He thought the best thing all round would have been if Peter had been hanged.

Along with the rest of his family, John had followed the general development of the case, which had anyway been virtually inescapable in the press and on radio and television. But, whenever possible, he had spared himself the details.

Neither his father nor his brothers and sisters were aware, for instance, that when Peter stood up in court and said he had been on his way home from work on the night that he killed Yvonne Pearson in Manningham, he had in fact just been helping Mick and his father move the heavier items of furniture into Rutland House. They wouldn't realise for more than a year – and only then when it was pointed out to them – that, within an hour or two of the end of his house-warming party at Heaton, Peter was attempting to saw the head off Jean Jordan's eight-day-old corpse in Manchester.

What Carl knew was mainly what his brother had told him on his first visit to see him in Armley. 'He said he hadn't done them all. He said to me, "They aren't really as bad as they say." He hadn't really ripped them to bits, he said.'

Asked why he had done it, Peter had looked at Carl and smiled, and said, 'I were just cleaning up streets, our kid. Just cleaning up the streets.'

33

Among the regular attenders at the Old Bailey during the first week of the trial was a tall, rather striking woman who every morning took her place in the back row of seats banked up steeply behind the dock and reserved for those with the right to stare most searchingly at the back of the Ripper's head.

By the time the verdict was announced, Anna Rogulskyj was back in Keighley, in the terraced house only a few hundred yards from where Peter Sutcliffe had stepped out behind her armed with a hammer on a warm summer night in July 1975, and which she had been able to buy out of the £15,000 that she had eventually received from the Criminal Injuries Board.

Sitting in an aluminium-framed garden chair in a room decorated with only a plaque dedicated to Our Lady of Lourdes and a few pictures torn out of magazines – John Travolta, the Pope, David Soul – she watched the news on a television wired to a meter which demanded more fifty-pence pieces than she was normally able to afford.

Dark-haired at the time of the attack, 'Joanna', as she now preferred to call herself, had become an ash-blonde and had particular reasons to be grateful for a thick growth of hair: it concealed the two ladle-sized craters in her skull, one below the crown and the other just behind the right ear, which, even after six years, she seemed compelled to ask people to thrust their hands into, as if this in some way alleviated the pain.

That John Sutcliffe should meet the woman acknowledged to be the first of the twenty victims claimed by his son, let alone explore her wounds with his fingers and invite her home to Sunday lunch, was something that seemed bizarre to everybody but John and Anna Rogulskyj herself. 'The depressions in her skull are horrific. You can get your fist into them. I mean, she was beaten and beaten and beaten. Her right hand is still deformed from trying to protect herself. He beat the hell out of her hand as well.'

It was only two years after she was attacked and left for dead that Anna Rogulskyj's name was added to the list of the Ripper's crimes, and the minute it was, the life she had been painstakingly rebuilding – after months in hospital, she had had to be taught how to walk and talk again – crashed about her ears. 'I don't go round the pubs. I never have done in my life. I'm not a gallivanting woman: I choose my men carefully, and they're few and far between,' she protested to anyone who would listen, but it wasn't enough: the phone never stopped ringing with heavy-breathers and people asking 'How much?' She was scared to get up in the morning in case another filthy letter had been pushed through the door, afraid to go out because of the pointing fingers and wagging tongues.

She became convinced that it wasn't the Yorkshire Ripper who had attacked her at all, but another man, whose identity she knew. And after the trial, she started to believe that the Ripper himself was the only person who could 'clear her name'. If his father could get him to put it in writing that he wasn't the man who beat her over the head, then perhaps at last she might be able to start getting back to being herself . . .

In the meantime she would go on taking her doses of Wyeth Ativan, without which her mouth dried and her nerve went and she was unable to face the world. 'If he takes me off them,' she said one cold night at the beginning of 1983, 'then I don't want to live.' While in London for the trial she had taken an overdose of her brother's blood-pressure pills and had had to be rushed into Edgware General to have her stomach pumped. It was only the latest in a series of attempts on her own life, and only one example of the illimitable misery which would continue to seep through the lives of countless others, like an unshakeable damp.

Through their common experience, Anna Rogulskyj and Olive Smelt had become friends, but it didn't make Mrs Smelt's day-to-day existence any more tolerable: she, too, was the victim of gossip and innuendo and, while never driven to attempt suicide, was vulnerable to sudden black depressions and amnesia. Linda, her oldest daughter, suffered a nervous breakdown whose roots, the doctors said, almost certainly lay in the assault on her mother.

Two years after Jayne MacDonald's death, in June 1977, her father died, so his wife believed, 'from a broken heart': 'He couldn't forget seeing her in the mortuary when he had to identify her,' Mrs MacDonald told the *Yorkshire Post*. 'All he could say was there was blood all over her beautiful hair.'

Doreen Hill firmly believes that if Jacqueline had still been alive her husband would still be alive as well. Jacqueline Hill was due to announce her engagement to Ian Tanfield, a Royal Air Force officer, on her twenty-first birthday, Friday, 22 May 1981, which happened to be the final day of Peter Sutcliffe's trial. Jack Hill had been seriously ill for some time with a tumour on the lung. 'But,' Mrs Hill said at her home in Ormesby, on Teesside, one Sunday afternoon near the end of Sutcliffe's second full year in jail, 'my husband lived to give Jacqueline away.'

A painting by Jacqueline, of the window in front of which Doreen Hill was sitting, hung on the fireplace wall. Below it, framed pictures of Jacqueline herself and of her fiancé stood at either end of the fire surround. Mrs Hill stared blankly at the piece of wall between these three objects for long periods, saying nothing. She no longer reads newspapers and tries to avoid the news on television and, asked whether she is bitter, says stonily: 'Of course. I've had my doubts about it for a number of years, but they're all settled now,' she says of the Bible. 'It's just one big fairytale.'

Simple imprisonment, she repeated, was too good for the man who had casually destroyed her life: 'Somebody has suggested putting him in a room and throwing away the key. Another person, who I was very surprised at, a doctor, suggested removing both his eyes, and giving them to somebody who needs them, taking away his kidneys for somebody who needs them, cutting his vocal chords and putting electrodes on his head. Perhaps the

337

best thing would be locking him in a room with thirty prostitutes and letting them loose.'

On 10 January 1983, Peter Sutcliffe was attacked with a broken coffee jar by another prisoner in F2, the hospital wing of Parkhurst, on the Isle of Wight. He sustained a deep laceration five inches long across his face, a two and a half inch-deep laceration at the upper part of his left eye and a laceration to his upper left eyelid, and lost more than a pint of blood. It took eighty-four stitches to repair the wounds and, when Sutcliffe gave evidence against the man who had attacked him – 'Glaswegian hardman Jimmy Costelloe' – at Newport Magistrates Court in November, the scars were clearly visible where his face wasn't covered in beard.

The incident was said to have occurred because of Sutcliffe's repeated defacing of the prison's copy of the *Sun*, which he described in court as 'trash'. Wearing a large gold crucifix on a thin chain fastened tightly round his neck, he railed against 'greed, immorality and depravity' and 'the declining moral values in society today'.

Peter only wrote infrequently to his family, but when he did this was also the tenor of his letters to them. 'These greedy moral-less scum' he wrote of his former 'so-called friends who have talked to the "gutter" press'.

'I may be classed as the number one criminal, but their behaviour disgusts me. They are real criminals, I'm not! (only by name and lack of understanding of why I had to do what I did) . . . I have a true and strong belief in God and the personal understanding I've had for years of his overall purpose for everything. Poverty, disease, famine etc – none of these are optional vices like immorality, corruption, greed . . . Look at the absolute moral decline of society. Every aspect of it is one of decay and corruption . . .'

To his father, this all seemed as divorced from the Peter he had known as the 'deranged' side of him that was now a matter of public record. 'You can't put them together,' John said. 'They're so poles apart. They're two completely different people, no doubt about it. When he was Peter he was Peter. He was one of the most natural-looking blokes in the world. There was nothing about him to make anybody suspect that he was in any way possessed by anything evil. He was merriment from the word go. But when he was this other guy he was somebody else altogether.

'You see, all this thing, it's so foreign to his nature. It's so unlike him. It's just incomprehensible that he could've done the things he's done, when you know him as we've known him. I'll tell you one thing: I wish that I had him back. They could put the other two in there, for me, and let me have him back. Because I got ten times more consideration from him in the space of one month than I got from either of the other two.

'Peter was everybody's favourite. He curried favouritism without trying. He would have made sure that his mother and I were looked after for the rest of our lives if it had been up to him. He is the one out of the whole family who, had his mother lived and had I lived on to any great age, I *know* would have looked after us. I can guarantee that.

'It's Peter who would have seen that we were all right. He'd have fetched and carried for us. He'd have taken us for days out and weekends out, run us over to Morecambe to see Anne and the kids . . . We'd never have been short of anything that he could have provided within his means. I know that. I couldn't say that about either Carl or Mick. They look after Number One. They look after themselves.'

Carl had to threaten to 'expose' them to the other papers before he got his money out of the *Daily Star*. But he finally received a cheque for £21,500 a year after the end of the trial, in 1982, and immediately invested it in a house in Gilstead that had belonged to Harvey Smith's uncle, and in a black MGB roadster that he saw as a 'collector's item'.

He shared the house with a succession of punks and other

drifters and immediately set out to alienate the neighbours, who he knew resented him moving in. 'They're all frightened of me, so I play it up,' Carl said one morning over the chatter of *Derek and Clive* on the video and the crackle of a CB receiver dangling from a wire in the middle of the room. 'When I walk up there, they all shoot inside. So one night I went out and started digging big holes in front garden. Another night I went and just sat there with me arms folded for an hour. When you come home at night you see curtains move, an' they all look. She spies on me over there. Silly old cow. I can't stand nosey people.'

Behind the bravado, though, and the showy good looks, Carl was still essentially withdrawn. He was embarrassed by the attentions of strangers and of 'females' eager to 'go with' him because of who he was and, for this reason, confined himself mainly to Bingley and a small, well-defined circle of pubs while constantly threatening to take off for South Africa to assume a new identity and start a new life.

Mick received a 'pay-off' of £5,000 from the *Daily Star* and disposed of it in a little over three months. He finally married Susan, the mother of his five-year-old daughter, in 1982, only to split up with her the following year a few months after being arrested for breaking into the house of the people next door while they were on holiday.

This, together with his drinking, led the rest of the family to virtually write him off. When she said she thought it would be 'a bloody miracle' if he made forty (he was thirty in 1982), Jane spoke for them all. 'Every time you see him he's staggering around, even at dinner-times now.' She felt the turning-point was his months with the *Star*.

Jane's reaction to Peter's arrest and conviction was perhaps the most conventional of all her family: she had nightmares for months, but in particular a recurring nightmare, which came every time she closed her eyes and had her believing for a long time that she was possibly going mad: 'I go to the prison and get permission to take Peter out. He's handcuffed to me and I take him to a cafe, then I bring him home. I cufflink him to the metal arm of the settee when I go to bed and take him shopping when I get up. When we get to the corner, though, the cufflinks suddenly drop, he says, "I've got to do it again," and disappears.' Her own screams, ripping through Priestthorpe Road, Carl's old address, where she had herself taken a bedsit, invariably woke her up.

By the middle of 1982, Jane had recovered sufficiently to take a 'front-of-house' job in a local hotel. When the manageress realised that 'Ellis' was only her married name, however, she was abruptly dismissed.

Soon afterwards she was persuaded to pose for some 'beauty' shots for a Sunday paper. One of the better prints hangs in a frame on her father's living-room wall, adjacent to the personally autographed picture of a Page Three girl that Jane acquired for him at the same studio session. The pictures of Jane which the paper chose to run as a centre spread, though, were not the most flattering that they took. She looked 'like Myra Hindley' in them, according to Mick.

Sonia had briefly reappeared in court to hear Mr Chadwin for the defence make his final appeal to the jury and Mr Justice Boreham begin his summing-up. Perched anxiously on the end of the third row of oak benches closest to the dock, she was in the perfect position to catch her husband's eye in the split second that it became level with hers during his hurried descent to the cells. And at lunchtime, and again at the end of the session, they exchanged shy smiles and shy, minimal waves of the hand which were the only acknowledgement either would make of the existence of anybody else in court. Nobody who witnessed these pathetic demonstrations of affection could question the truth of the 'I still love him' and 'I stand by him' headlines which followed the verdict.

Sonia pledged herself to visit Peter for the rest of his life, no matter where in the country he was, and reconciled herself to a future in which she would be an object of curiosity at best and, at worst, an object of fear and derision.

Quite soon after the trial she moved back into what she had always thought of as her 'dream house' on a street now bristling with 'For Sale' signs, and defiantly repainted the exterior wood-work a glossy black-and-white and replaced the boards covering the shattered front windows with neat lace curtains. Shunned by her neighbours, she was much sought after by the sightseers who had singlehandedly transformed Garden Lane from a quiet backwater into a busy thoroughfare.

Trade at the Quarry Arms, the pub in Clayton where the Sut-cliffes had held their wedding reception, was also boosted by people wanting to be photographed against the flock-wallpaper and the carriage lamps which had formed a backdrop to the much-reproduced pictures from the 'Ripper's' wedding album.

The widely anticipated onslaught on Bingley cemetery, how-ever, never happened. Most holiday-makers negotiating the Bin-gley stretch of the Leeds–Liverpool canal do so without realising that the small, sun-dappled graveyard across the other side of the valley from Five-Rise Locks is the site of the white crucifix-shaped headstone marking what the men now working in the cemetery know as 'the talking grave'.

The 1982 season was no better for L. J. Tussaud and G. Nicholson Ltd, of Morecambe, than any other season in recent memory. The bodies still weren't coming in to see the bodies, as Mr Nicholson would have it, and this despite the addition of a new model which he might have expected to really draw the crowds. The trouble, as with another of his notorious exhibits, was that its delicate nature precluded brash advertisement.

Unlike Mick, who had discussed it with nobody, Maureen was unaware of the fascination that 'Madame Tussaud's' held for Peter. She was also unaware that a waxwork of Peter had recently gone on display. Coming across it unprepared a little over a year after he had been sent to prison, she stood transfixed for a few seconds, simultaneously fascinated and repulsed, and then ran for her life.

'I was with a friend and she said, "Let's go in here. They've got

342

a Billy Connolly." She's from Glasgow. So we went in, saw Billy Connolly, an' there were this little turnstile . . . She said, are you all right? Oh it were awful. I just walked round corner an' it were first room upstairs. I'd only ever been in once before, an' it were years and years and years ago. I'd no idea they'd got him. And then we just walked round this semi-circle, turned right, an' there he were. I felt me heart go. I thought I were goin' to die . . . I felt right sorry for 'im, though, that were thing.'

Wearing a black velvet jacket and tan stacked-heel boots, 'The Ripper' stands at the entrance to the Chamber of Horrors in a chickenwire-fronted box with front pages from the 'gutter' press pasted to the walls. Only two dozen paces and two large antique cabinets separate the effigy of Peter from the images of feculence and moral lassitude that he was so drawn to.

When Carl made a visit, though, quite independently of his sister, it wasn't this strange irony which exercised him, or even the fact that he had stood on the exact spot with Peter where Peter was now immortalised in wax. What genuinely fired him was that, with its tight little shoulders and thin little arms and iron-filing hair and beard, the 'dummy' seemed such a travesty of the original.

Carl asked to see the manager, and Mr Nicholson came sauntering cheerfully along, but he took some convincing that the young man running down a piece of work he had only recently spent £1,200 on was who he said he was and not just some joker. He took in the denim jacket with its family of Robertson's 'Gollies' on the pocket and Ban-the-Bomb badge, the jeans and 'trainers' and dark, darting eyes, and looked for some sign that might tell him this was the brother of the Ripper. He saw instead a lanky youth who, once beyond the doors, would melt invisibly into the holiday crowds shuffling along the prom.

PART FOUR

Afterword

A small boy, Asian, aged about seven, wearing a flat-top hair-cut and bright, baggy clothes in the style known as Manc (after Manchester, their city of origin) or Acid House, is playing on his own in Garden Lane.

He cycles along the crown of the road, from his own gate to the electricity sub-station abutting No. 6 and back, home and back, over and over. But, either because he has been forbidden to do so by his parents or because he is merely following some childhood superstition, like not stepping on cracks in the pavement, he is careful never to cross the invisible line which would mean entering the space occupied by the Ripper's house.

Even on the warmest day, such as today, No. 6 Garden Lane seems to stand in deep shadows of its own making. It projects a cold-field several yards into the road which children are not alone in being reluctant to enter.

It's a Saturday. The second Saturday of the 1990 Wimbledon fortnight, drenched in the familiar sights and sounds of an English summer – a *traditional* English summer, that is, as opposed to the summers-in-spring and summers-in-winter, the freak Februarys and Novembers, of recent years.

Garden Lane appears almost exaggeratedly still and suburban. The slab hedges, baize lawns and caravans and motor homes waxed and cleaned out ready for the season add up to what may seem an over-emphatic expression of contained and orderly lives, of normalcy and unremarkableness untainted by the grim events associated with the narrow house which still stands sentry at the eastern end of the street.

The curtains of a number of houses are drawn against the sun; windows are open, and the sounds of Martina Navratilova pounding her way to a record ninth Ladies' Singles title – grunt-and-pock, grunt-and-pock, punctuated by explosions of applause – reverberate in the nearly empty street.

(When did she win her first Wimbledon title? 1974? 1975? What stage of her life had Jean Jordan or Yvonne Pearson or Helen Rytka or Jayne MacDonald or Josephine Whitaker or Barbara Leach or Jacqueline Hill reached then? It is the kind of calculation the friends and families of the women murdered by Peter Sutcliffe must find themselves making dozens, perhaps hundreds, of times a year, every time something happens to trigger the recollection that there was another life, once, when such considerations were irrelevant.)

At the end of Garden Lane furthest away from the Sutcliffe house, two teenagers in formal suits and chafing shirt-collars tape ribbon to the bonnet of a car in preparation for a wedding.

As they step back to admire their handiwork, a bowler on the elevated playing-field directly opposite makes his short approach and releases the ball. The thunk of wood on leather is followed by a smattering of applause from the spectators sitting in deck-chairs in front of the small, weatherboarded pavilion.

A timeless Saturday, in other words. A Saturday out of time – tangible evidence of an order that has been violated and yet persists, somehow larger and more enduring than the depraved acts of a single individual. That's the message.

It's a message that has been put across with commendable energy by Bradford city council in the years since Sutcliffe's arrest, and with positive results. Six million people now apparently visit Bradford every year, to see the National Museum of Photography and Europe's largest collection of David Hockney paintings, or to join the industrial heritage or 'culture and curry' trails, or the TV tours to *Emmerdale Farm* country.

Although it wasn't the sole intention, the promotion of Bradford as a 'Great British City' has done some of the work of enhancing the negative image of red-light areas, drug-dealing and bottom-of-the-barrel squalor with a more up-beat one of inner-city regeneration, tourism and enterprise.

348

The fact remains, however, that for many – perhaps most – people, Bradford remains the city of the Ripper.

His father, now retired, his sisters, both remarried, and his brothers (Mick intermittently in trouble with the law; Carl training as a photocopier repair-man) still live within a few streets of each other in Bingley, rarely venturing out into the wider world.

More problematically, as far as any municipal public relations exercise is concerned, Sonia Sutcliffe continues to live in the house she shared with her husband in the years when he was bringing terror to the whole of the North of England.

Ten years after his arrest, No. 6 Garden Lane, and no less the woman in it, remains a target of abuse, an object of curiosity and a source of boundless speculation.

Taxi drivers have been known to make voluntary detours between the city centre and the airport in order to offer their passengers the frisson of 'the Ripper's house'. There is a steady stream of tourist coaches throughout the summer, in addition to the year-round traffic of family groups posing for pictures on the steeply raked drive, mugging against a backdrop of scratchy plants and dim-leaved, curtaining trees.

And yet Sonia stays on. More than stays on – has fought defiantly in the courts over the years for the right to go on living in what she evidently still regards as her 'dream house'.

'Plainly that is not the ideal place for her to live, and a move to a fresh address, on her own evidence . . . would be likely to remove some of the continuing strain in which she is obviously living and might well assist in lifting the depression from which she is still suffering through the events which came to light in 1981,' Judge Gilbert Hartley announced at Bradford County Court in 1986.

The judge had just ordered that the house in Garden Lane be sold in order that Peter Sutcliffe's half-share of the proceeds be paid as compensation to Maureen Long, Marilyn Moore and Mrs Irene MacDonald, Jayne MacDonald's mother, who had been awarded a total of £25,722 in damages against him four years earlier.

No. 6 Garden Lane was put on the market in January 1987, at an asking price of £45,000. Eight months later it was announced that Sonia had bought the remaining half-share after borrowing £25,000 from 'a friend'.

'It's my home, and I have worked to make it beautiful,' she once had told this same friend – actually a woman journalist with a Sunday paper – who would also be her companion on a much-publicised holiday in Greece. 'Nothing bad has ever happened to me here. No grisly murders were committed here and no bodies buried. It is not a house of horrors but a very nice home.'

This, of course, was to ignore the evidence: the knife which had been used to murder Helen Rytka and then returned to the kitchen drawer where her husband had found it; the blood-spattered clothes he washed in the kitchen sink; the screwdriver he worked to a vicious point on the garage floor and introduced into the vagina of Josephine Whitaker – 'one of the most fiendish weapons you have ever seen' in the words of Sir Michael Havers; and the trousers Sutcliffe was wearing when he attempted to decapitate Jean Jordan on the night of the house-warming party at Garden Lane, which he later burned in the garden.

'I think the person harbouring the Ripper is as bad as he is,' the stepfather of Josephine Whitaker told *Newsnight* in 1980. 'I can't understand the mentality of anybody who can co-habit with such a loathsome creature.'

The mentality of Sonia Sutcliffe is only slightly less of a mystery now than it was on the day almost a decade ago when her husband was revealed as the Yorkshire Ripper. She has vehemently denied any awareness of Peter Sutcliffe's activities, but otherwise has kept her own counsel, only emerging from her self-imposed seclusion when necessary to defend her position in the courts.

She tried to get an injunction to stop this book being published in 1984, having already fought Sutcliffe's case at bankruptcy proceedings, following books borrowed from a lawyer.

She was awarded an undisclosed sum in damages by a Yorkshire newspaper in 1983 and caused a public outcry in 1989 when she was paid a record £600,000 in damages against the satirical magazine *Private Eye*. The magazine alleged that she had signed a £250,000 deal with the *Daily Mail* for her story.

The case eventually went to appeal and Sonia, unemployable on her own admission – 'No one seems to want to employ anyone who is the wife of someone as notorious as my husband' – settled for £160,000 plus costs for that and other claims she had against *Private Eye*.

In 1984, apparently still hearing voices and said to be suffering from paranoid schizophrenia, Peter Sutcliffe was transferred from a conventional prison to Broadmoor, the secure hospital for the criminally insane in Berkshire, where his wife still makes regular visits to see him.

In January 1987, a senior detective from outside West Yorkshire was appointed to investigate allegations that the hoax tapes in the Ripper case were made by a policeman.

By April, Detective Chief Superintendent Tony Fitzgerald was able to report that he was satisfied that there was no substance to the allegations.

In September 1988, the Law Lords threw out Mrs Doreen Hill's application to sue West Yorkshire Police for negligence in not catching Peter Sutcliffe earlier.

On Saturday, 7 July 1990, the day Martina Navratilova won her record ninth championship at Wimbledon, the front page of the Bradford *Telegraph and Argus* carried the following story:

> A teenage girl who was savagely battered in the red-light district of Bradford was today fighting for her life in hospital. Doctors say that the 17-year-old girl is drifting in and out of consciousness 48 hours after the attack.
>
> Julie Baxter, who is from the Meanwood area of Leeds, lay undiscovered for more than seven hours in the alley behind Hallfield Road and Peel Square, Bradford. She was suffering from exposure, serious head injuries and broken cheek-bones.

A 13-year-old boy told today of his horror when he spotted the battered girl. He said: 'I heard a moaning noise and then I saw a leg sticking out from behind a dustbin. I went closer and saw the girl. She was covered in mud and she had blood all over her legs.'

A man was arrested the following day.

Acknowledgements

Most of those who, through their co-operation, enabled me to write this book did so on the understanding that it was to be a fair and honest attempt to establish the truth about Peter Sutcliffe and the events surrounding his life.

Fact and fiction had become hopelessly blurred in the weeks and months following Sutcliffe's arrest, largely as a result of newsmen offering hard cash for 'good copy'. And many of those who talked to me did so in the hope of setting the record straight. No money was ever offered for information; money, with one or two notable exceptions, was never asked for, and none was ever paid.

As the text will show, I am particularly indebted to John Sutcliffe, his sons Michael and Carl, and his daughters Mrs Maureen Holland and Mrs Jane Ellis for allowing me into their lives for what, in the end, turned out to be almost two years, for their unfailing hospitality during that time and for their willingness to confront what must have often been distressing, embarrassing or unsettling for them.

It is to their credit that they set no conditions on what might and might not be talked about and were prepared to submit to long, frequently circuitous interviews conducted, in some cases, over a period of several months.

A number of people who helped in my research prefer to remain anonymous, and real names have been replaced by pseudonyms in the cases of 'Allan Wright' and John Sutcliffe's oldest daughter, Anne, in order to protect the privacy of her family.

Among those whose assistance was invaluable, though, and whom I can name, are: Laurie Ashton and Cath Ashton; Ronald Barker; Mrs Marie Bell; Mrs Barbara Brown; Anthony Davies;

Mrs Marion Dean; Sammy Foulds; Mr and Mrs Jack Hawkes; Robin Holland; Gary Jackson; Douglas Mctavish; Louie Melgram; Dr Hugo Milne; Bill Moore; Eric Robinson; Mr and Mrs Rex Squires; Keith Sugden and Doreen Sugden.

I owe a particular debt of gratitude to Mrs Doreen Hill and her solicitor, Mr Anelay Hart, and to Mrs Anna Rogulskyj.

I would also like to thank Mrs Margaret Davies and the staff of Bingley library for their knowledge and their patience; Peter Holdsworth, librarian of the Bradford *Telegraph and Argus*, and Julie O'Hare and Clive Entwistle of Yorkshire Television.

Many people, through their generosity and friendship, made the researching of this book a far pleasanter experience than it would otherwise have been. In addition to many of those already mentioned, I would particularly like to thank Terry Jackman and his staff at the Fleece Hotel, Bingley; Shawn and Gill Smith; Fred and Margaret Carby; Denise and Billy Bailey; Sam Bailey, and Peter Carrington.

The *Sunday Times* 'Insight' team generously made their files on the case available.

Louise Bloomfield and David Robson read the book at proof stage; and Richard Simon, Vivien Green and David Godwin believed in it when everybody else didn't.

Belief – and unstinting support and encouragement – is something for which I would also like to thank John Tennant, Paul Green and Bruce Bernard. Carol Gorner's contribution is too enormous ever to be set down on paper, so I would just like to thank her for her wisdom, companionship and love.

Also by Gordon Burn

ALMA COGAN

Winner of the Whitbread Award for Best First Novel

In his debut novel, Gordon Burn takes Britain's biggest-selling vocalist of the 1950s and turns her story into an equation of celebrity and murder. Fictional characters jostle for space with real-life stars – from John Lennon to Doris Day and Sammy Davis Jr. – as Burn, in a breathtaking act of appropriation, reinvents the popular culture of the post-war years. As beautifully written as it is disturbing, *Alma Cogan* remains a stingingly relevant exploration of the sad, dark underside of fame.

'An extraordinary, unprecedented novel. Audacious, innovative and totally compelling.' William Boyd

'No other novel has displayed the originality and power of Gordon Burn's *Alma Cogan*. This is my book of the year, because it is the one I desperately wish I had written.' Hilary Mantel

'A novel to treasure. As a dark meditation on fame and its undertow, as a dangerous and loving vision of post-war England, as a ruthless antidote to nostalgia, it's unlike anything I've ever read.' Michael Herr

www.faber.co.uk

ff

THE NORTH OF ENGLAND HOME SERVICE

In a forensic dissection of Britain's souring landscape, Gordon Burn tells the tale of Ray Cruddas, a light entertainer effecting a semi-dignified retreat from his fading career, who returns to the unnamed northern town of his youth.

'Elegiac, grave and affectionate . . . The history he presents, at times wielding an Orwellian eloquence, is worth the price of the book itself.' Sean O'Brien, *Independent*

'It is a book that feels as if it were written on foot, every sentence exhibiting a lifetime of close observation and streetwise wit . . . Nothing, not a joke or a jogger, is let off lightly.' Tim Adams, *Observer*

'Burn carves a tale of mutual dependence between two also-rans – Ray, once a successful Geordie comedian, and Jackie, an almost made-it boxer . . . It is a book about ageing, about the long haul between what you hoped your life might be and acceptance of what it is – and about the loneliness of men.' Anna Raeburn

www.faber.co.uk

ff

Also by Gordon Burn

POCKET MONEY

1985, and following 'that' final between Dennis Taylor and Steve Davis, Britain suddenly found itself in the grip of a new sporting obsession. Snooker, or 'Coronation Street with balls', was big business, and with TV looking to cash in, 1986 was to be a crucial year. In one corner was Barry Hearn and his Romford mafia – Davis, Taylor, Griffiths – and in the other were the bad boys – Higgins, White, Knowles – threatening the game's good name and its earning potential.

For one year, Gordon Burn travelled with this snooker circus. With unprecedented access to the leading personalities, *Pocket Money* offers a unique snapshot of 1980s Britain.

'A classic.' Frank Keating, *Guardian*

'Unputdownable.' *The Face*

'Funny, incisive and hugely entertaining.' *Time Out*

www.faber.co.uk

ff

Also by Gordon Burn

FULLALOVE

Norman Miller used to be one of Fleet Street's finest. Now he's a middle-aged, burned-out hack with a gift for the sensational story, the shouting tabloid lead. But as he reports on a series of brutal murders and sex crimes, he's forced to wonder whether he is just a witness – or part of some deeper pattern of cause and effect . . .

'Remarkable . . . Devastating . . . Required reading for anyone interested in what British fiction should be doing today.' *Esquire*

'Prescient, compelling, enthrallingly written and profoundly disturbing . . . *Fullalove* is an extraordinary, gripping and chilling book which lingers disquietingly in the mind, like the echo of a nightmare, long after you have put it down.' *Financial Times*

'Extraordinary . . . One of the year's most richly imagined and provocative novels.' *New Statesman*

ff

Also by Gordon Burn

BEST AND EDWARDS: Football, Fame and Oblivion

In *Best and Edwards*, Gordon Burn looks at two of football's brightest talents. United by the club they played for, but divided by the tragedy of Munich, they came in very different ways to embody their respective generations. In plotting the course and trajectory of these two careers, Gordon Burn has produced a brilliant and startingly original look at football and British culture.

'Immaculately written, inspiring, sad, elegiac.' *Daily Telegraph*

'A remarkable piece of work . . . A non-fiction book with the scope of a Don Delillo . . . Superbly evocative.' Taylor Parkes, *When Saturday Comes*

'Compelling . . . It transcends the routine one-size-fits-all approach to sports writing and is a splurge of ideas sets free.' *The Times*

www.faber.co.uk

ff

Also by Gordon Burn

HAPPY LIKE MURDERERS: The True Story of
Fred and Rosemary West

In this controversial and seminal work of reportage, Gordon Burn reveals the strange inner dynamic of Fred and Rosemary West's relationship. Based on meticulous research, this dark history is told in a powerful, compelling narrative.

'With his forensic commitment to get behind the tabloid headlines . . . Burn brilliantly reinvents reportorial writing . . . Startlingly original.' Matt Seaton, *Esquire*

'Brilliant, bleak, unflinching.' Deborah Orr, *Guardian*

'One knew . . . that if a book of merit could be written about these crimes, Gordon Burn would be the man to do it. His achievement rests on two pillars – the novelist's acute glance at apparently inconsequential detail, and the researcher's bold determination to immerse himself in the fetid world it is his task to explain . . . It is brave, and by no means easy, to do this without prurience . . . A book of record.' Brian Masters, *Spectator*

www.faber.co.uk

Also by Gordon Burn

BORN YESTERDAY: The News as a Novel

Born Yesterday does what the media do every day: blurring the boundaries between what is real and what is invented.

Summer 2007 was an extraordinarily rich time for news. Floods. Foot and mouth. The disappearances of Tony Blair and Madeline McCann. The arrival of Gordon Brown. Terror attacks in Glasgow. In this powerful and electrifying novel, Gordon Burn takes the news from that year and weaves the strands together into an essential story for our time. The characters in these long-running reality soaps are presented here in three dimensions, their stories told through revealing glimpses and startling insights.

'Gordon Burn is right. The news is now a novel.' Mark Lawson

'Wonderful . . . poignant, hilarious, and at times, uncomfortably true.' *Evening Standard*

'Original . . . [and] highly sophisticated . . . No one has written more shrewdly and knowingly about popular newspaper culture than Burn, but with this novel he taps into something more profound and sinister.' William Boyd, *Guardian*

www.faber.co.uk

ff

THE GORDON BURN PRIZE

The Gordon Burn Prize was established in 2012 to celebrate the legacy of one of literature's great innovators. Gordon Burn's writing was precise and rigorous, and often blurred the line between fact and fiction. He wrote across a wide range of subjects, from celebrities to serial killers, politics to contemporary art; his works include the novels *Alma Cogan* and *Born Yesterday: The News as a Novel*, and non-fiction including *Happy Like Murderers: The Story of Fred and Rosemary West*, *Best and Edwards: Football, Fame and Oblivion* and *Sex & Violence, Death & Silence: Encounters with Recent Art*.

The Gordon Burn Prize, run in partnership by the Gordon Burn Trust, New Writing North, Faber & Faber and Durham Book Festival, seeks to celebrate the work of those who follow in his footsteps: novels which dare to enter history and interrogate the past; non-fiction adventurous enough to inhabit characters and events in order to create new and vivid realities. The prize is open to works in English by writers of any nationality or descent who, at the time of entering, are permanently resident in the United Kingdom or the United States of America.

MEMBERS

FABER

Become a Faber Member and discover the best in the arts and literature.

Sign up to the Faber Members programme and enjoy specially curated events, tailored discounts, and exclusive previews of our forthcoming publications from the best novelists, poets, playwrights, thinkers, musicians and artists.

ff

Join for free today at faber.co.uk/members